I0810586

IMAGES
of America

CLARK COUNTY

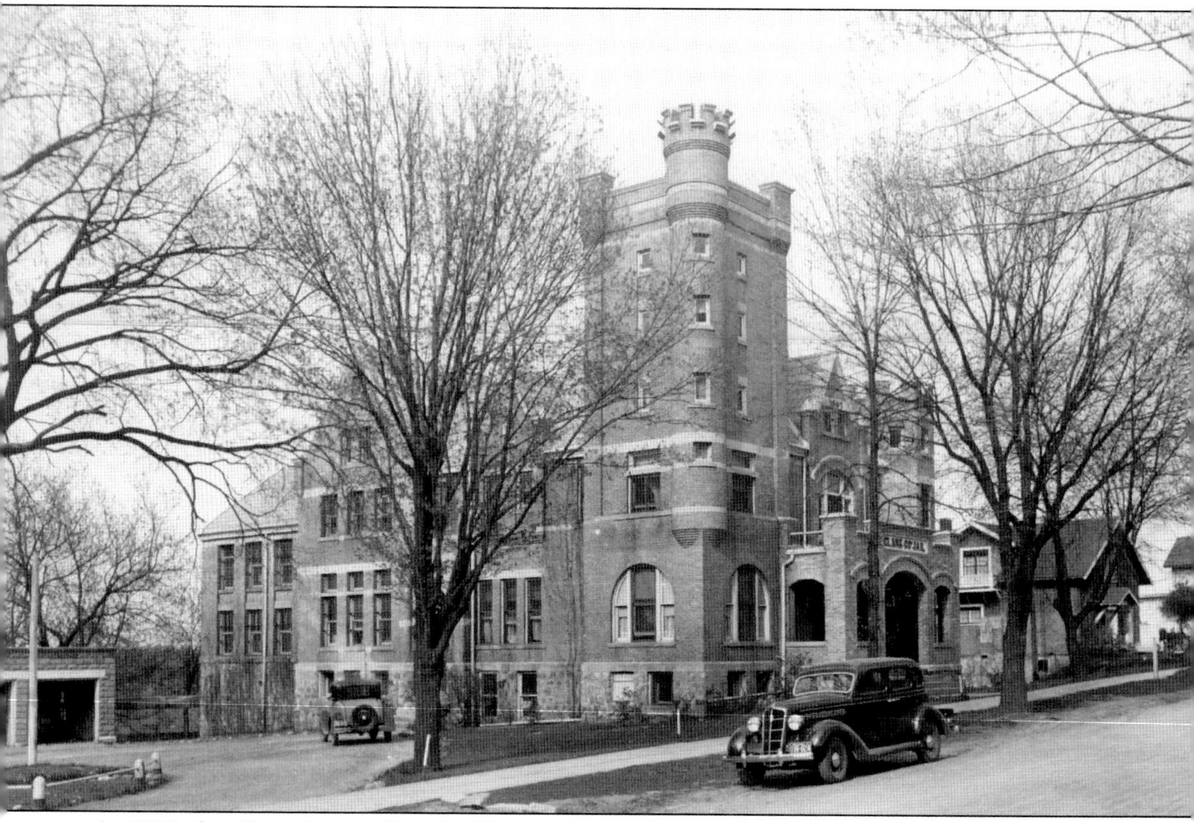

In 1897, the Clark County Board of Supervisors authorized the construction of the third county jail and sheriff's residence, seen here. Built at a cost of $15,000, it housed each sheriff and his family in the front residence, with the prisoners and the sheriff's department in the back. In 1978, when the sheriff's department moved into its new facilities, the 1897 jail stood vacant. Rather than see the building demolished, the Clark County Historical Society made arrangements with the county to lease the structure and make improvements, and by 1980, they were able to open the new 1897 Clark County Jail Museum. In 2008, the 1897 Clark County Jail Museum Inc. was separately incorporated, and it continues to operate and maintain the museum. Listed in the local, state, and national registries of historic places, this building is one of the many historic structures in Clark County. (Courtesy of the 1897 Clark County Jail Museum Inc. and the Clark County Historical Society.)

ON THE COVER: Two young men ride their ponies on Hewett Street in downtown Neillsville in 1909. Woelffer's Drug Store, in the background, has picture postcards displayed in the front (left) window. Some of those same images may also be in this book.

IMAGES
of America

CLARK COUNTY

Natalie K. Erpenbach and Stephen J. Roberts

ARCADIA
PUBLISHING

Copyright © 2013 by Natalie K. Erpenbach and Stephen J. Roberts
ISBN 978-0-7385-9898-7

Published by Arcadia Publishing
Charleston, South Carolina

Printed in the United States of America

Library of Congress Control Number: 2012951876

For all general information, please contact Arcadia Publishing:
Telephone 843-853-2070
Fax 843-853-0044
E-mail sales@arcadiapublishing.com
For customer service and orders:
Toll-Free 1-888-313-2665

Visit us on the Internet at www.arcadiapublishing.com

To Delores "Dee" Zimmerman, and to all the people, living or remembered, who kept the history of Clark County alive and well for all of us to enjoy

Contents

Acknowledgments

We are grateful to the 1897 Clark County Jail Museum Inc. for giving us full access to their photographs and resources. Because of their efforts and the efforts of the Clark County Historical Society these past 35 years, the Jail Museum's collections are available for visitors to see, and for anyone who would like to research Clark County's history. They are all a testament to how much small groups of dedicated people can accomplish.

Everyone mentioned below has offered their assistance, knowledge, support, and, especially, their photographs for this project. We appreciate all of you very much. Future generations will truly appreciate all of our efforts! We hope you enjoy reading this book. If you do, please make sure to support your own local historical society, museum, library, or educational facility in whatever way you choose.

Our thanks and appreciation to:

The 1897 Clark County Jail Museum Inc. and its membership, the most dedicated group of volunteers we know.

The Clark County Historical Society and each of its local historical societies and members. The work you have done and the artifacts you have preserved over the years are nothing less than outstanding.

The Clark County History Buffs, at www.wiclarkcountyhistory.org, the best local history website and group of website volunteers in the country.

Delores "Dee" Zimmerman: you are simply amazing.

Each of the people and organizations who offered their photographs for this book; we could not have done this without you.

The good people of Clark County, living or remembered, who made this a wonderful place to live, work, and raise a family.

And finally, to our families, who allowed us the time to work on this project. We appreciate your love and support.

Unless otherwise noted, all photographs appear courtesy of the 1897 Clark County Jail Museum Inc. and the Clark County Historical Society.

INTRODUCTION

The Wisconsin state legislature authorized the creation of Clark County on July 6, 1853, and named the county after Revolutionary War hero Gen. George Rogers Clark, who spent most of his career in the western frontier, known as the Northwest Territory, which includes present-day Ohio, Indiana, Illinois, Michigan, and Wisconsin. Together with his troops, he helped secure possession of these lands for the United States of America, and provided aid to American settlers in these territories. Over time, the US government made treaties—the most important one in 1838—with the various Indian tribes who lived in the Northwest Territory. On May 29, 1848, Wisconsin was admitted to the Union as the 30th state.

The earliest pioneers, in the 1830s, used the Black River as their first "road" into what is now Clark County. Looking for lumber to cut and land to settle, they found dense forests of white pine and hardwoods, plenty of wildlife to hunt and fish, and, in general, friendly Indian neighbors. Soon, lumber camps were set up, sawmills were built, and permanent settlers arrived. In the early 1840s, men like James and Henry O'Neill, William and Samuel Ferguson, E.L. Brockway, and Samuel Cawley arrived and began carving their new homes out of the wilderness.

In 1841, a group of Mormons also made their way into the Black River area. Arriving from Nauvoo, Illinois, they had heard of the excellent timber available in the area, and came to get the lumber they needed to build a new tabernacle back home. They had a sawmill near Black River Falls and lumber camps farther upriver, in what are now the Neillsville and Greenwood areas. They operated these camps until 1844, when they were called back to Nauvoo by their elders. The Mormon lumber camps were abandoned, and for years afterwards, these areas in the woods were known as the Mormon Clearings by the local residents.

By the 1850s, lumbermen and loggers began arriving from east coast states like Maine, Vermont, New York, and Pennsylvania. Many of these men brought their families with them as well, and the communities of Clark County began to take shape. Merchants opened shops and stores, a school was built, and county officials were elected. Over the next 25 to 50 years, the land itself changed as well. By the 1890s, the lumber industry was in its final days in southern and central Clark County, and lumbermen had to make a choice. They could move to the west coast, where the lumber industry was booming, they could move their lumber camps farther north in Clark County or beyond, or they could start a business or settle into retirement.

Agriculture and dairy farms became the next economic force in the county. As sections of land were cleared of timber and the tree stumps were removed, more families settled in the rural areas of the county. Clark County has been one of the largest producers of crops and dairy products in the country for more than 100 years. Excellent farmland for crops and green pastures for dairy herds were underneath all of those dense forests, and county residents wasted no time in putting the soil to good use.

Businesses, county government, schools, and churches have changed through the years as well. Livery stables were replaced by car dealerships, the county government now operates with a multimillion-dollar budget, and the one-room schoolhouses have been replaced with centralized school districts. Along the way, the citizens of Clark County have found ways to enjoy each other's company and all of the great natural resources within the county's borders.

We hope you enjoy the photographs in this book and the history surrounding each of them. May we always take the time and find ways to remember our past, share it with our children, and preserve it for future generations.

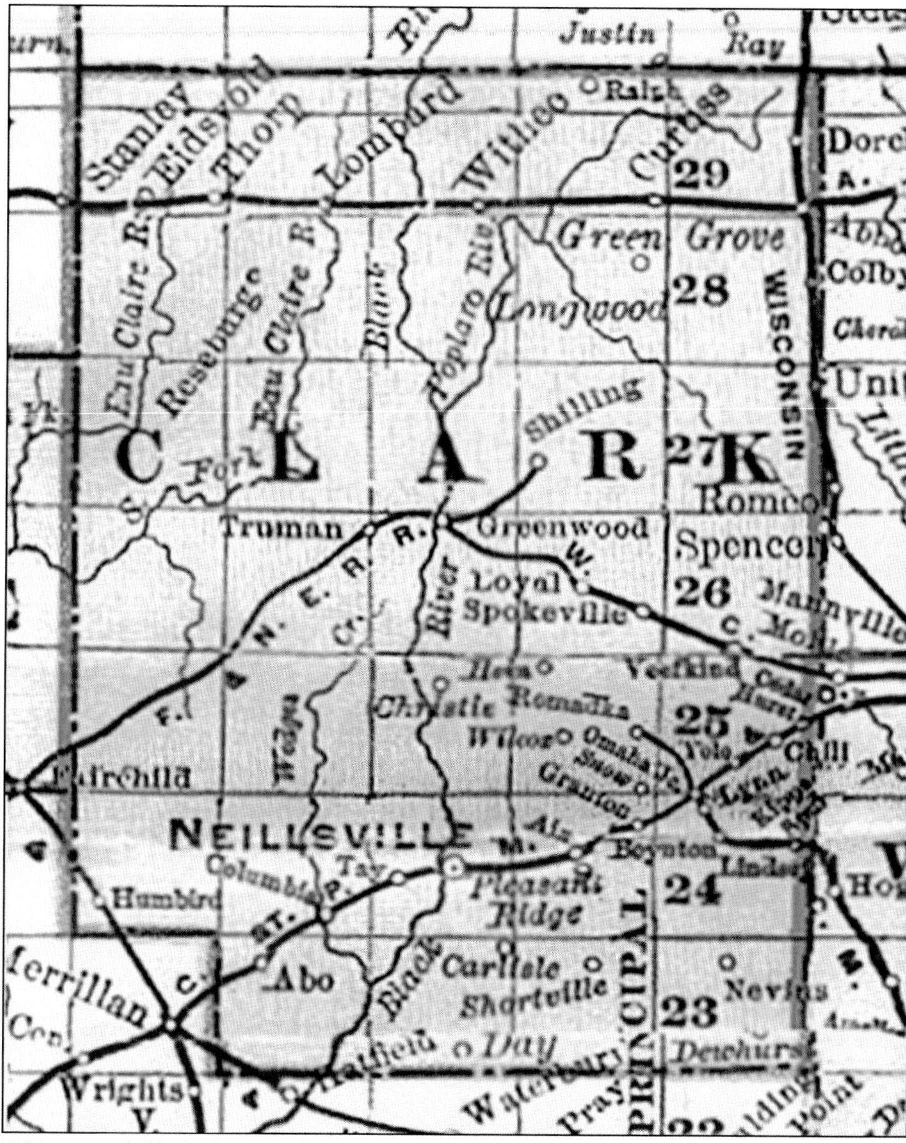

This 1901 map of Clark County shows where the major cities, villages, rivers, and creeks were located at that time. Most of the communities are still thriving and retain their historic charm. Others, like Columbia, Pleasant Ridge, Spokeville, and Tioga exist only in the stories and memories of past generations. (Courtesy of Clark County History Buffs.)

One

The Lumber Years and Clark County's Founders

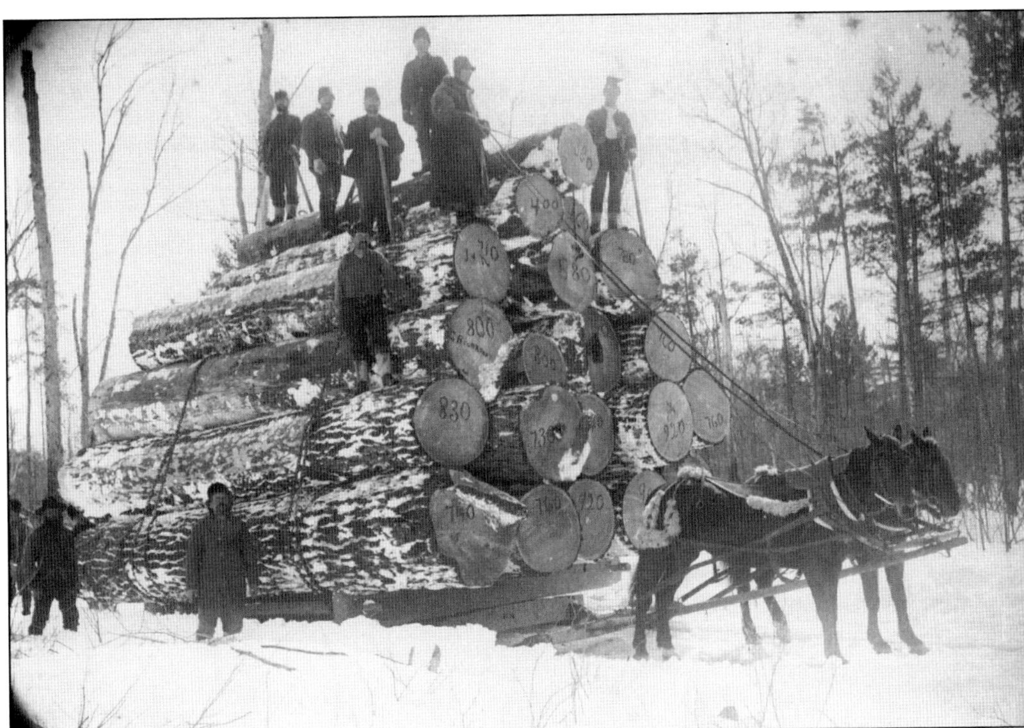

In this 1890 photograph, lumbermen from the John Pietenpol camp stand on a load of logs cut near Cunningham Creek. Located about two miles south of Neillsville, this tributary of the Black River received its name in the early 1840s when a Mormon named Elijah Cunningham drowned in it. Thereafter, the creek has borne his name. (Courtesy of the Dick and Joanne Tibbett collection.)

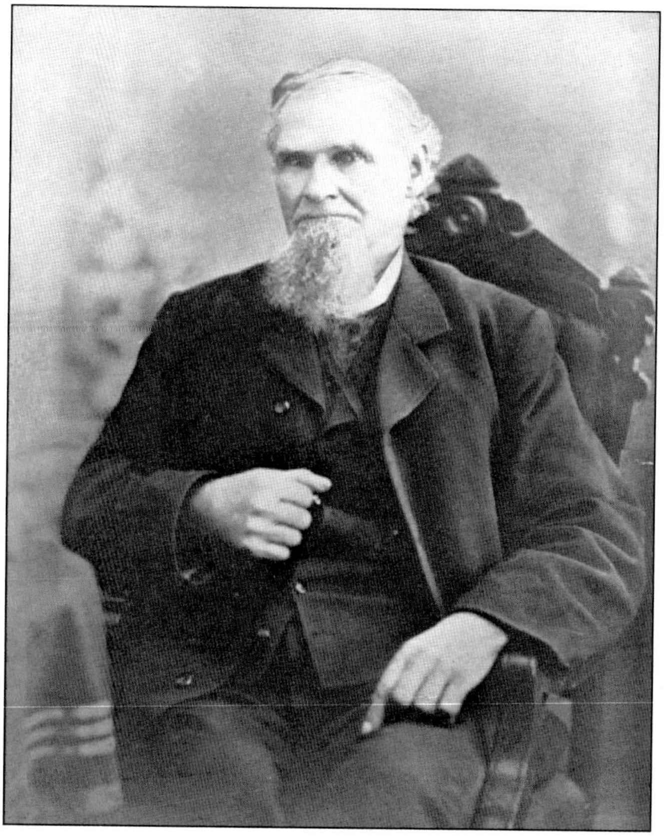

James O'Neill, seen here in his later years, was born in Lisbon, St. Lawrence County, New York, in 1810. At age 26, he left home and traveled west to Wisconsin. By 1839, he and his brother Alexander had built a successful sawmill south of Black River Falls, and in 1845, he and another brother, Henry, moved their base of lumber operations to an area that would eventually bear his name: Neillsville.

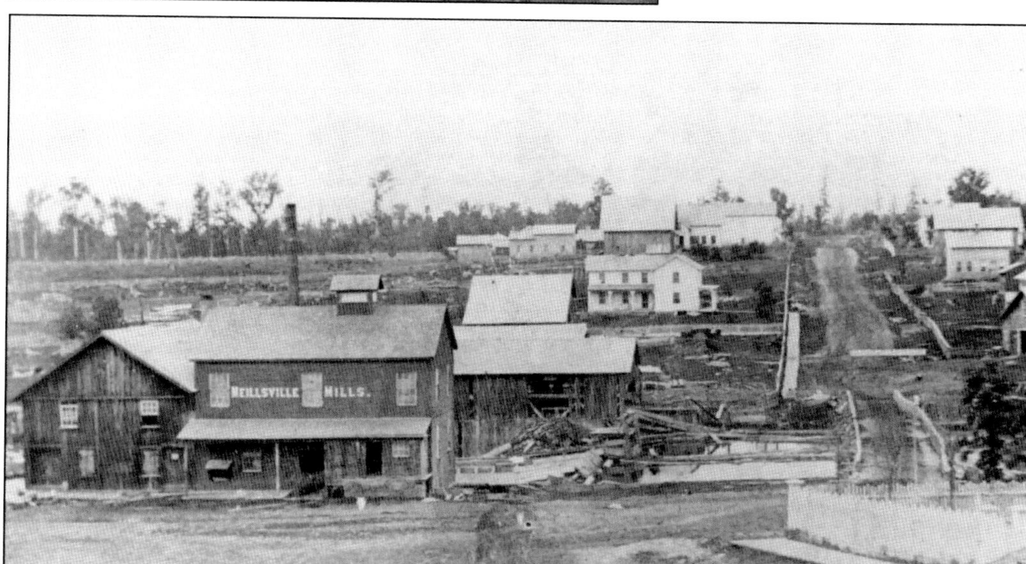

By 1865, Neillsville was a growing community. This photograph shows Main Street (later Hewett Street) looking north towards Staffordville and Christie. By this time, the Neillsville Mills stands where the O'Neill sawmill stood in 1845, and the surrounding land has been cleared for homes and businesses. The white picket fence in the bottom right was in the front yard of James O'Neill's house, which he built after he married and had a family.

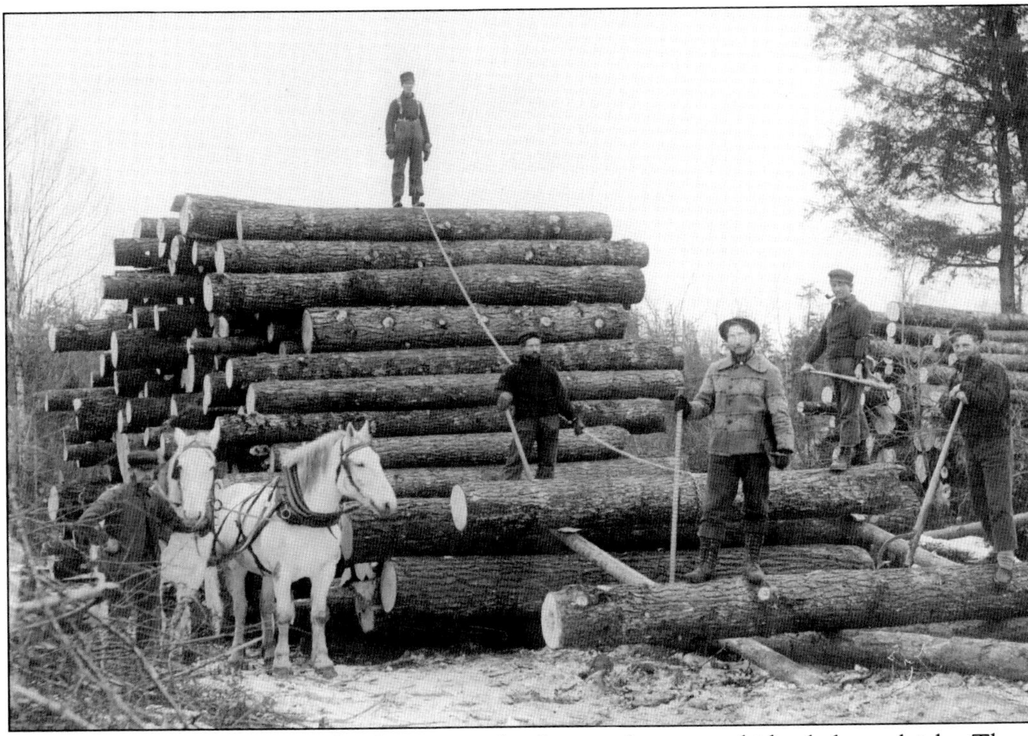

Moving timber to the nearest landing meant loading cut logs onto skids, sleds, or sleighs. These men are using horses, chains, and cantor hooks to roll logs onto the top of the load in the late 1890s. (Courtesy of the Loyal Area Historical Society, Bertz Collection.)

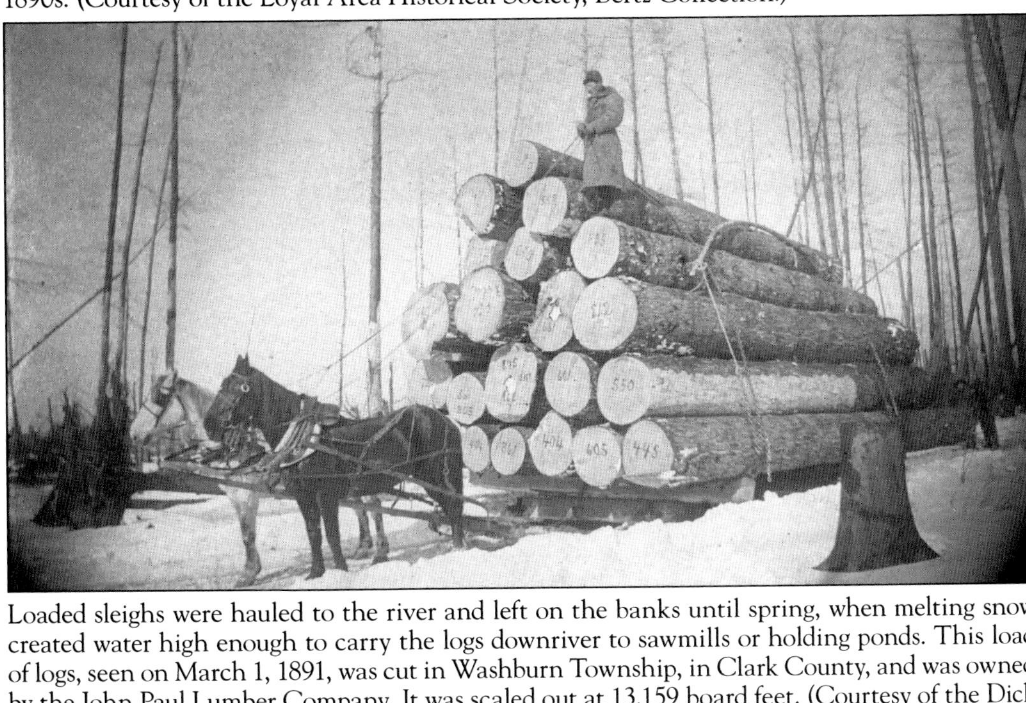

Loaded sleighs were hauled to the river and left on the banks until spring, when melting snow created water high enough to carry the logs downriver to sawmills or holding ponds. This load of logs, seen on March 1, 1891, was cut in Washburn Township, in Clark County, and was owned by the John Paul Lumber Company. It was scaled out at 13,159 board feet. (Courtesy of the Dick and Joanne Tibbett collection.)

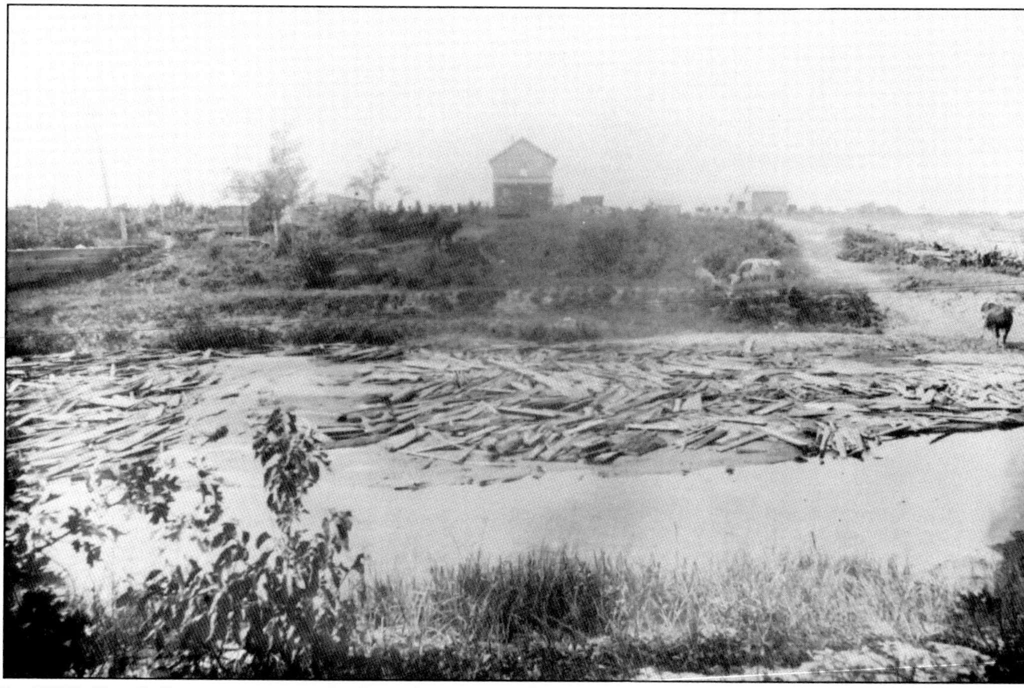

In 1895, Frank Farning operated a boardinghouse (background, center) along the banks of Wedges Creek near Columbia. Lumbermen and loggers were frequent visitors to the Farning boardinghouse. In the foreground, lumber from the nearby mill floats in the creek.

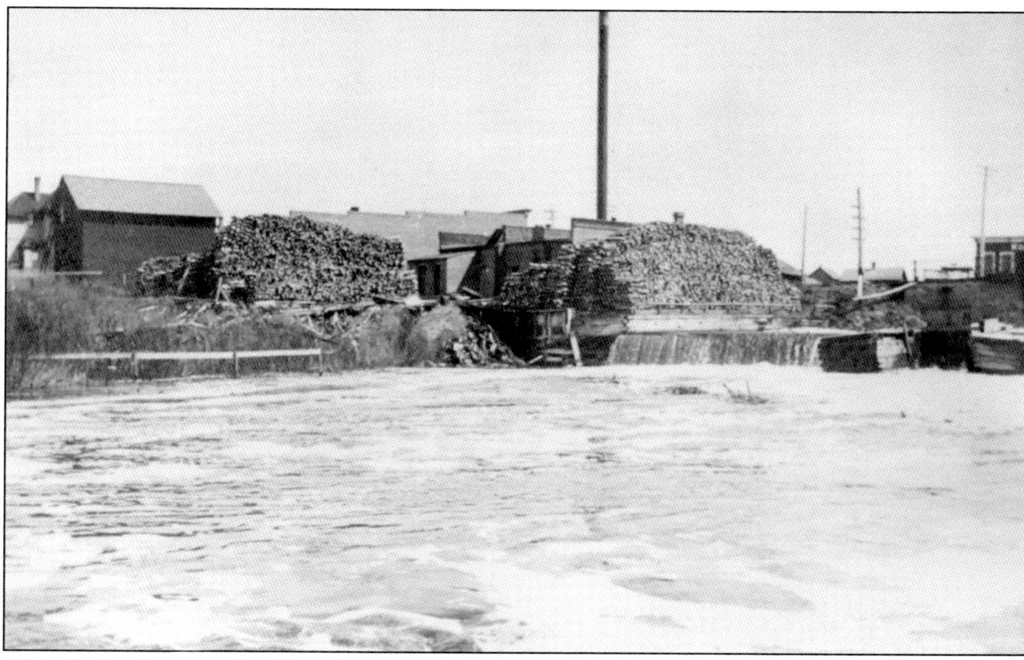

O'Neill Creek meets the Black River at the northwestern corner of Neillsville's city limits. This photograph, taken around 1900, shows stacks of planed lumber on the north side of the creek, just below the dam at the Hewett Street Bridge. The Wolff & Korman wagon shop is on the extreme right.

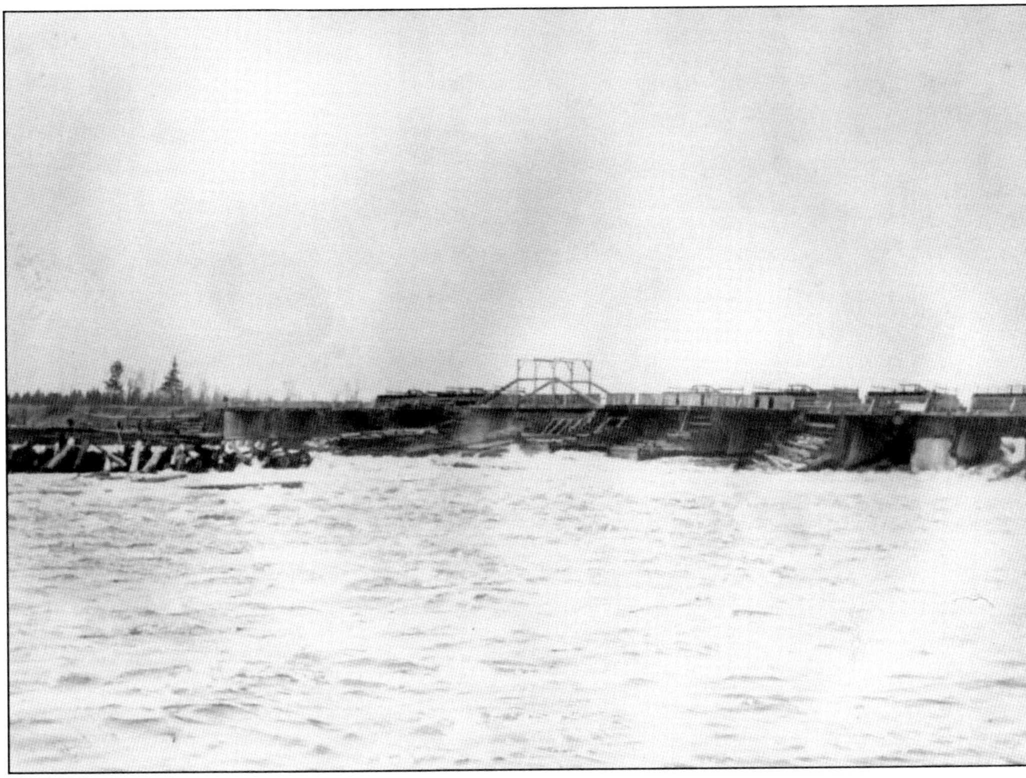

In 1879, a dam was constructed at Dells Dam by the Black River Improvement Company. Located between Neillsville and Hatfield, it was constructed to prevent flooding on the Black River and to control water flow for loggers. The great flood of 1911 broke the levees of Dells Dam, and repairs were made, but the flood of 1914 was so damaging that it took out the dam completely.

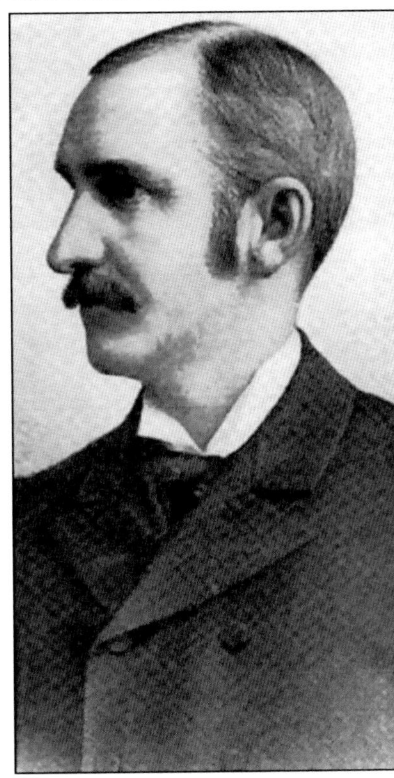

James L. Gates was born in New York and came to Clark County in 1856 with his parents, Daniel and Jane (Hewett) Gates. His family managed a boardinghouse on Wedges Creek for years, and they later moved to Neillsville. Married four times, Gates became a rich, powerful lumberman, owning thousands of acres of timberland and becoming a leader in selling cutover land in northern Wisconsin.

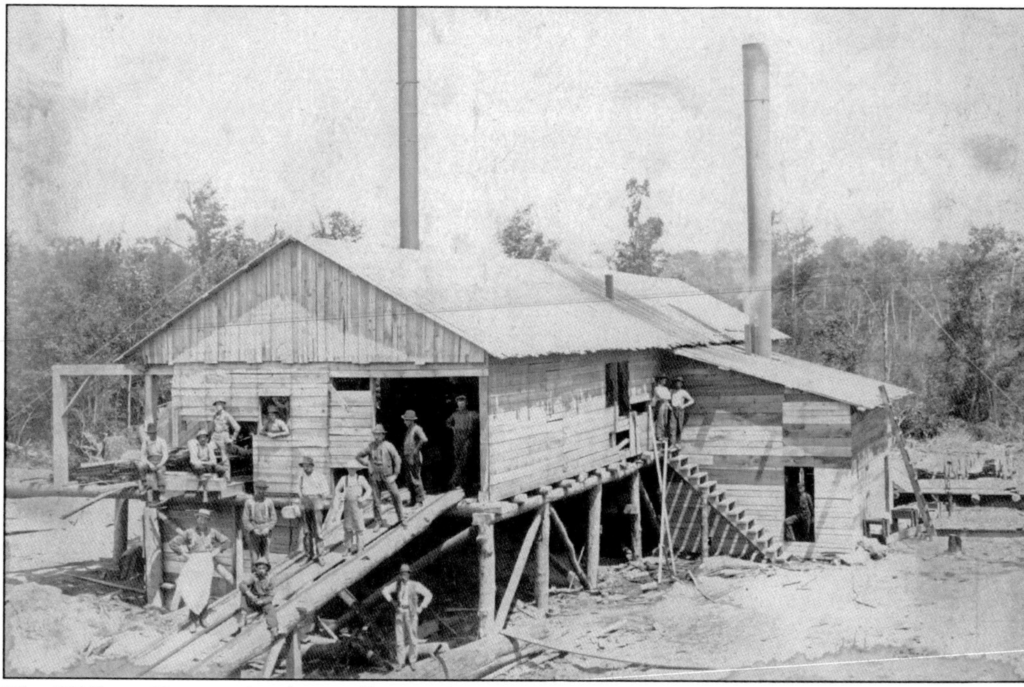

The William Farning lumber mill, seen here in 1895, was at the junction of Five Mile Creek and Wedges Creek near the village of Columbia. Farning also owned a lumber mill in Weston Township, as well as other lumber interests. In total, his operations produced more than two million board feet of lumber each year, and employed many mill workers.

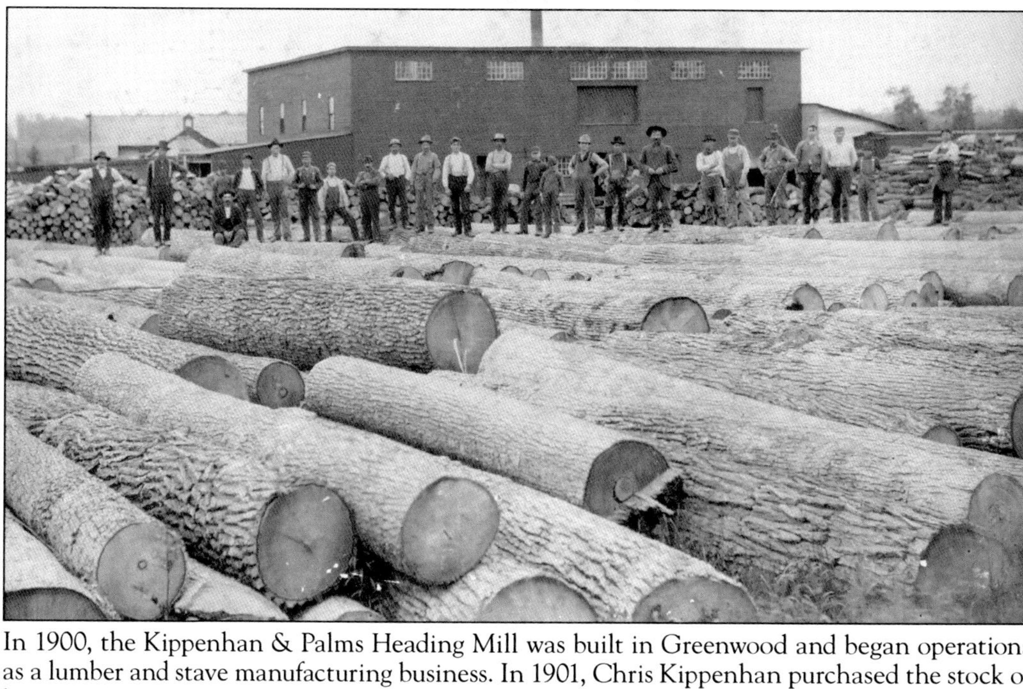

In 1900, the Kippenhan & Palms Heading Mill was built in Greenwood and began operations as a lumber and stave manufacturing business. In 1901, Chris Kippenhan purchased the stock of his partner, George Palms, and renamed the company Kippenhan Heading Mill. Here, employees pose for a photograph in front of the mill between 1900 and 1905.

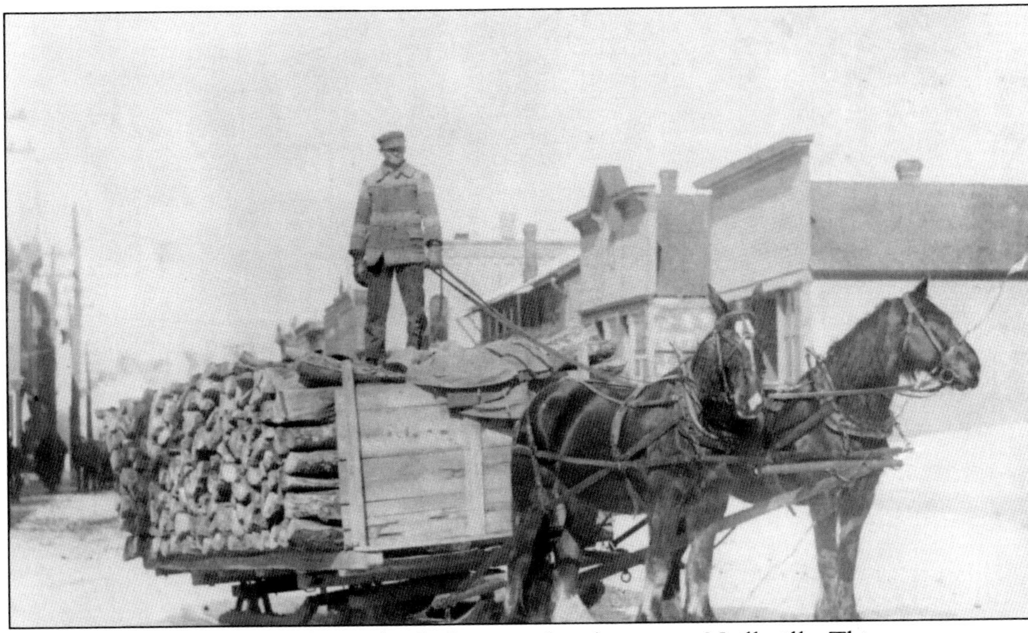

This unidentified man stands on a load of cut wood in downtown Neillsville. This was a common sight in the late 1800s and early 1900s. Wood was delivered to homes and businesses to fuel kitchen stoves, potbellied stoves, and fireplaces. In some instances, the delivery of cut wood was bartered for charges at local businesses.

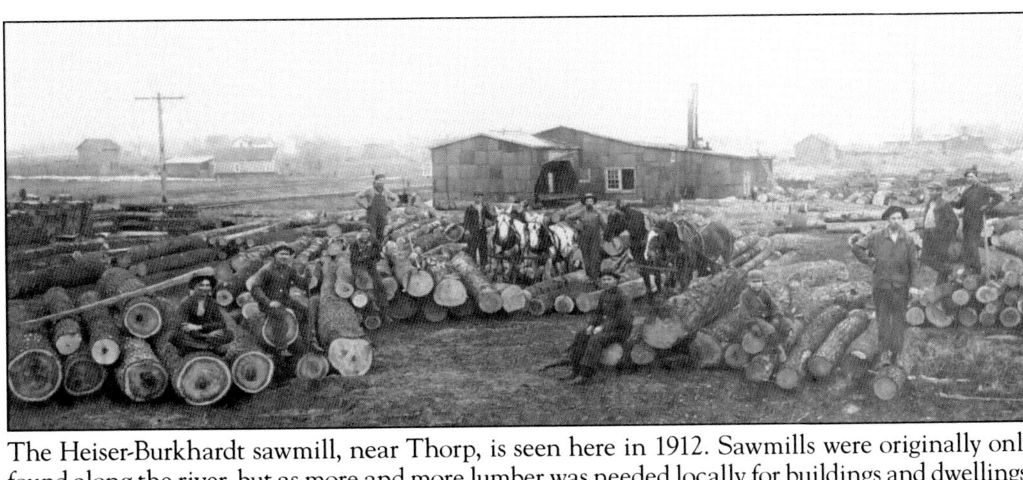

The Heiser-Burkhardt sawmill, near Thorp, is seen here in 1912. Sawmills were originally only found along the river, but as more and more lumber was needed locally for buildings and dwellings, they became common throughout the county. Peter Heiser also had a portable sawmill that could be taken directly to a worksite to saw logs for the customer to use immediately.

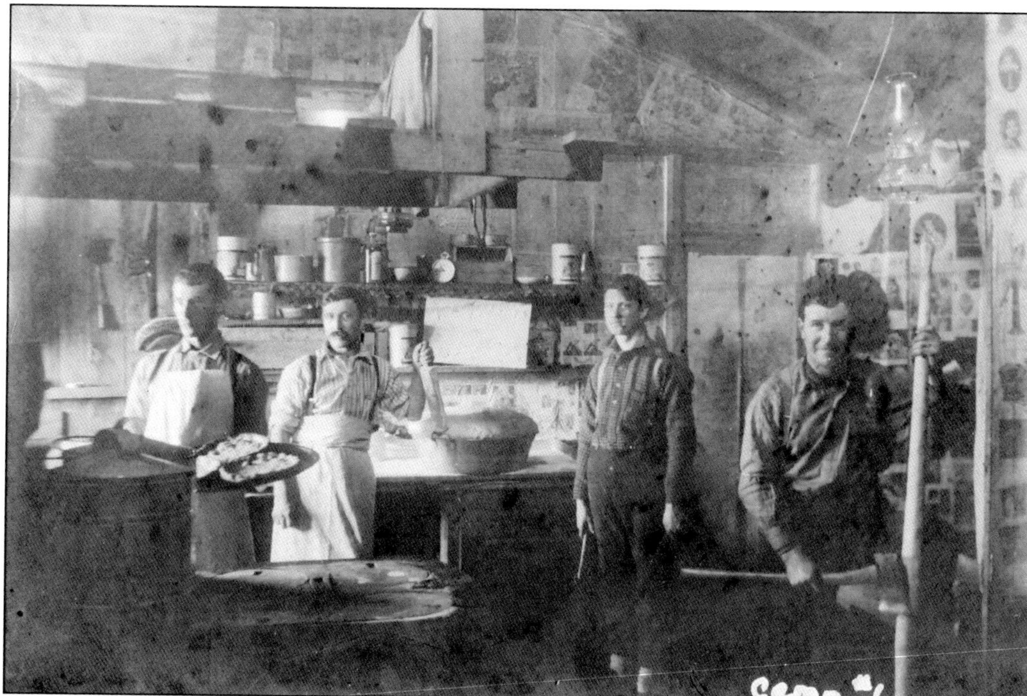

This lumber camp in northern Wisconsin, run by William Tibbett in 1925, was certainly more comfortable than the camps of 40 and 50 years before, but it was still a makeshift home in the woods. Above, four men prepare a meal in the camp kitchen, also known as the cook's shanty. There is bread dough rising in the large pan on the stovetop. Below, men gather outside of the bunkhouse on what appears to be a day off. The men sitting on the far right are each holding puppies, and the man sitting in the chair in the center is wearing an apron and receiving a haircut. (Both courtesy of the Dick and Joanne Tibbett collection.)

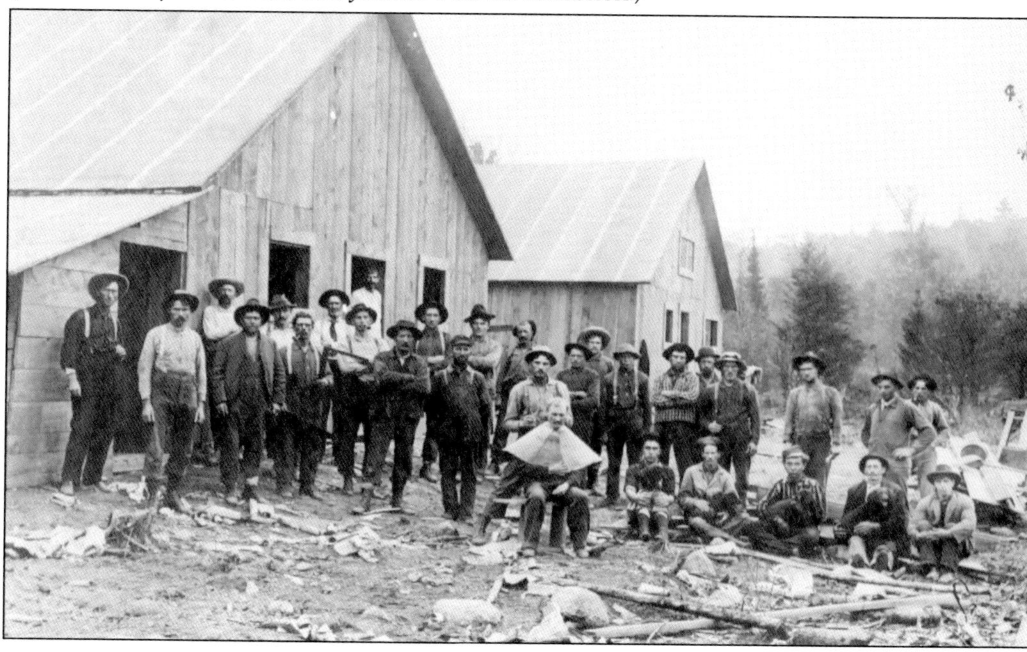

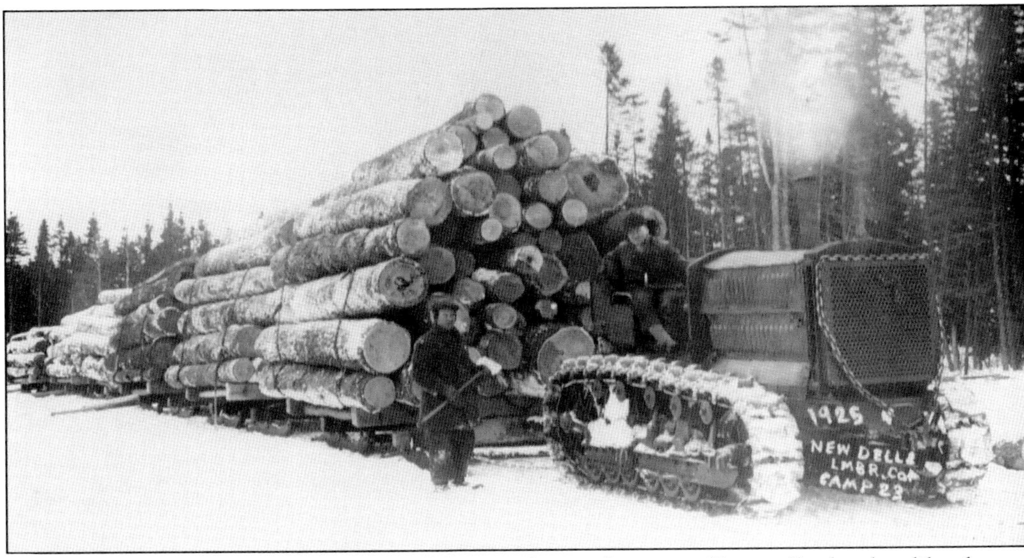

By 1925, the way logs were moved out of the woods was changing. Caterpillar haulers like the one above were replacing horses as the preferred method of moving skids of logs out of the deep woods. Above, two men and one hauler move six skids of logs at the New Dells Lumber Company's Camp 23. Railroads were replacing creeks and rivers as the primary method of moving logs to the mills, and were becoming the new "highways" of the lumber industry. Below, a group of men lay logs and steel as they build a new section of railroad track. Lumbermen built many miles of railroad track, or spurs, on their own land and at their own expense, in order to connect with the central railway systems. (Both courtesy of the Dick and Joanne Tibbett collection.)

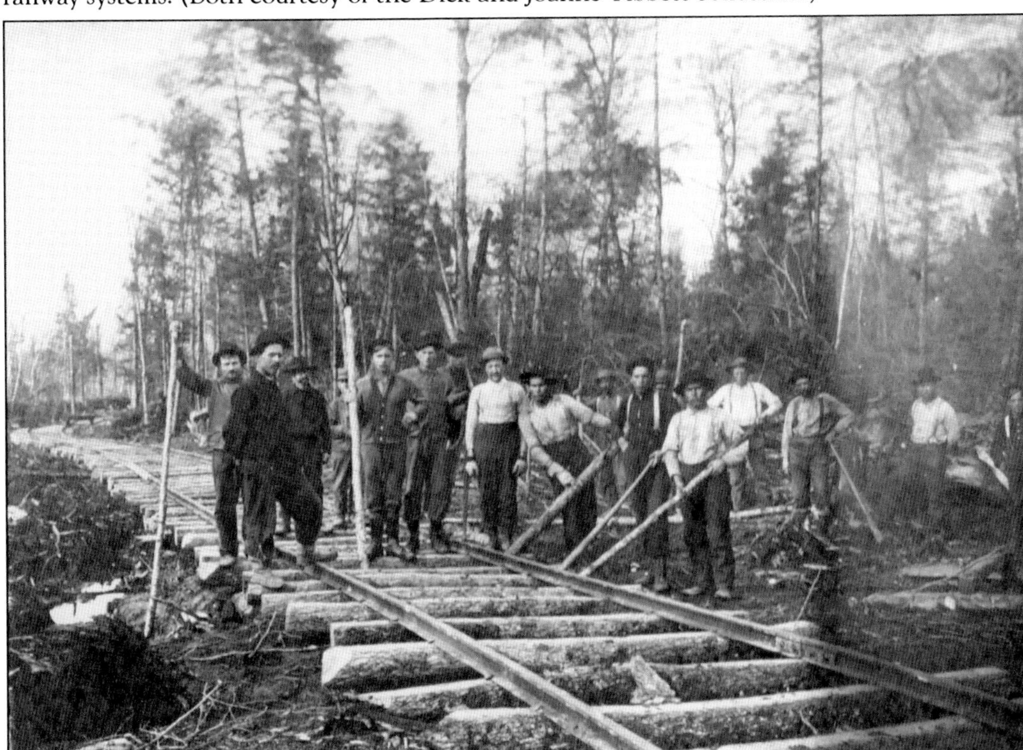

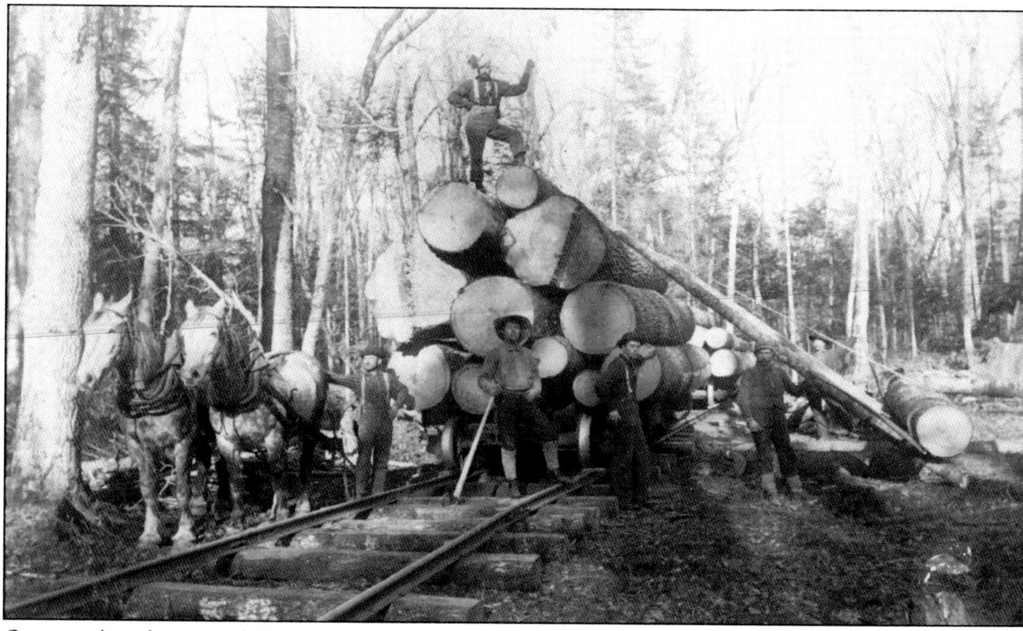

Once railroads arrived, horses like the ones seen here around 1890 still moved the cut logs in the woods and helped load the flatbeds, but train engines and the railroad system, not the river, moved the logs from that point on. Regardless of how the loads were moved, lumbermen enjoyed having their photograph taken with a large, or "star," load of logs. (Courtesy of the Dick and Joanne Tibbett collection.)

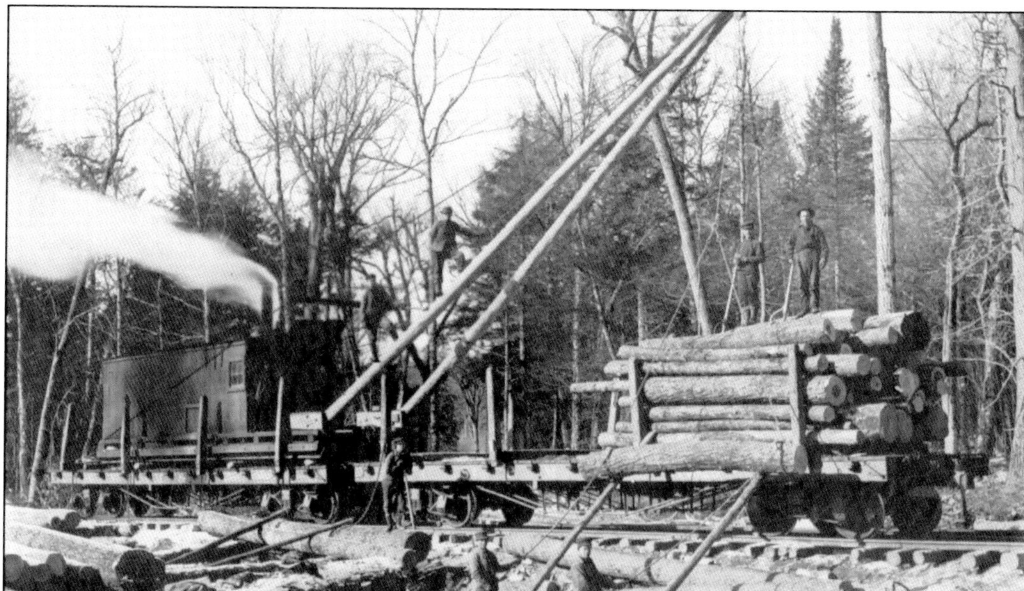

In the later years of the lumber industry, loggers used steam-powered log loaders, or jammers, like the one seen here. This equipment could be operated from a flatbed, which made it easier to move from one log-loading site to another. (Courtesy of the Dick and Joanne Tibbett collection.)

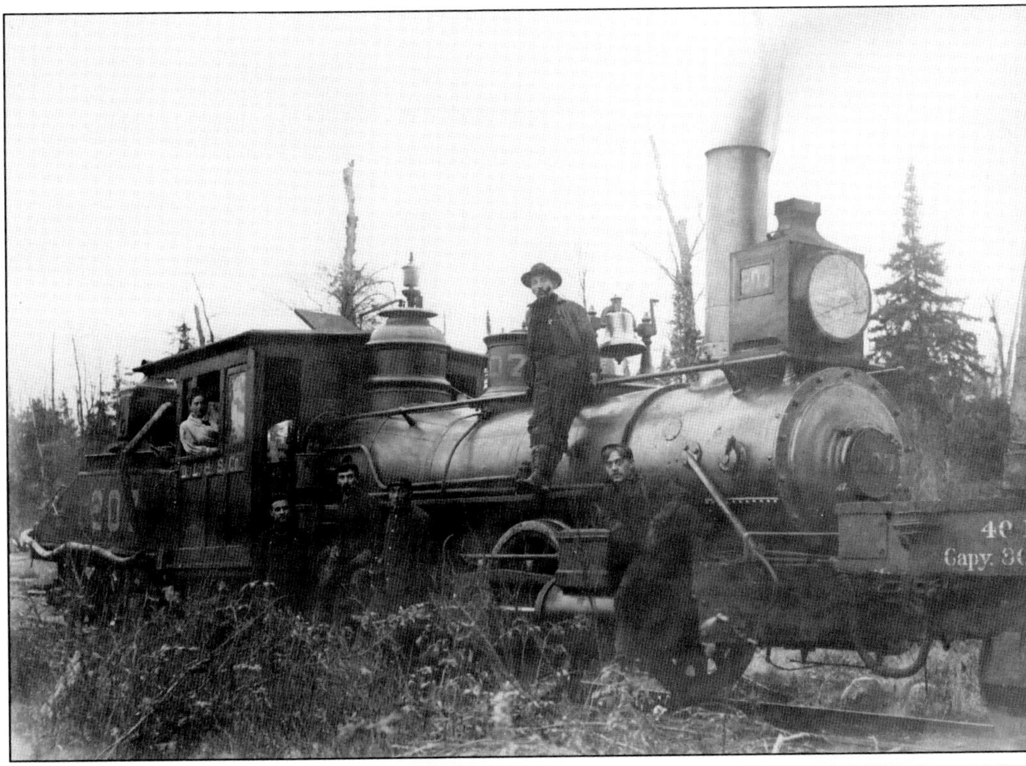

This steam engine was used in logging camps run by William Tibbett in northern Wisconsin in the 1920s. The D.L. & S. Company used the engine, No. 207, to haul logs, equipment, or supplies out of the woods or between camps. This man and woman (in the engineer's seat) have stopped and posed for the photographer. (Courtesy of the Dick and Joanne Tibbett collection.)

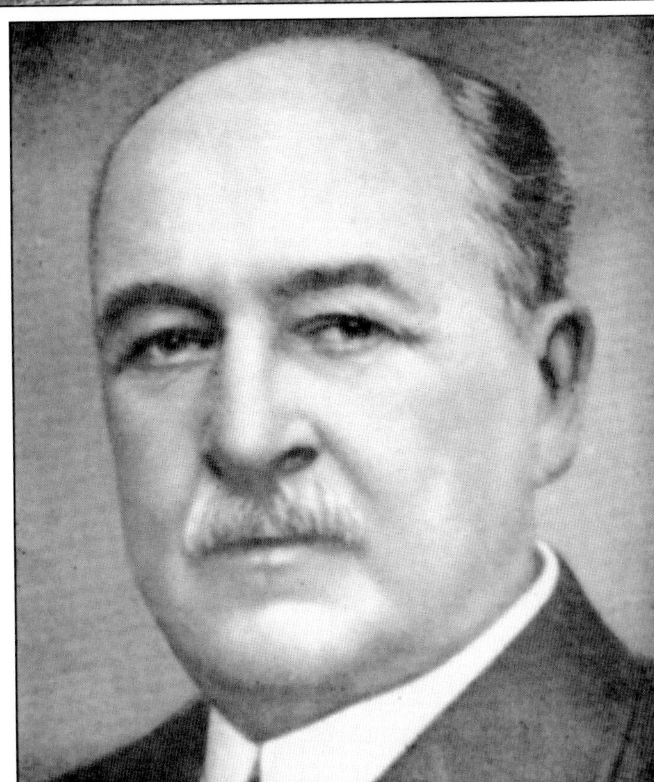

In the 1890s, John S. Owen owned at least 30,000 acres in northern Clark County and elsewhere. He was also an owner of a multi-location retail lumber business, the O&N Lumber Company. As timber was cleared from the land, he and other lumbermen and communities began to actively promote the sale of this cutover land to people looking for homesteads or farmland.

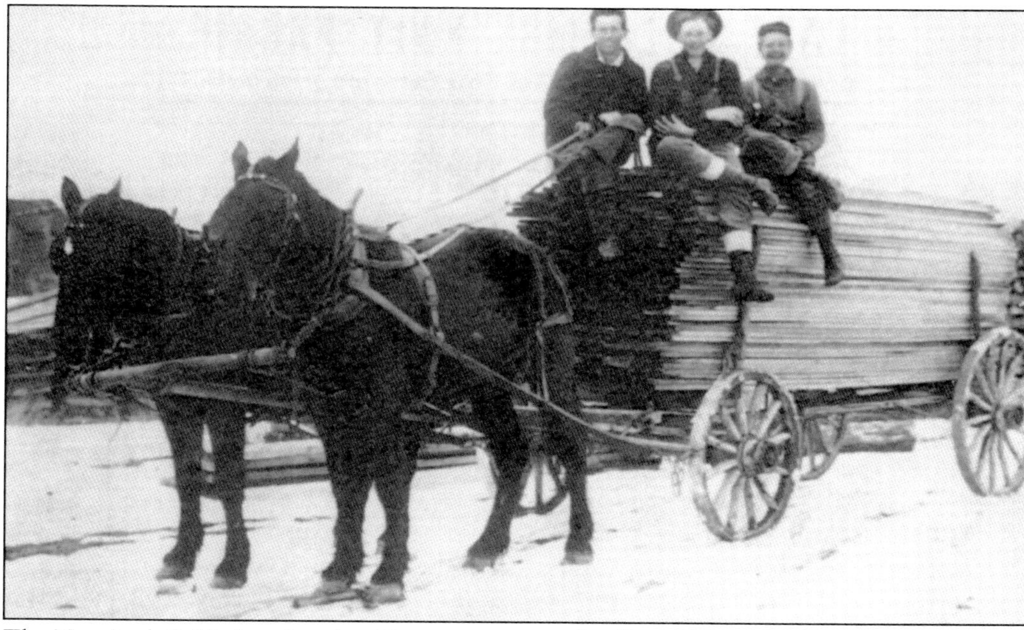

The Nye, Lusk & Hudson Lumber Company operated mills in Eidsvold, Thorp, and Stanley, in the township of Thorp. Fire destroyed the Eidsvold mill in 1899, but a new mill was built within 90 days. In 1907, these men are making a delivery of cut lumber. On top of the wagonload are, from left to right, Alfred Kass, George Eiler, and Martin Eiler. (Courtesy of the Stanley Area Historical Society.)

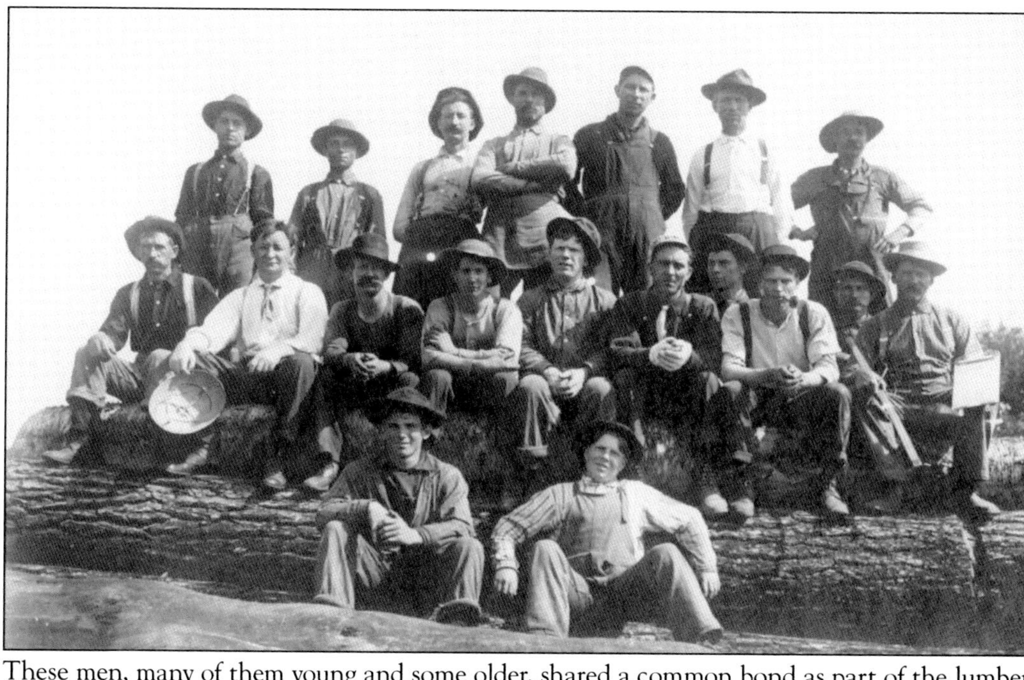

These men, many of them young and some older, shared a common bond as part of the lumber history of Clark County. They all cut dense forests of lumber, hauled logs out of the woods, and sent logs down the Black River or over the railroad system. They all knew what it was like to be a lumberman, and had the stories to prove it.

Two

Communities and Their Citizens

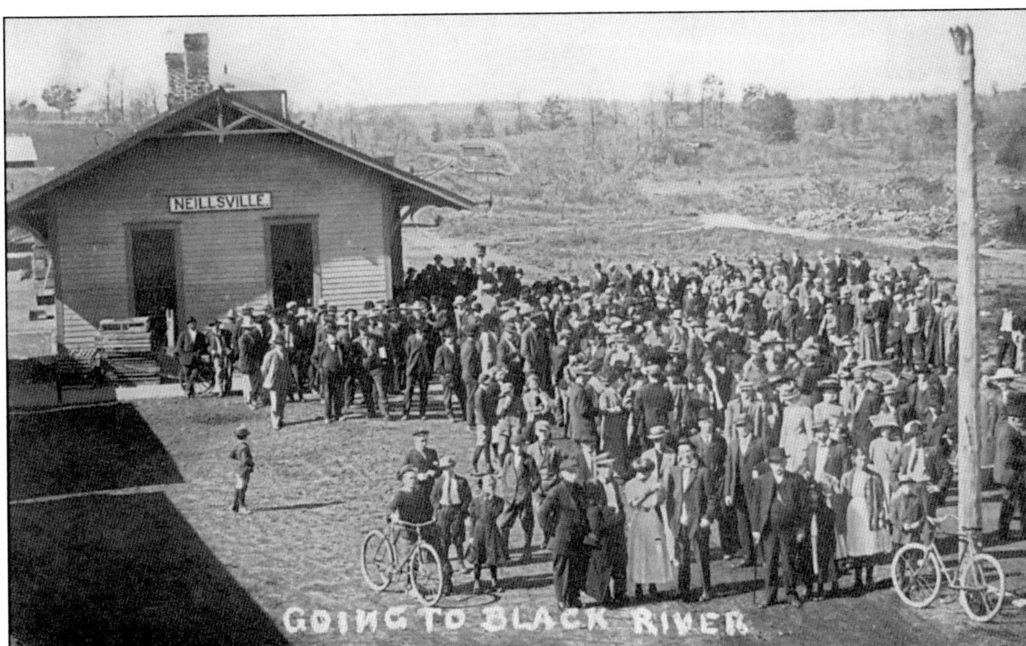

On October 6, 1911, the Black River flooded its banks, and dams up and down the river were damaged or destroyed. The city of Black River Falls received the worst treatment, as it was nearly swept away by the high waters. News of the devastation quickly spread, and people like the ones seen here at the Neillsville station made their way to Black River Falls to see the damage and offer help.

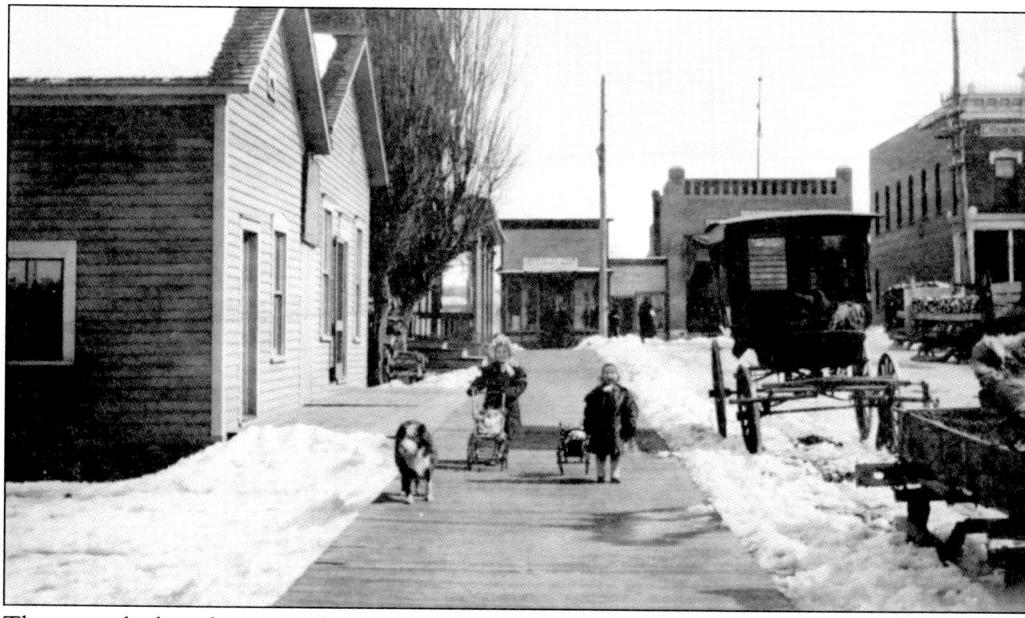

These two little girls are out for a walk in Neillsville with their dog and their dolls on a sunny day in the winter of 1904. As they walked on the wooden sidewalk on Seventh Street, just west of the Merchant's Hotel, there were carriages and wagons parked in the street. Directly behind the girls, on Hewett Street, is a confectionery store that they may have just visited.

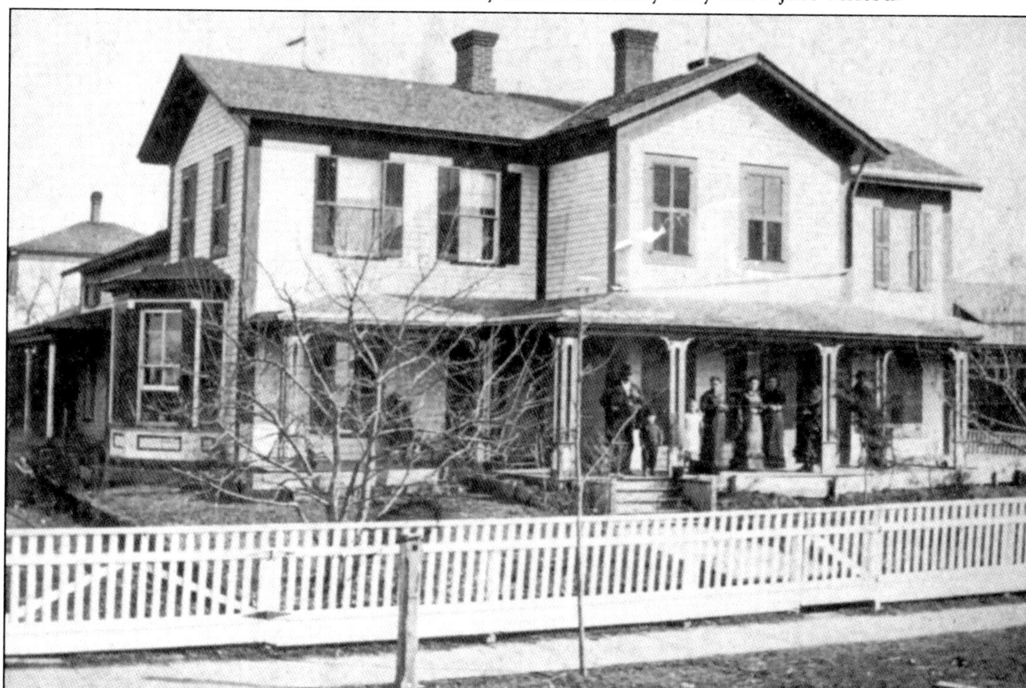

This house, on the northeast corner of Hewett and Fourth Streets in Neillsville, belonged to B.F. French and his family. French was a lawyer who also studied medicine and worked as a lumberman. He was active in early government and civic activities. Standing on the front porch around 1875, the French family included, from left to right, B.F., Edwin, Dimple, Elizabeth, Rosenette, Elva, and Viola.

Robert J. McBride was born in Philadelphia in 1847 and came to Neillsville in 1866. He found work with a lumber company and studied law with B.F. French. In 1870, he married Addie Gates, the daughter of Daniel and Jane (Hewett) Gates. McBride was a successful attorney, a county judge, and a state legislator. In 1894, he was appointed the United States counsel to Edinburgh, Scotland, by Pres. Grover Cleveland.

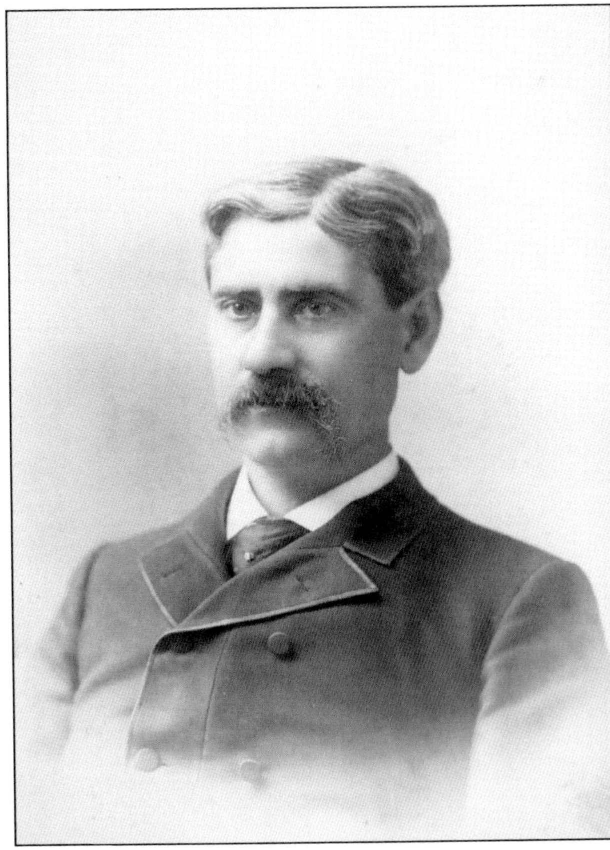

The clothes worn by these young people around 1905 were typical for the times. Everyone is wearing a hat, which was the fashion, and the men are all wearing ties. Among this fun-loving group of friends, the following people were identified, in no particular order: Jess Snyder, Hazel Wood, Bige Selves, Ernie Snyder, Placido Hommel, Maude Bruley, and Herb Brown.

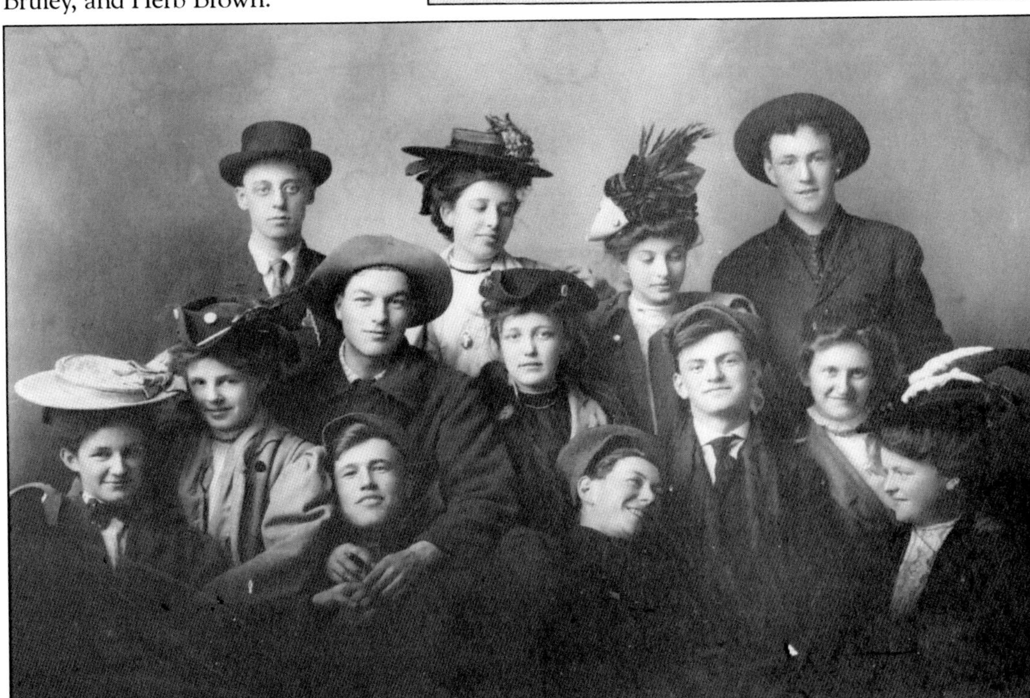

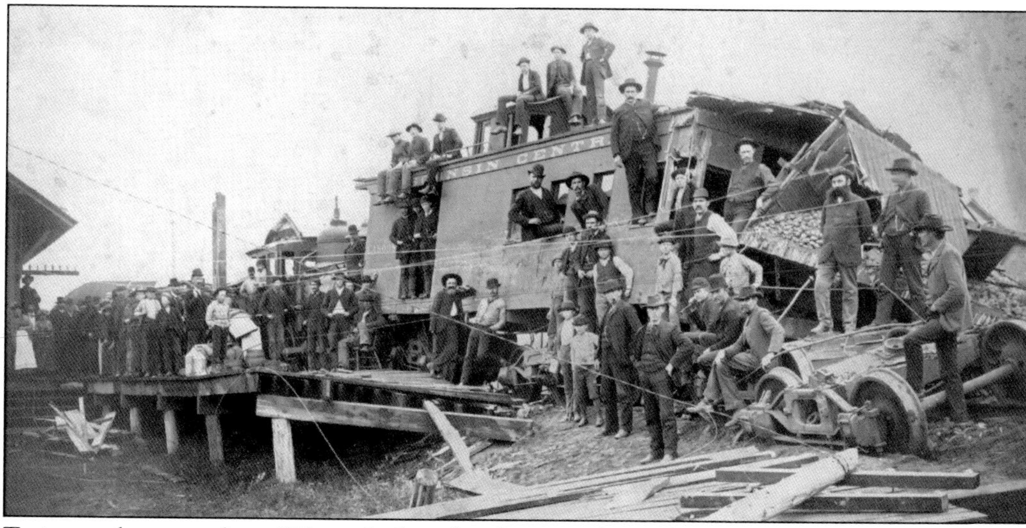

Train wrecks were a fact of life, and when they happened, people arrived from points near and far to view the damage. This train wreck occurred in Greenwood, near the depot. There is no record of the accident's actual date, but train service first arrived in Greenwood in 1891, and based on the people's clothing, the photograph appears to be from the 1890s.

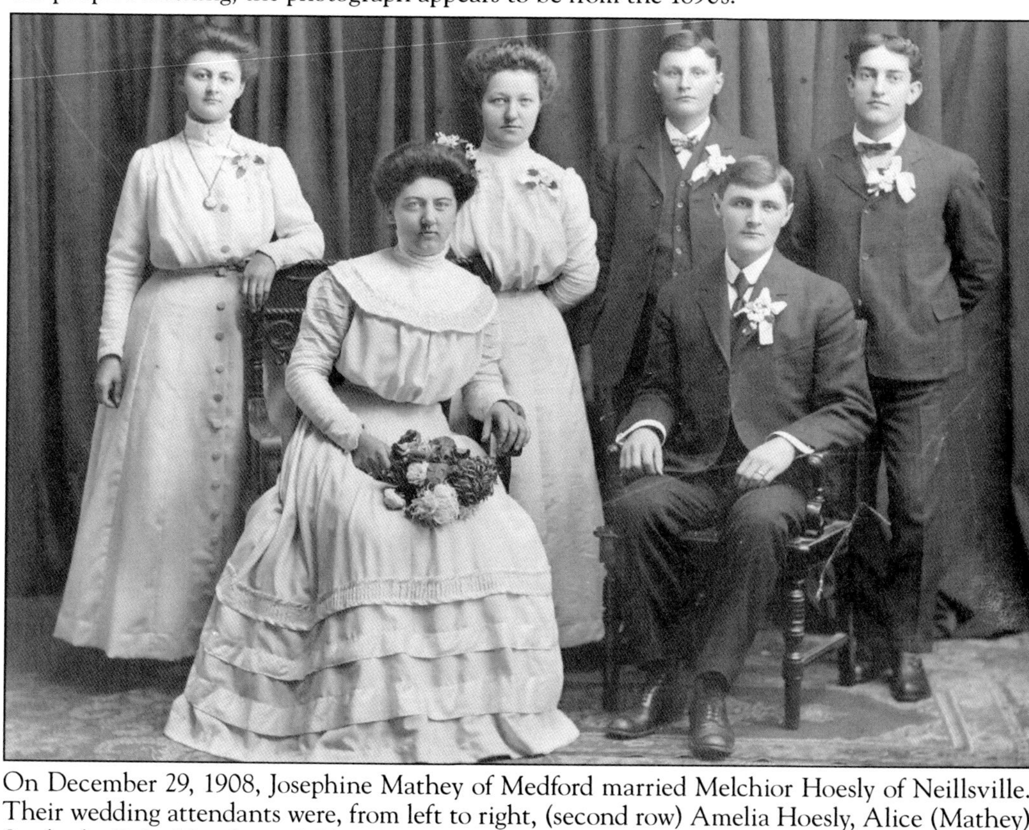

On December 29, 1908, Josephine Mathey of Medford married Melchior Hoesly of Neillsville. Their wedding attendants were, from left to right, (second row) Amelia Hoesly, Alice (Mathey) Swaboda, Baltz Hoesly, and Alex Cretton. The newly married couple farmed for several years before moving to Neillsville in 1920 with their three children, Alice, Ellen, and Melchior Jr., where Melchior Sr. operated the Ford garage.

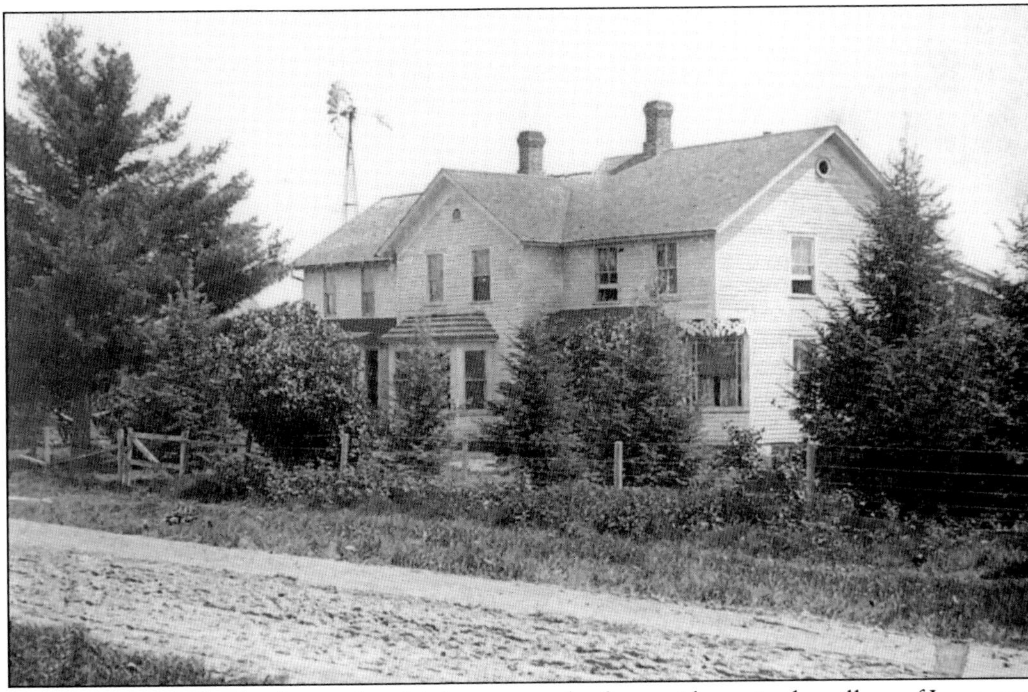

Built in 1858 by Charles Sternitzky, this house was the first residence in the village of Lynn, and remained in the family for more than 100 years. The home was frequently used as a boardinghouse, as a resting spot for a hot meal, and as part of the stagecoach route. (Courtesy of Kay Buettner.)

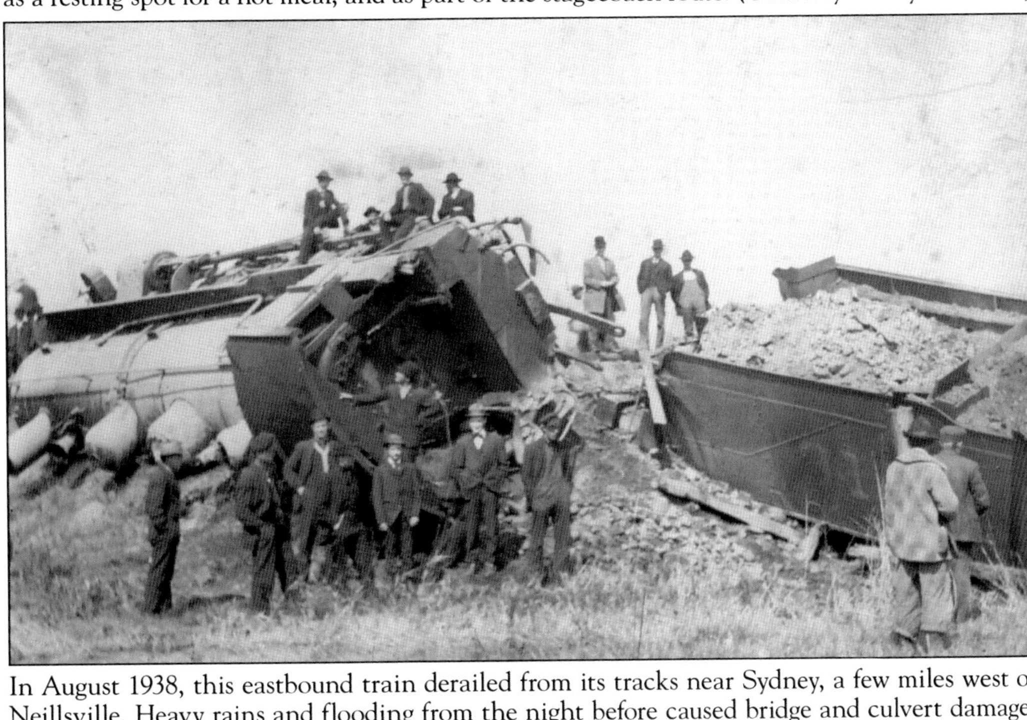

In August 1938, this eastbound train derailed from its tracks near Sydney, a few miles west of Neillsville. Heavy rains and flooding from the night before caused bridge and culvert damage. The tracks were washed out, resulting in the train wreck. The engineer and a few passengers were injured, but none severely. Hundreds of people drove out to see the damage the next day.

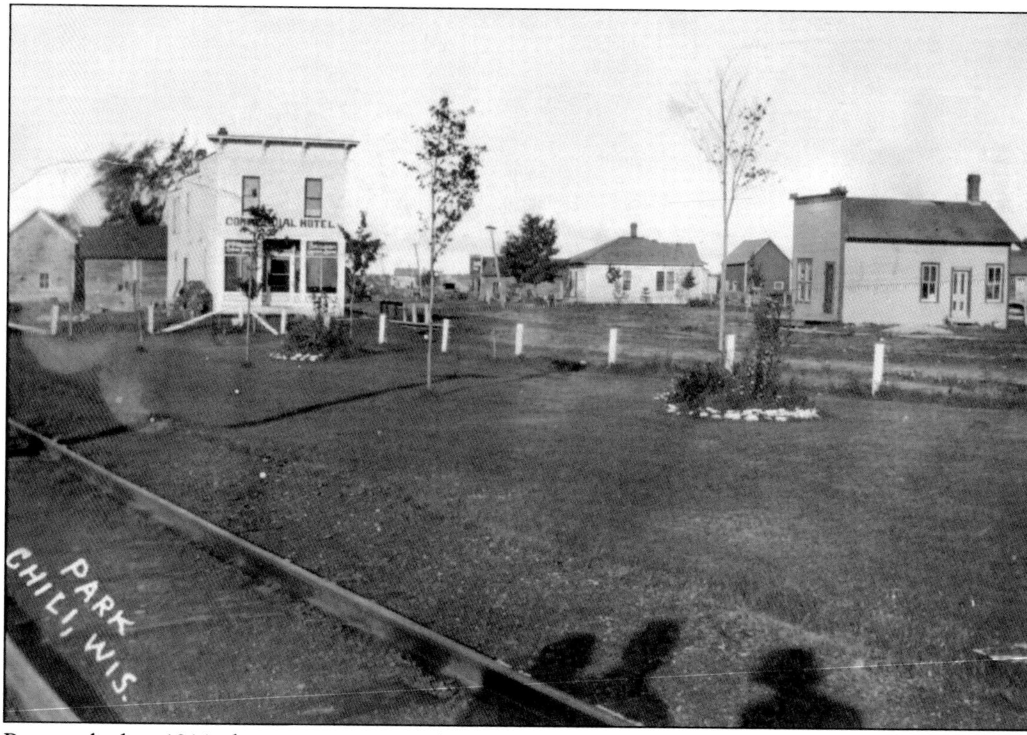

Postmarked in 1914, this picture postcard of the village of Chili was probably taken by someone sitting on a passenger train that was parked on the railroad tracks. The village was platted in 1891, right after the Omaha railroad route was completed in 1890. The Commercial Hotel and the village park are seen here, as well as several other buildings, homes, and barns.

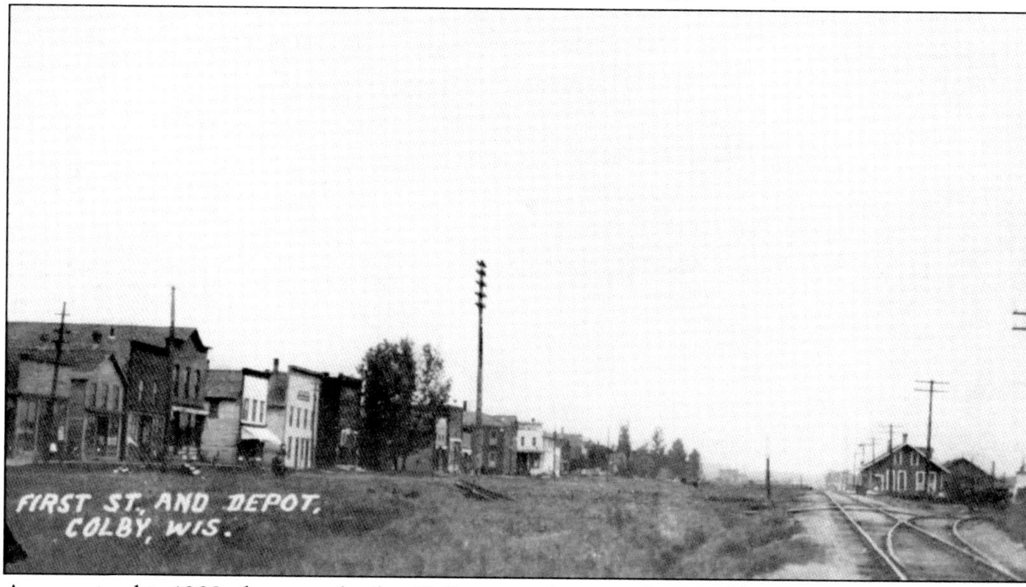

As seen in this 1909 photograph, the Colby train depot and several businesses were located on First Street. The Wisconsin Central Railroad (later the Soo Line) tracks were first built around 1873. Colby, a small community on the county line with Marathon County, had rail service before most other cities in Clark County.

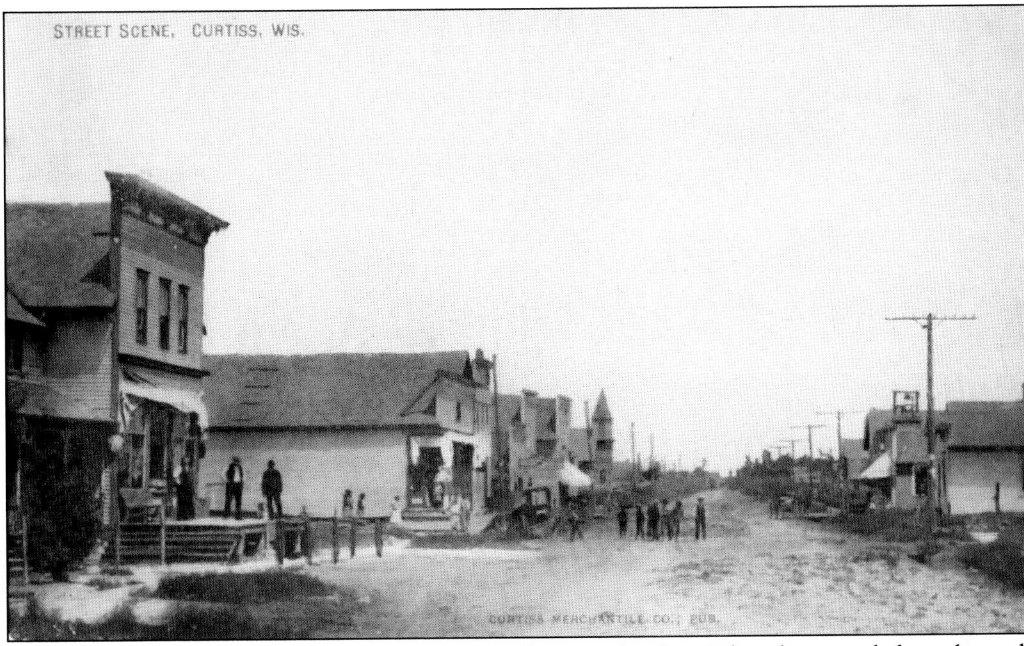

The village of Curtiss is on the Hoard and Mayville Township line. This photograph from the early 1900s shows a busy Main Street with merchants, saloons, a bank, a harness shop, a blacksmith, and a church at the end of the street. The village, platted in 1883, had a sawmill, a planing mill, a creamery, and a cheese factory.

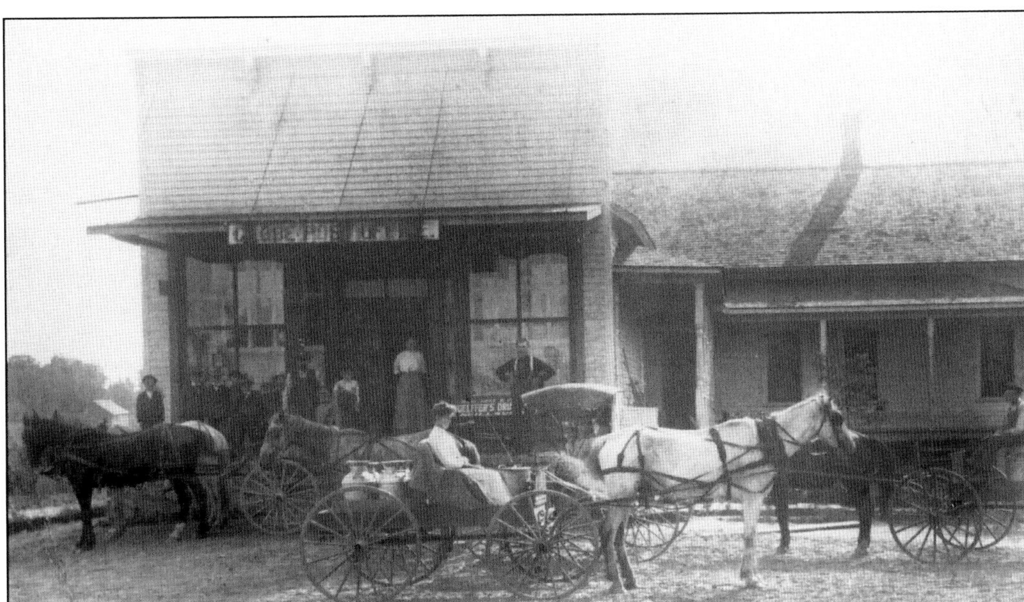

The Globe store, seen here around 1900, was about 10 miles northwest of Neillsville, at the corner of county trunk highways H, O, and G, and was known locally as HOG Corners. The Globe store also served as the post office and the home of the owner, George Rupperecht. The store was torn down years ago, and the only reminder of Globe today is the German Lutheran church.

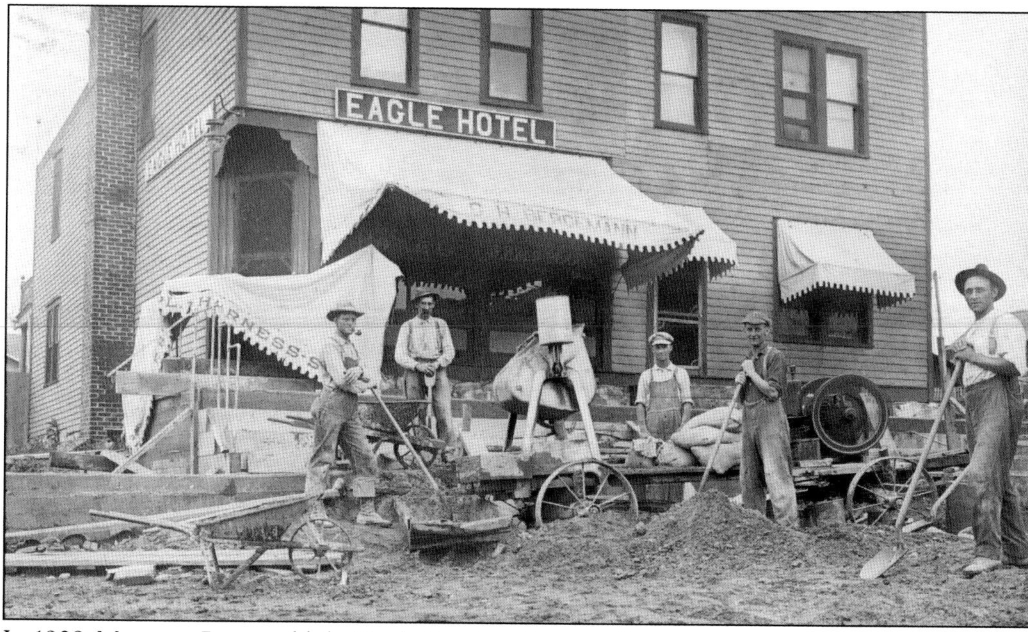

In 1908, Margaret Peters sold the Eagle Hotel to Gustave Bergemann, a man with hotel industry experience. He moved his wife and three sons to Granton from southern Wisconsin, and they had a fourth son, John, a few years later. In 1913, these men were building steps using forms and a cement mixer. They are, from left to right, Leslie Todd, Frank Gardner, Clarence Sulsbury, Delbert Gardner, and "Gus" Bergemann.

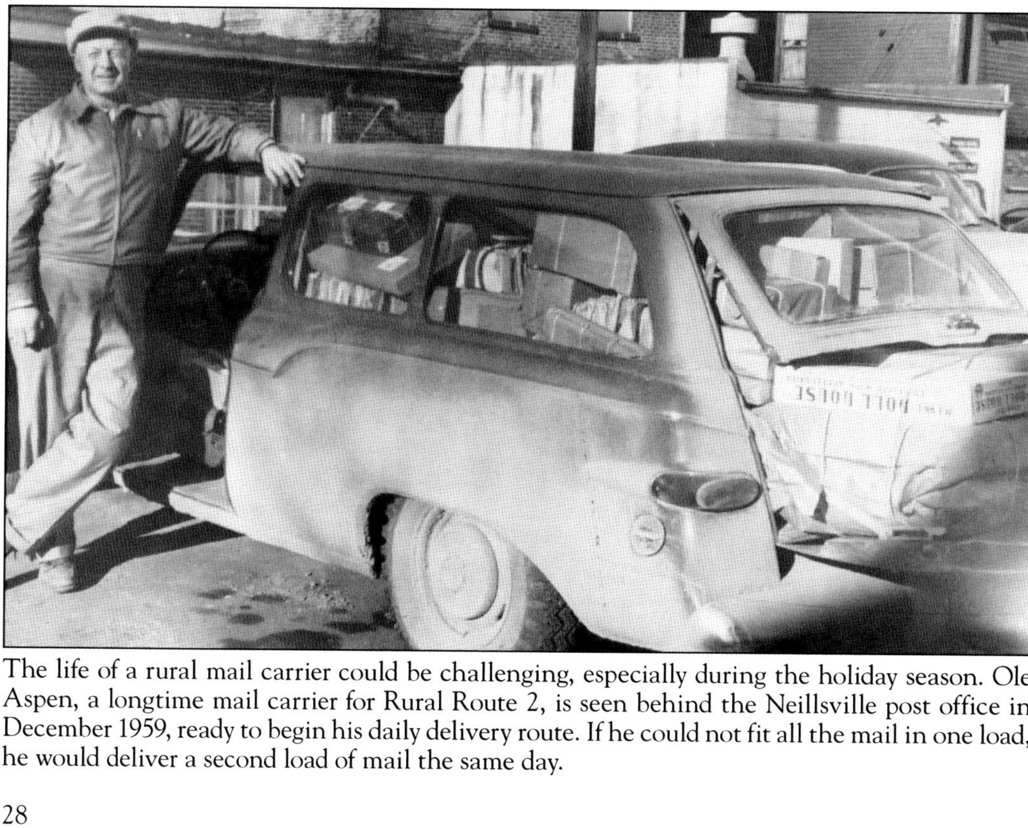

The life of a rural mail carrier could be challenging, especially during the holiday season. Ole Aspen, a longtime mail carrier for Rural Route 2, is seen behind the Neillsville post office in December 1959, ready to begin his daily delivery route. If he could not fit all the mail in one load, he would deliver a second load of mail the same day.

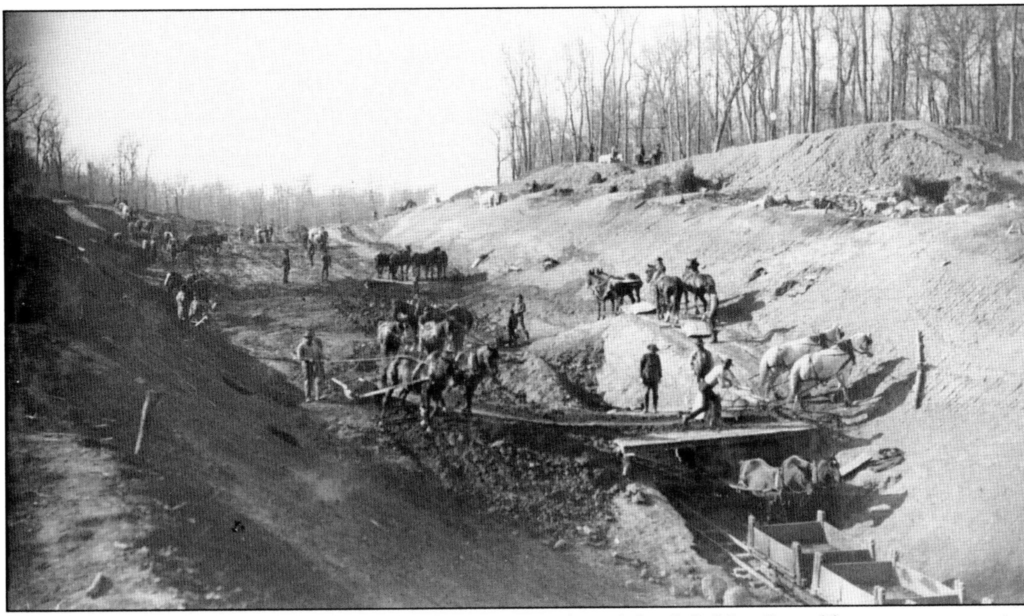

In 1886, the Wisconsin Central Railroad train route from Marshfield to Loyal began construction on a new railroad track from Loyal to Greenwood. Three miles west of Loyal, workers had to deal with a section of land called the Big Cut, seen here. It reportedly took 100 workers, 50 teams of horses, and more than three months to excavate this section of land for a train bed.

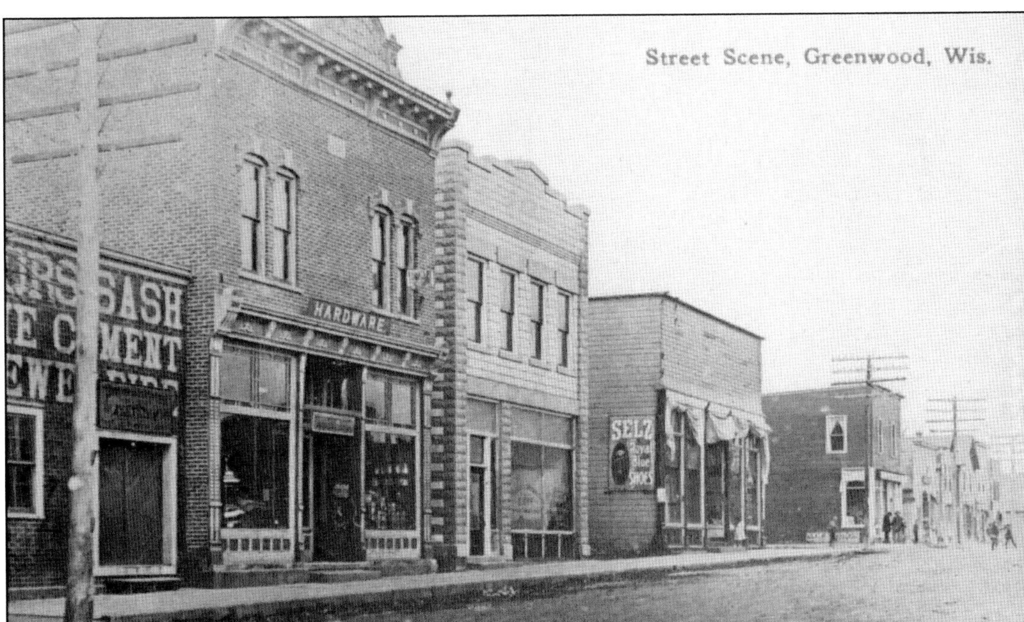

Seen here in 1910, Division Street in Greenwood had a busy group of merchants. Businesses included, from left to right, a sash, cement and sewer pipe store, the A.M. White hardware store, Farmers and Merchants Bank, the John Arend Grocery, and the Volk Bros. tailor shop.

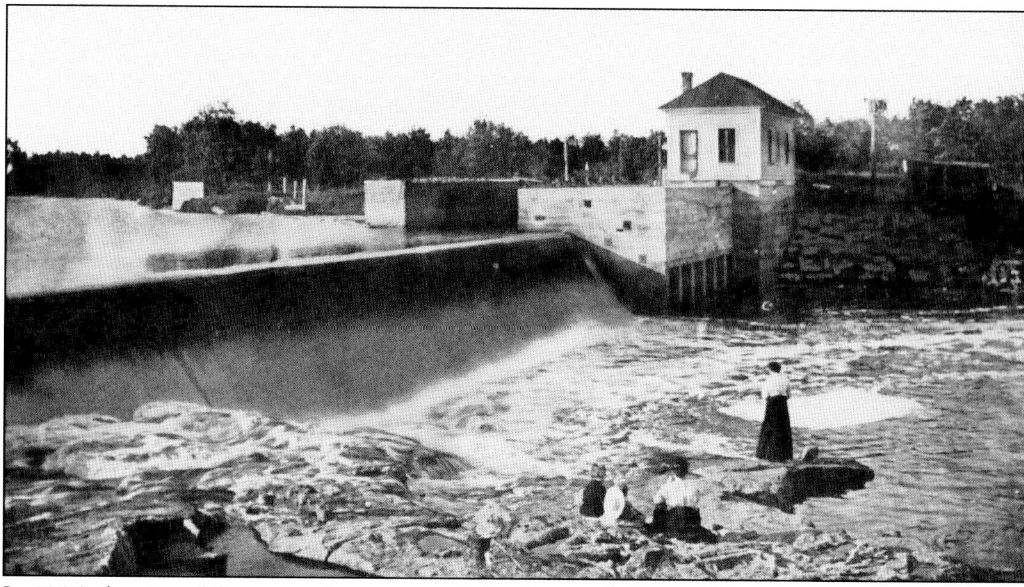

In 1906, the city of Greenwood constructed this dam and electrical power plant across the Black River. In 1914, high floodwaters caused the sandy soil around the plant to wash out, leaving the building in the middle of the river. Repairs were made, and the 60-kilowatt plant continued to serve the area until 1919, when the Northern States Light and Power Company brought service to Greenwood.

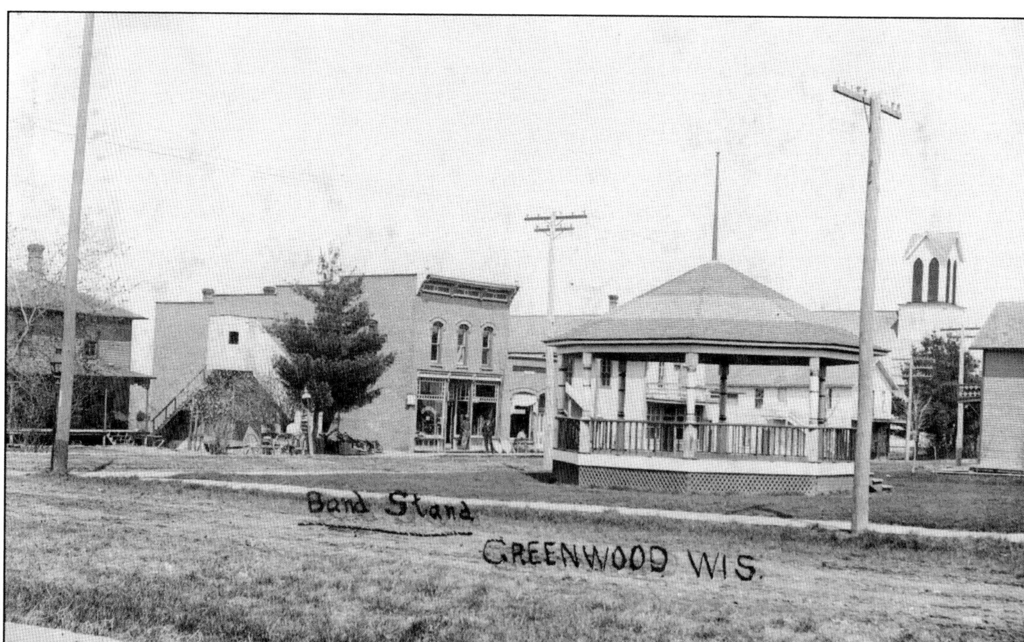

This lovely community bandstand was in downtown Greenwood. Seen here around 1910, the bandstand held many open-air concerts, usually in the summer months, and was used in conjunction with picnics and parades. The Greenwood High School band program provided many fine musicians, many of whom played at this community gathering place.

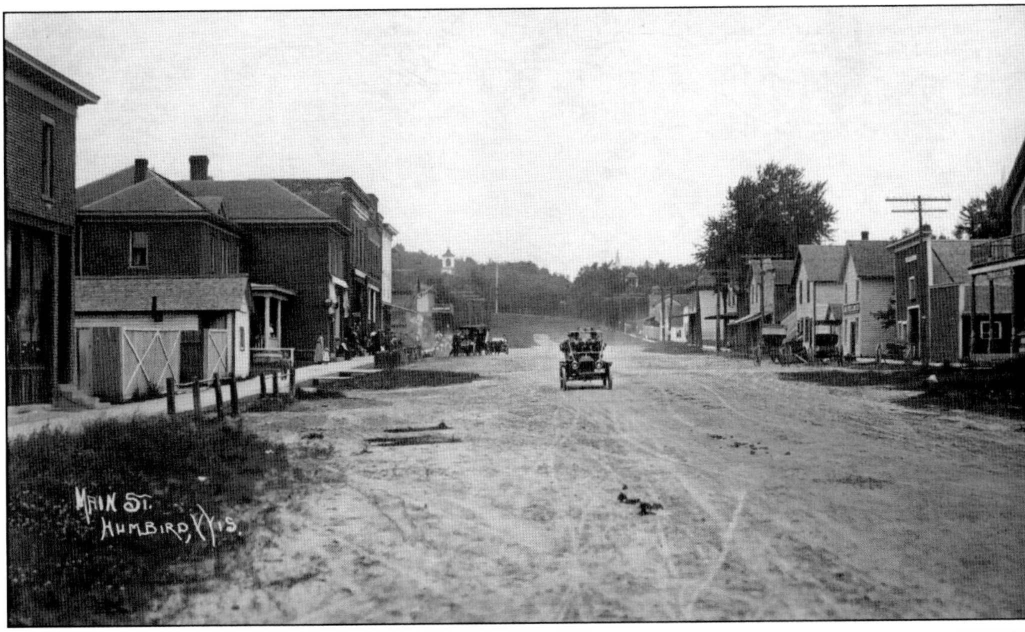

In 1869, the village of Humbird was already a busy community. In 1872, when the railroad came through town, it became a major hub of commerce. Merchants sold goods and services to citizens and to the many lumber camps in the area, while hotels and shops met the needs of the many train passengers. This photograph from around 1915 of Humbird shows the many businesses lining Main Street.

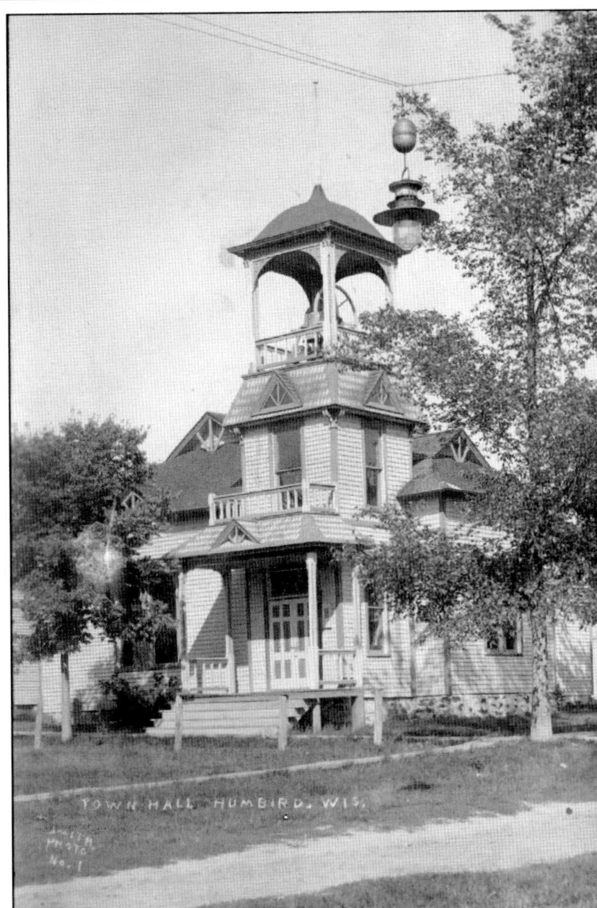

The village of Humbird was a vibrant community in the early 1900s, with many merchants, churches, and schools. The town hall, seen here, was the gathering place for almost all town events in that time. Besides holding local government meetings, it also hosted community events, funeral services, and dances.

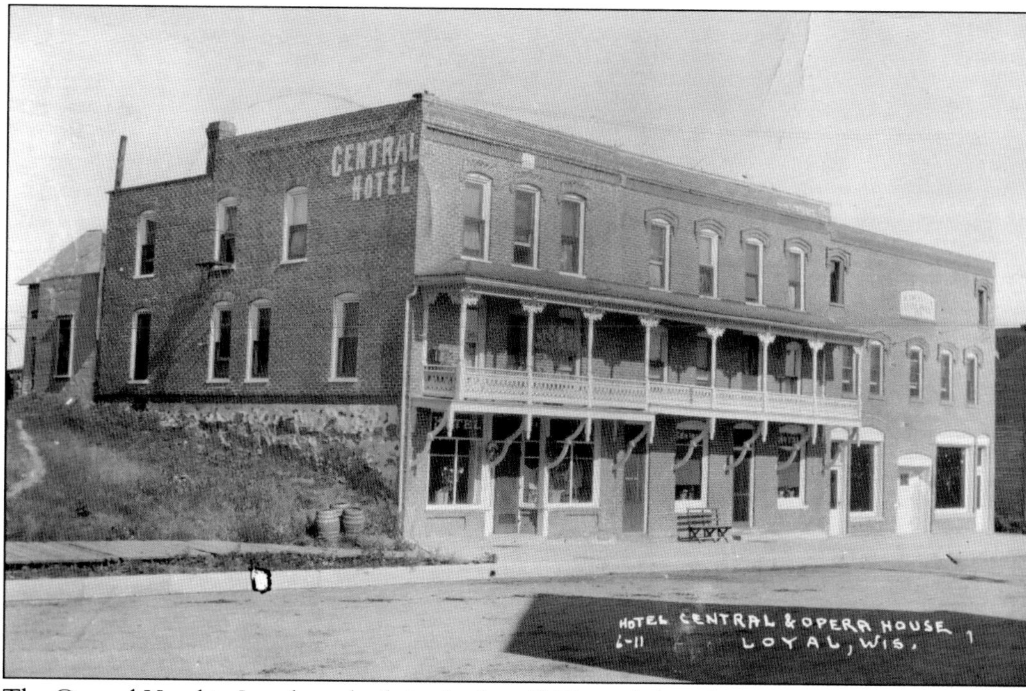

The Central Hotel in Loyal was built in the late 1800s, and the adjoining opera house was built around 1910. In 1914, Fred and Mary Voight bought both properties from Aaron Blumenstein. The Voights operated the hotel for several years, but the opera house burned to the ground in 1924. After the fire, the vacant lot was made into a pretty flower garden that was enjoyed by everyone.

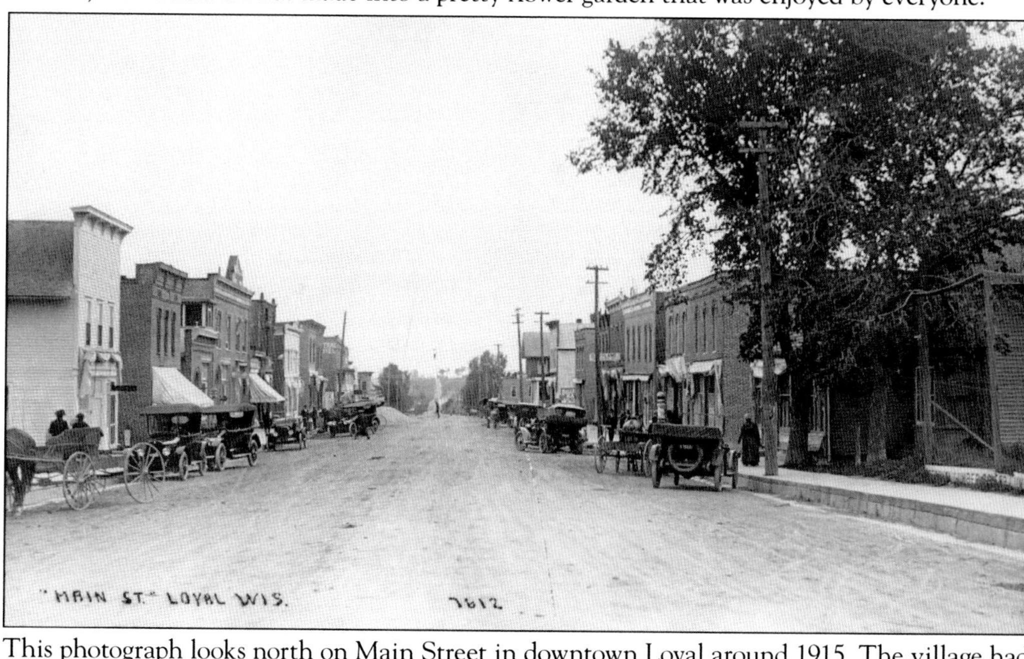

This photograph looks north on Main Street in downtown Loyal around 1915. The village had nice sidewalks and a wide variety of businesses, including a hardware store, the hotel and opera house, a general store, a barbershop, and a millinery shop. Customers to the downtown businesses arrived on horses and wagons or in their new automobiles.

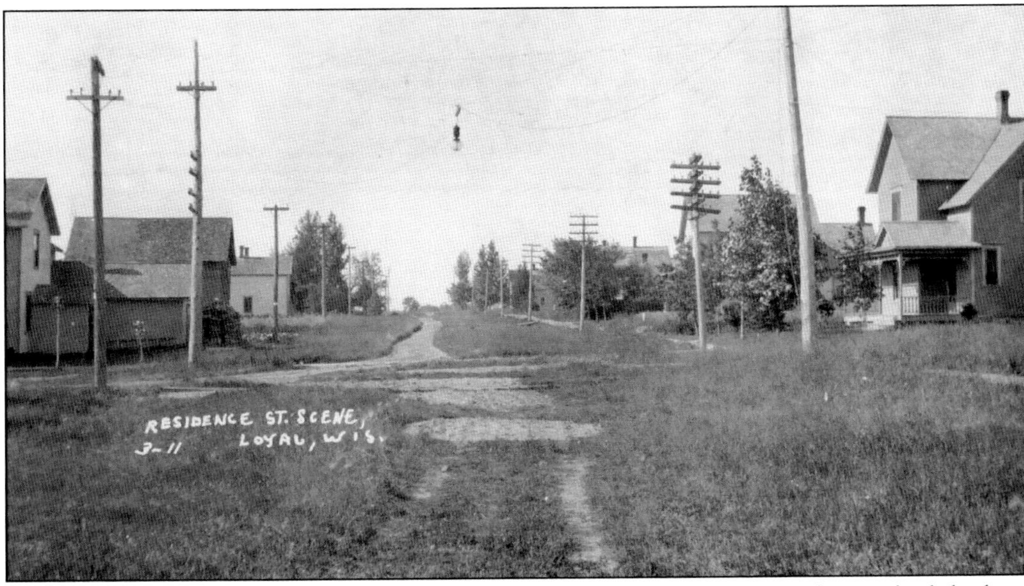

This view of a street in the village of Loyal around 1915 shows many nice houses built by local residents. Electrical service was available for homes, and the neighborhood even had a streetlamp over the intersection. Judging by the dirt trail down the center of the street, it is easy to imagine how many times the same path was taken by horses, buggies, and automobiles.

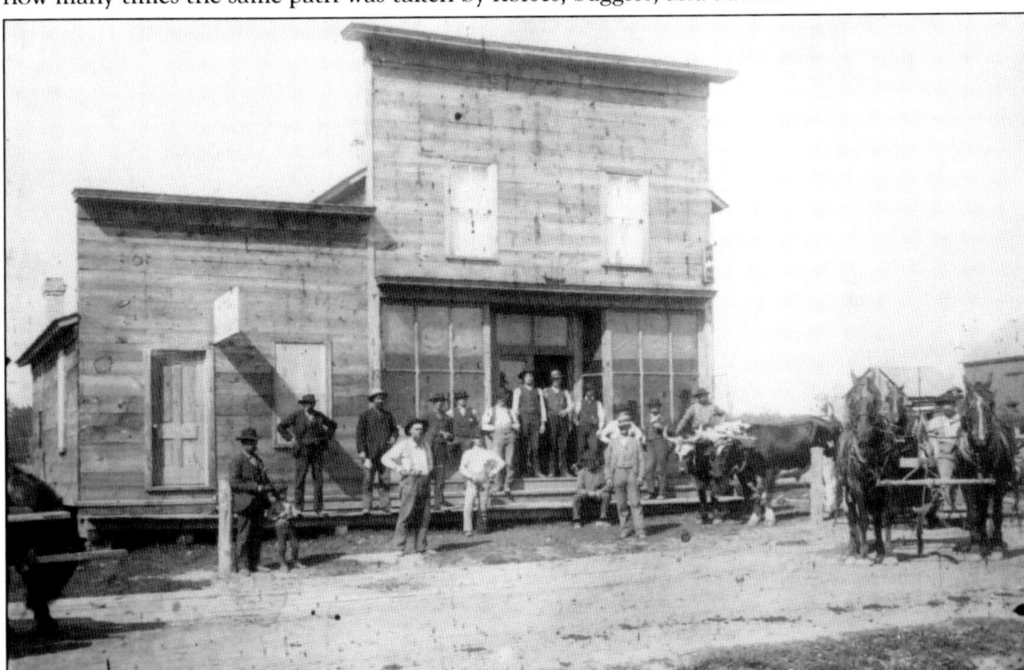

In 1866, the tavern in Lynn was owned by the McConnel brothers, seen here in the saloon doorway. Frequent customers were workers from two area railroad companies, each constructing a railroad line that would intersect at Omaha Crossing. One group was building a west-to-east line, and the other was building a south-to-north line. The group that reached the intersection last would pay the cost of construction for the intersection crossing.

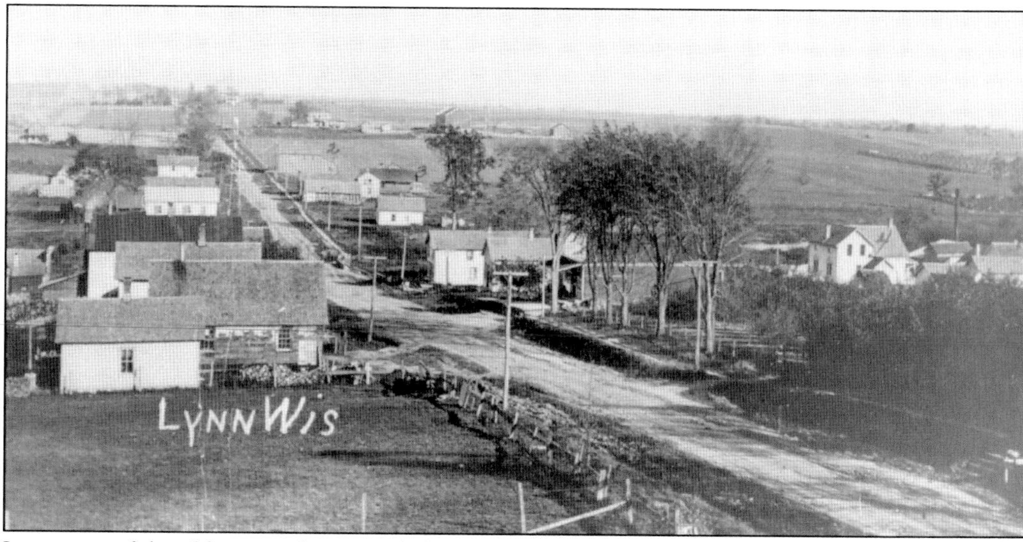

Lynn, one of the older townships in Clark County, was first settled by families like the Sternitzkys, Kleinschmidts, Yankees, Marshes, Nelsons, Levis, and Brookses. This photograph looks east in Lynn in March 1912, towards Chili and Marshfield. The white building on the far right was the Lynn Dairy.

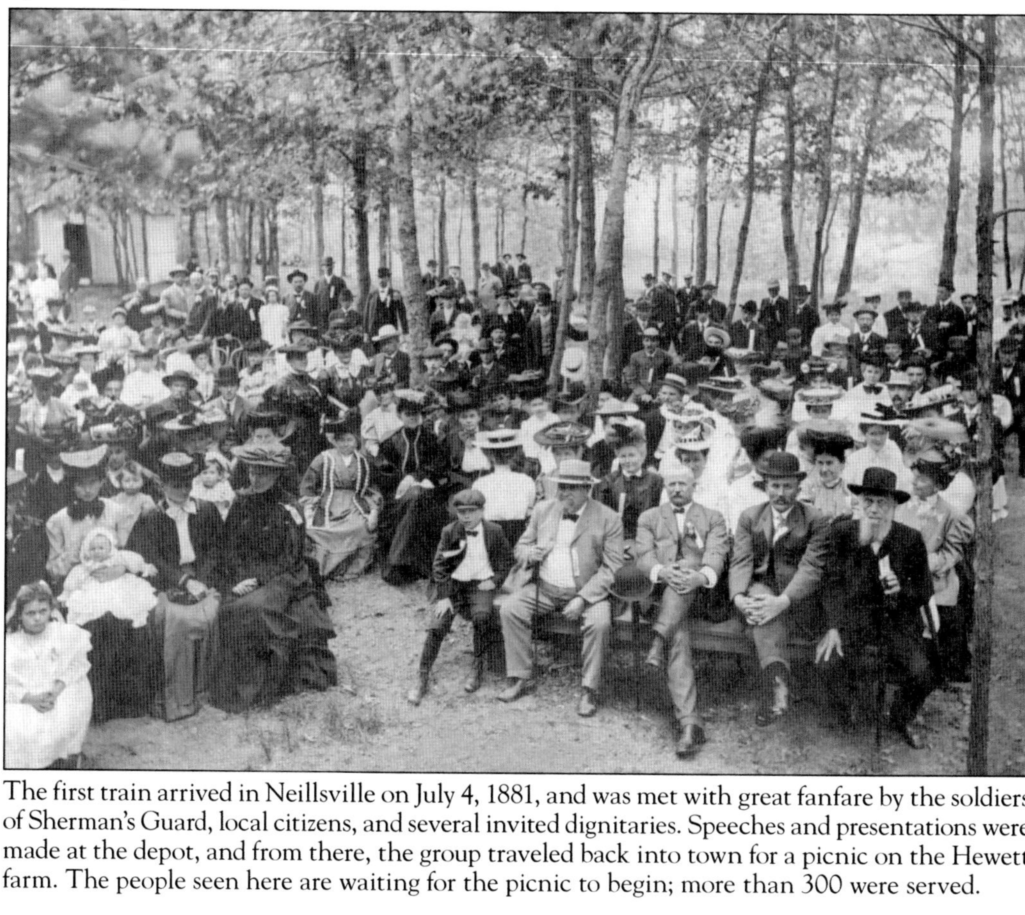

The first train arrived in Neillsville on July 4, 1881, and was met with great fanfare by the soldiers of Sherman's Guard, local citizens, and several invited dignitaries. Speeches and presentations were made at the depot, and from there, the group traveled back into town for a picnic on the Hewett farm. The people seen here are waiting for the picnic to begin; more than 300 were served.

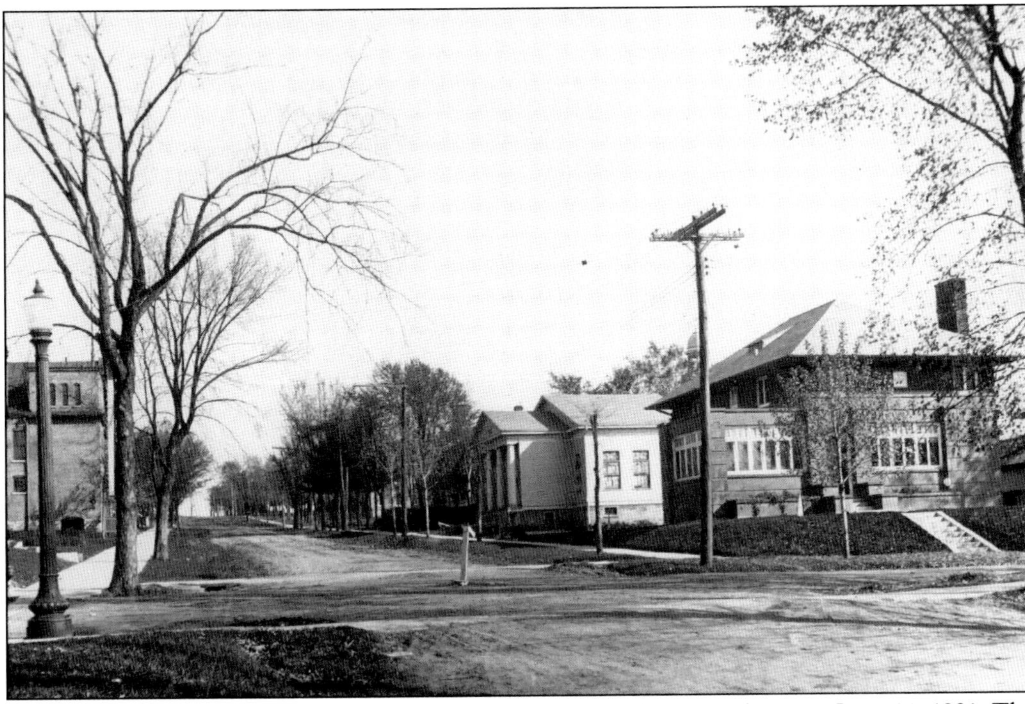

The intersection of Hewett and Fourth Street in Neillsville is seen here on June 14, 1921. The house on the right belonged to Charles C. Sniteman, the local pharmacist. He commissioned Chicago architect George Awsumb to design his new home in a style that would complement the Neillsville Carnegie Library, across the street, which Awsumb also designed.

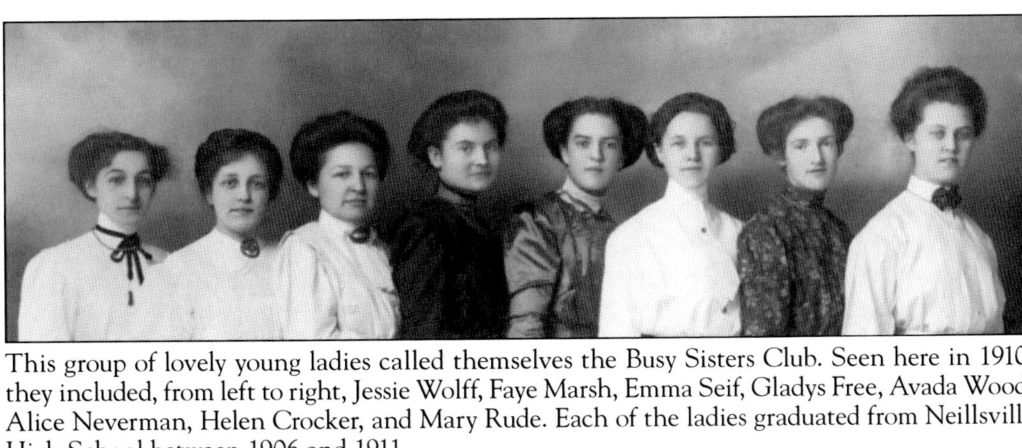

This group of lovely young ladies called themselves the Busy Sisters Club. Seen here in 1910, they included, from left to right, Jessie Wolff, Faye Marsh, Emma Seif, Gladys Free, Avada Wood, Alice Neverman, Helen Crocker, and Mary Rude. Each of the ladies graduated from Neillsville High School between 1906 and 1911.

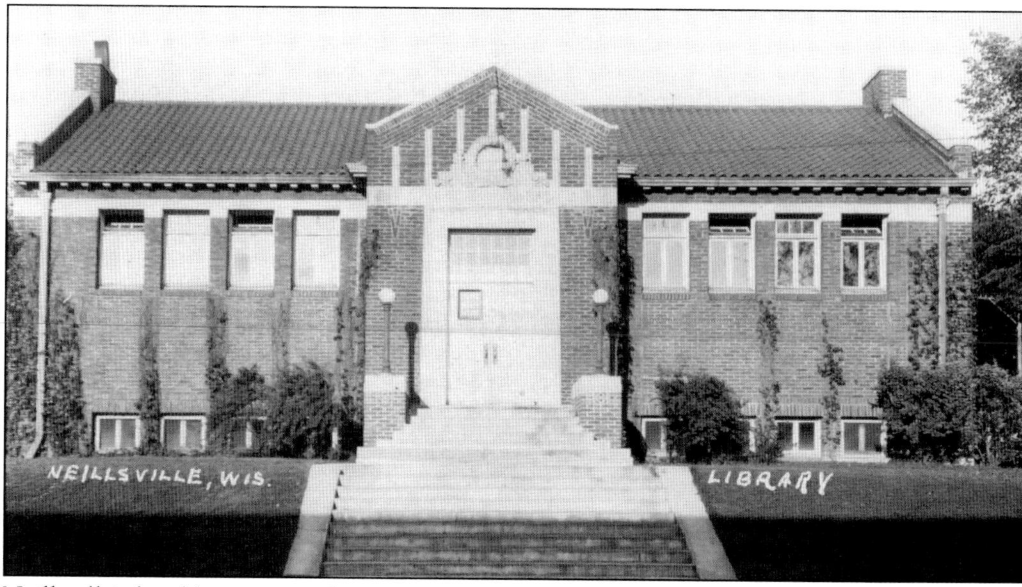

Neillsville's first library opened in 1897, and operated out of Neillsville High School until 1914. Ida Hommel, a resident of Neillsville and a former Carnegie family daughter-in-law, sent word that $10,000 could be received for a new Carnegie public library if the city agreed to pay $1,000 per year to maintain the library. The new library was completed in 1914 and is still used today.

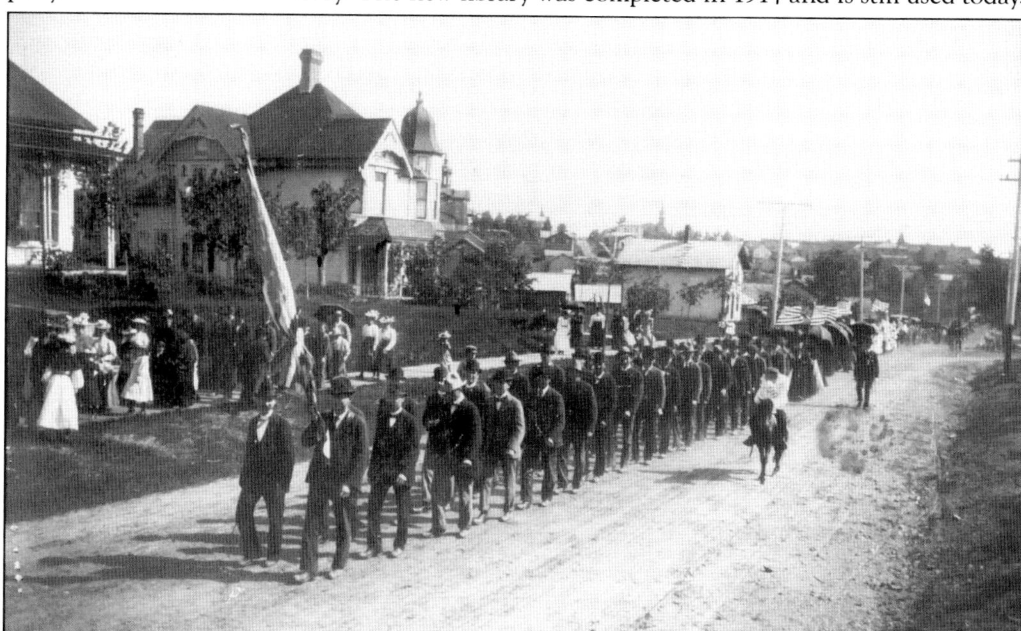

Funerals of beloved citizens usually involved the entire community. This long line of mourners walks north on Hewett Street near Twelfth Street, towards the Neillsville Cemetery. Though the deceased was not identified, the fourth man in line, wearing a white hat, was most likely J.W. "Tom" Hommel, the husband of Ida Hommel and the commander of the local National Guard unit.

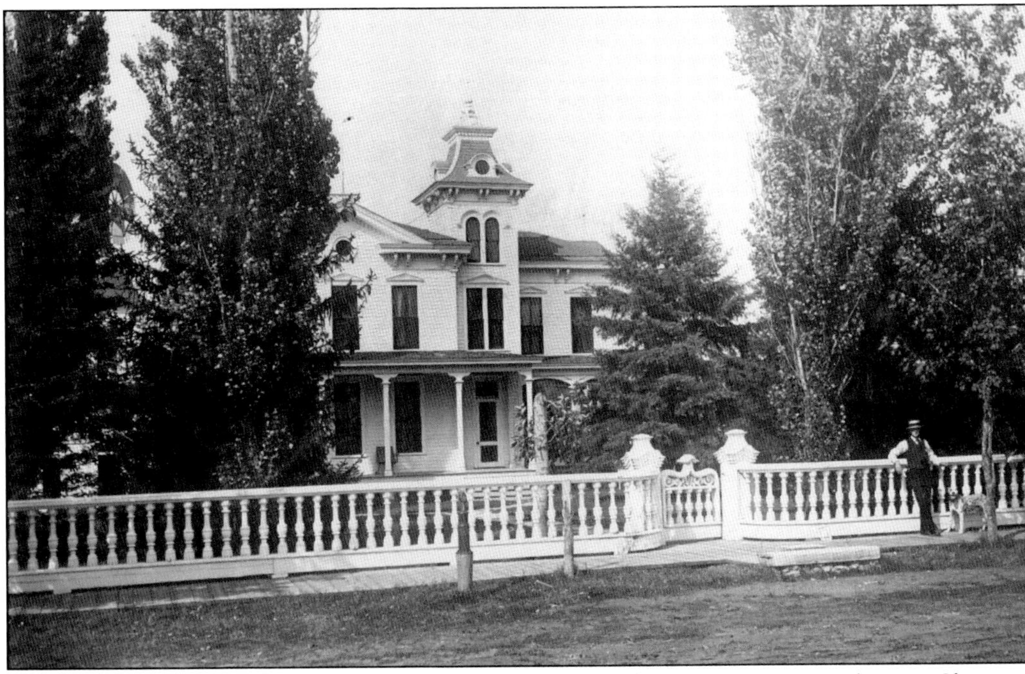

In 1874, James Hewett built this home at a cost of about $10,000. Years later, his son Sherman "Frank" Hewett and his family made it their home as well. Unfortunately, in the late 1940s, the grand home was destroyed by a fire that started in the third-floor turret. St. John's Lutheran Church later built a new church on this same lot, on West Fifth Street in Neillsville.

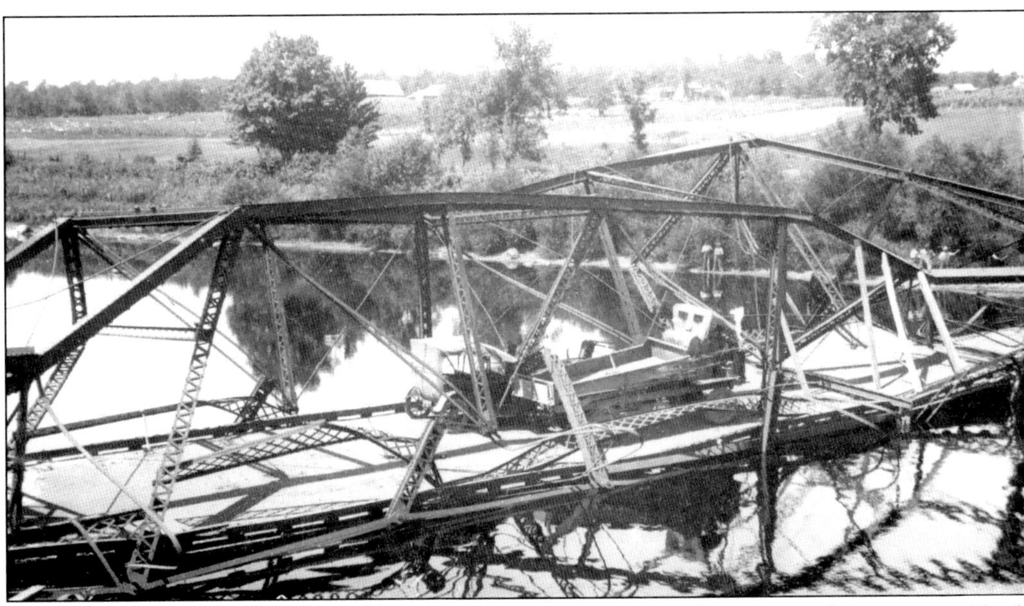

On August 2, 1920, the Black River Bridge, north of Neillsville on Grand Avenue, suddenly collapsed. Three of the vehicles on the bridge were able to escape damage, but a fourth was struck by falling debris, which instantly killed the driver. Some very early bridges could not handle heavy loads or multiple vehicles, since they were originally built for horses, wagons, and buggies.

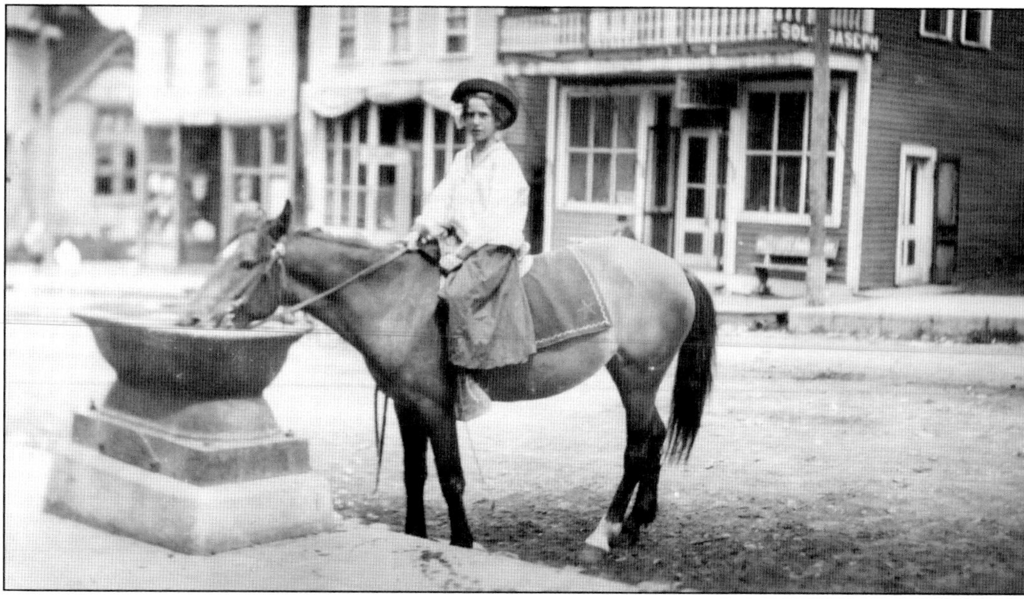

Ruth Whitcomb waters her horse at a public water trough outside the Neillsville city hall, on West Fifth Street, around 1900. Whitcomb was a talented violinist, performing in the local Whitcomb Orchestra at many area weddings and social events. Later, as a young woman, she moved to Nebraska, playing with different orchestras as a lead violinist.

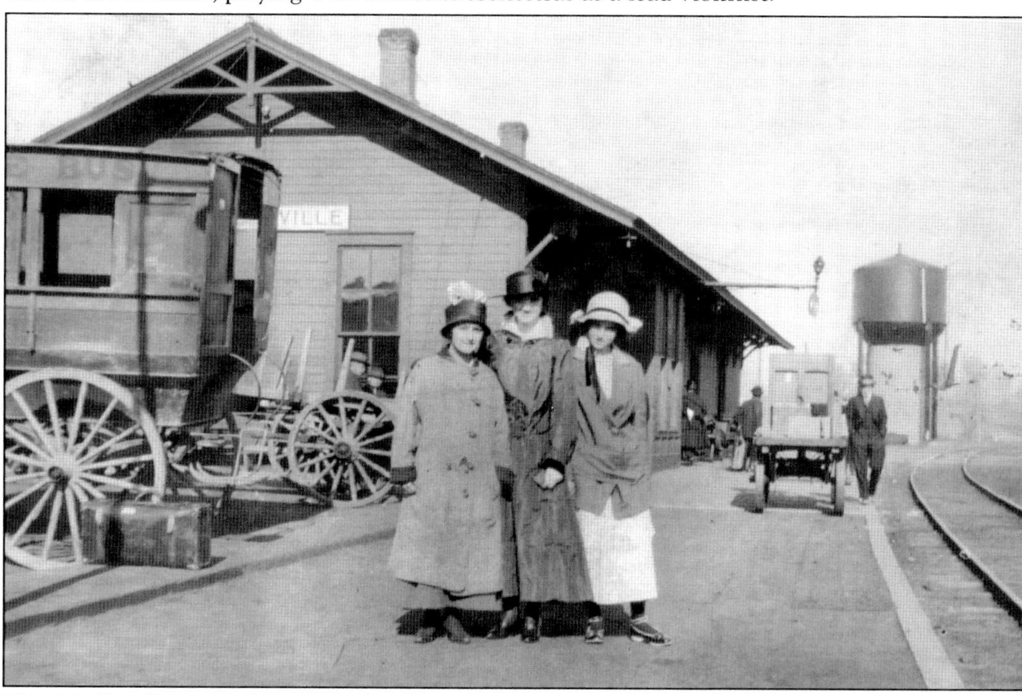

The Neillsville train depot saw freight and passenger cars arrive several times a day in the early 1930s. Isabelle (Helwig) Pietenpol (center) is seen here awaiting the next train with two unidentified friends. The bus on the left was available to transport people wherever they needed to go, while baggage handlers helped with luggage and packages as needed. (Courtesy of the Dick and Joanne Tibbett collection.)

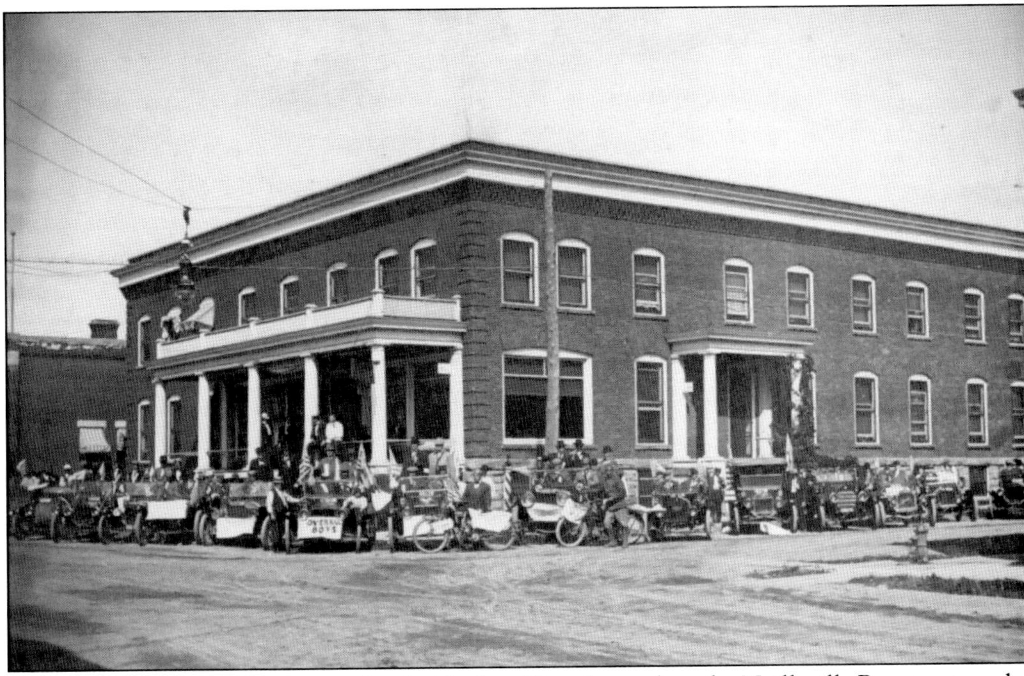

On September 12, 1912, a group of individuals calling themselves the Neillsville Boosters traveled from town to town encouraging their fellow county citizens to attend the upcoming Clark County Fair. Seen here outside the Woodland Hotel in Owen, the boosters, in their decorated automobiles, appear to be enjoying their afternoon ride.

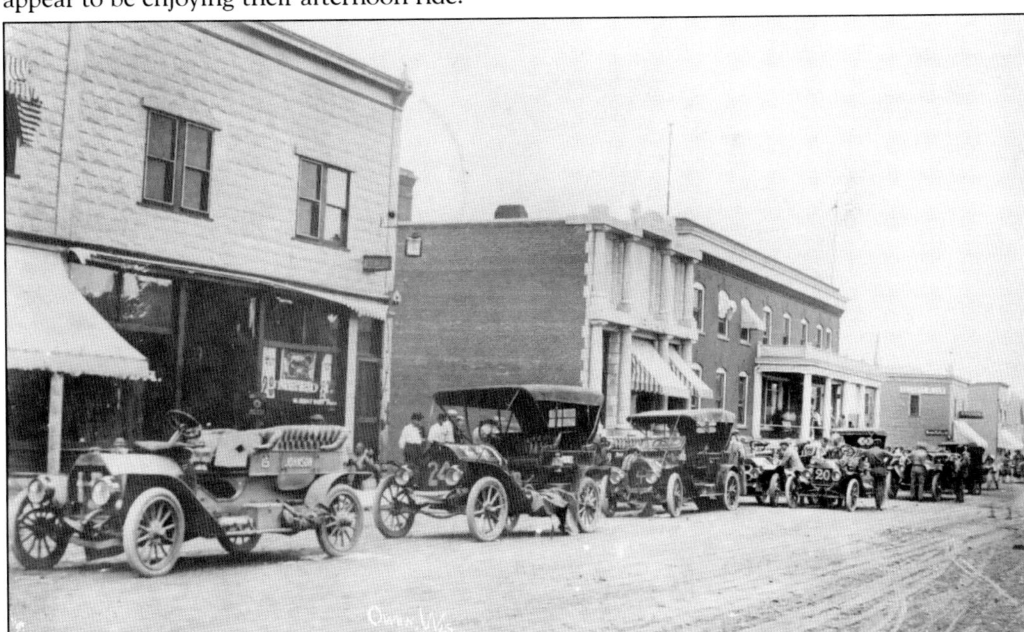

These automobiles were parked in Owen in 1911, as their drivers stopped for a break. Each automobile was labeled with a number and a name, like the "15 Johnson" written on the first car on the left. In those days, it was common for friends to race as they drove their open-style touring cars on sunny days. If it did start to rain, drivers were glad for windows or a roof.

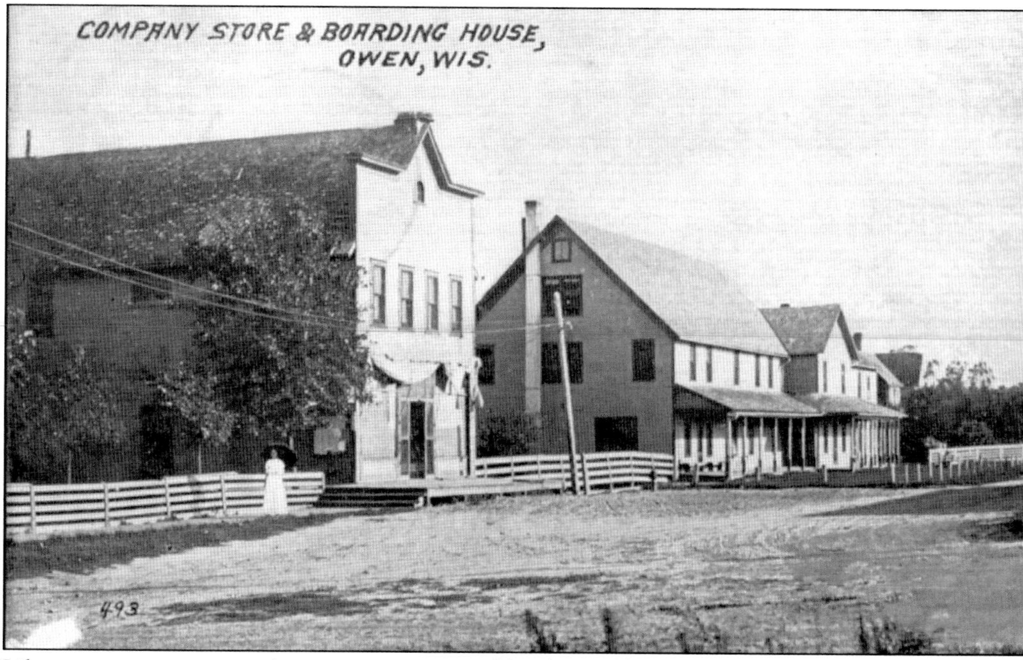

Like many communities that sprang up around lumber mills, the village of Owen had a company store and a boardinghouse for the mill workers to use. The John S. Owen Lumber Company store and boardinghouse is seen here. After working long hours with little time off, the mill workers usually bought what they needed at the company store and lived in company housing.

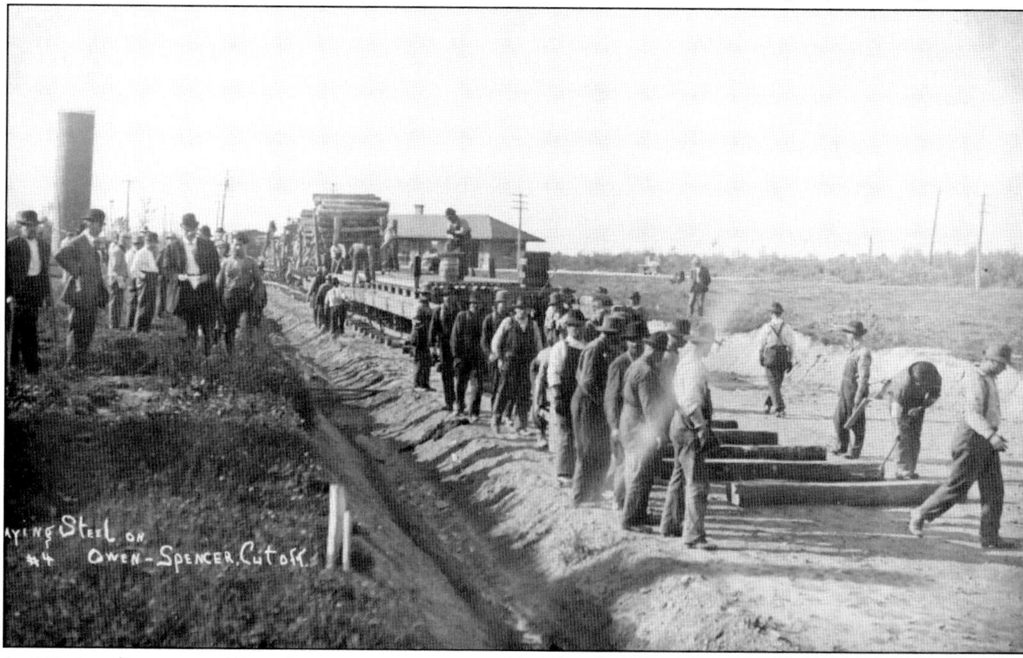

In 1910, a direct cutoff, or shortcut, route was added by the Wisconsin Central Railroad between Owen and Spencer. This new track allowed trains from the Minneapolis-St. Paul or the Duluth-Superior routes to bypass Abbotsford and run directly into Spencer. These men prepare the railroad track bed and lay logs and steel for the tracks. (Courtesy of the David Jankoski collection.)

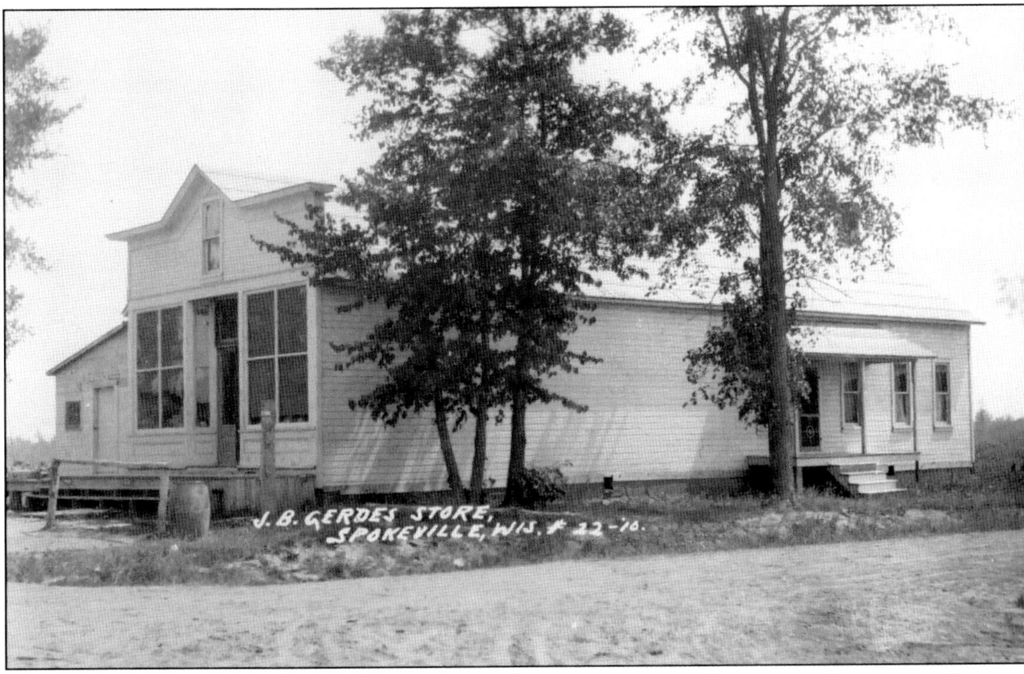

Spokeville, just a few miles southeast of Loyal, was a stagecoach stop on the way to Spencer in the early 1900s. The John B. Gerdes store, seen here, was built in 1909 and carried general merchandise and supplies. The community also had a saloon, a creamery and cheese factory, an elevator, a school, a church, and a spoke mill.

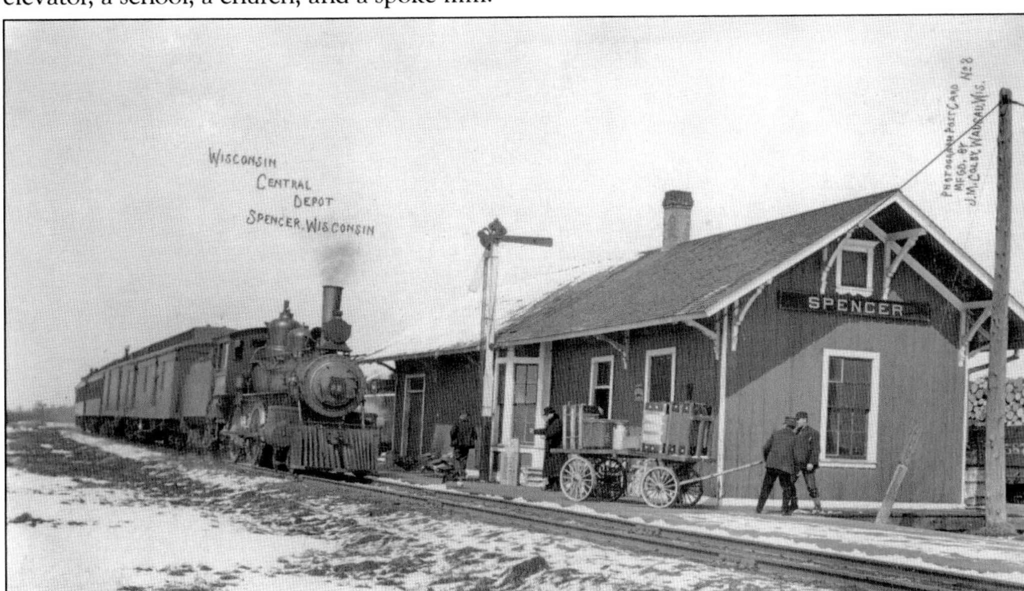

Spencer's first settlers arrived in 1871, when the Wisconsin Central Railroad extended the line from Stevens Point. Families and businesses soon followed, and by 1874, Spencer had schools, churches, and a new city government. The addition of the Owen-Spencer cutoff route in 1910 also brought changes to the city. Improvements and additions were made to the railroad depot, and Spencer continued to grow.

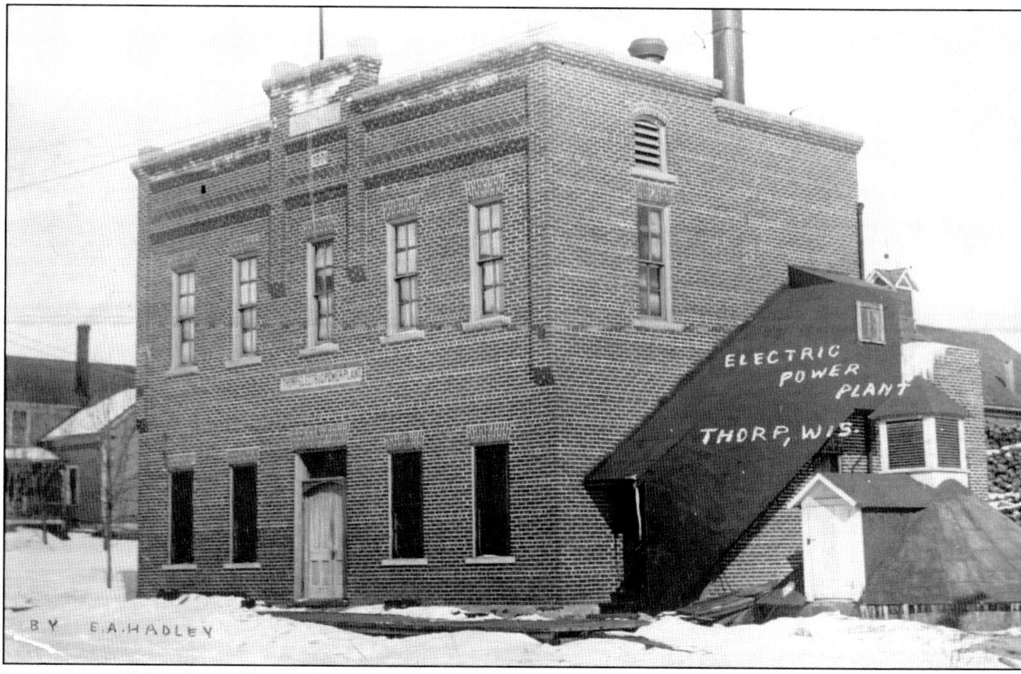

In August 1901, the village of Thorp started building a new electric power plant. Seen here, the plant's powerhouse was a 30-foot-by-50-foot brick building with an attached boiler room in the back. Crews began setting the power poles and installing the lines, and service to area citizens and businesses began in early October 1901.

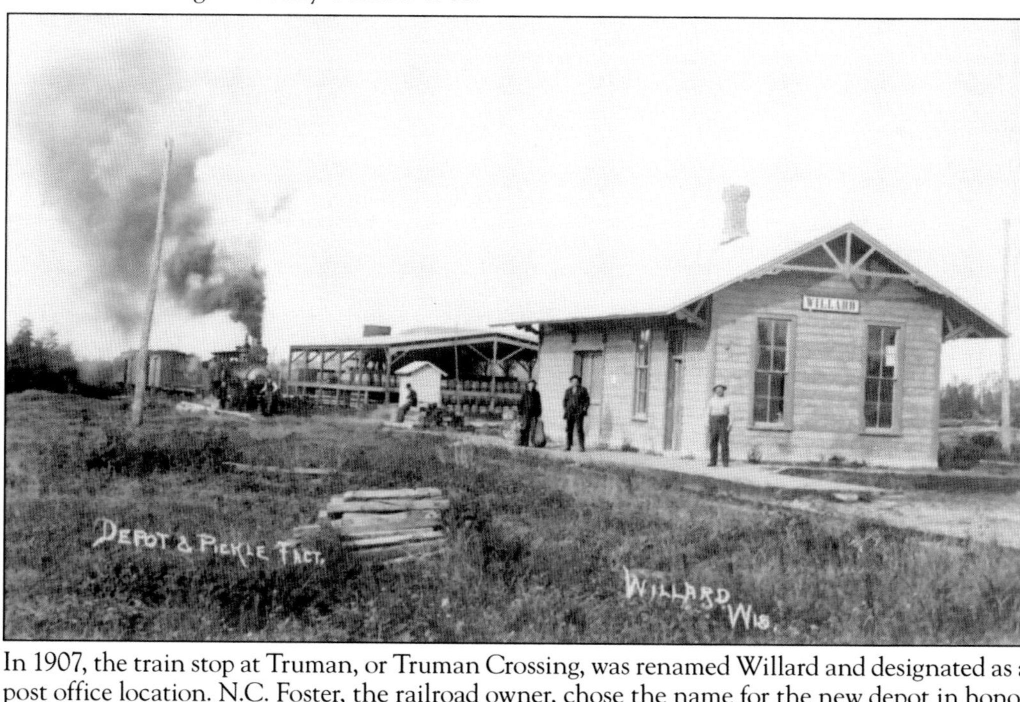

In 1907, the train stop at Truman, or Truman Crossing, was renamed Willard and designated as a post office location. N.C. Foster, the railroad owner, chose the name for the new depot in honor of his oldest son. Here, around 1910, an inbound train passes the pickle factory as it pulls into the new Willard depot. (Courtesy of the Willard Historical Society.)

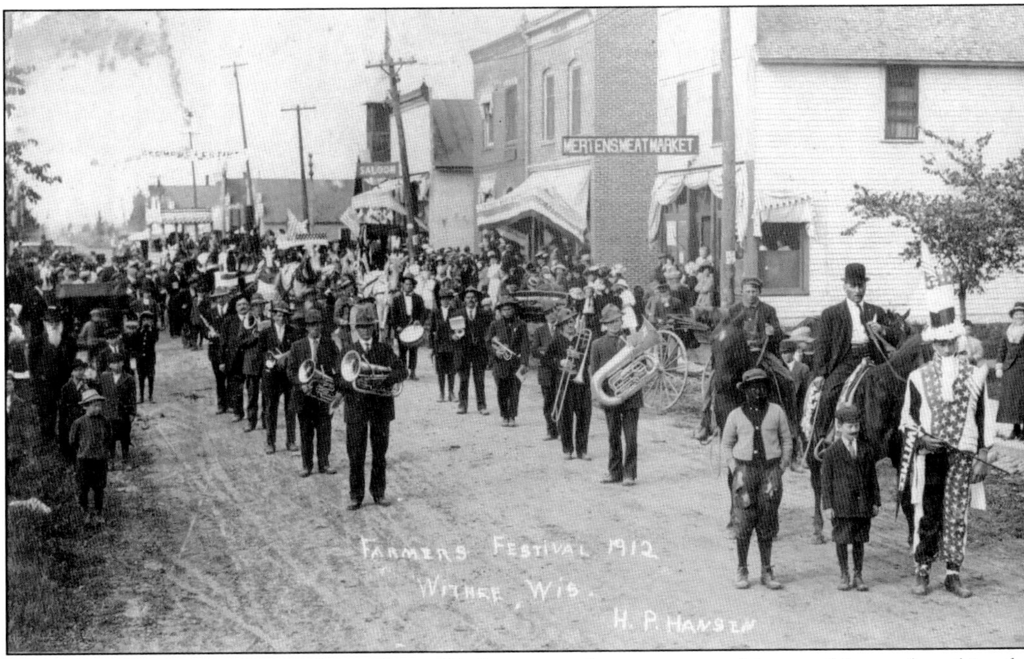

In 1912, the Farmer's Festival parade in Withee was a huge success. Men and boys played in the marching band, and floats were decorated in grand style. Community events like this one usually included a fun parade, good food, and visiting with friends. On the right, spectators watch the parade from the front stoop of Mertens Meat Market. (Courtesy of the David Jankoski collection.)

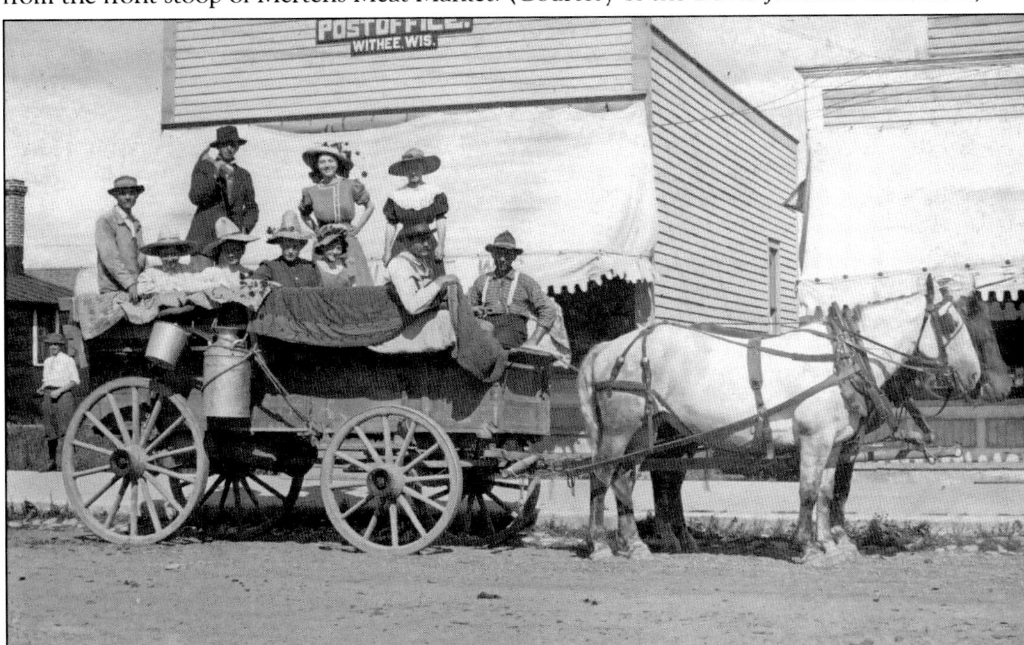

This group of young people had everything they needed to go berry picking on a summer day in the 1930s. The ladies had hats to protect them from the sun, milk pails and cans to put picked berries in, and probably a picnic lunch. However, the most important part about picking berries was knowing the location of the best berry patches.

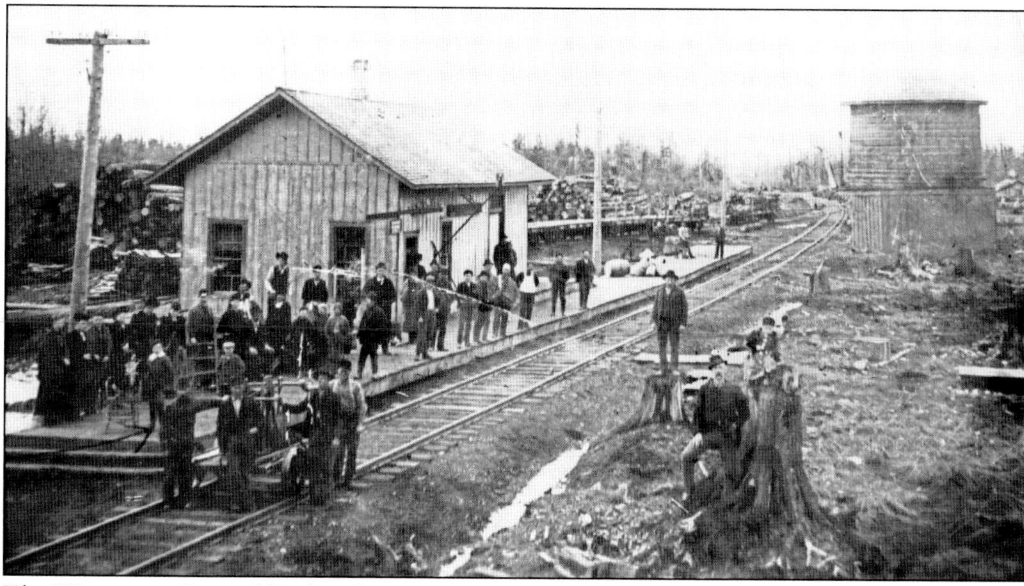

The Wisconsin Central Railroad train route from Chippewa Falls to Abbotsford first stopped in Withee on November 23, 1880. At that time, train engines were powered by steam, so depot agents needed to make sure that water and cut wood were available as trains arrived. In this 1893 photograph, the man standing on the far left of the tracks, in front of the handcar, is identified as Christ Jensen, the section foreman.

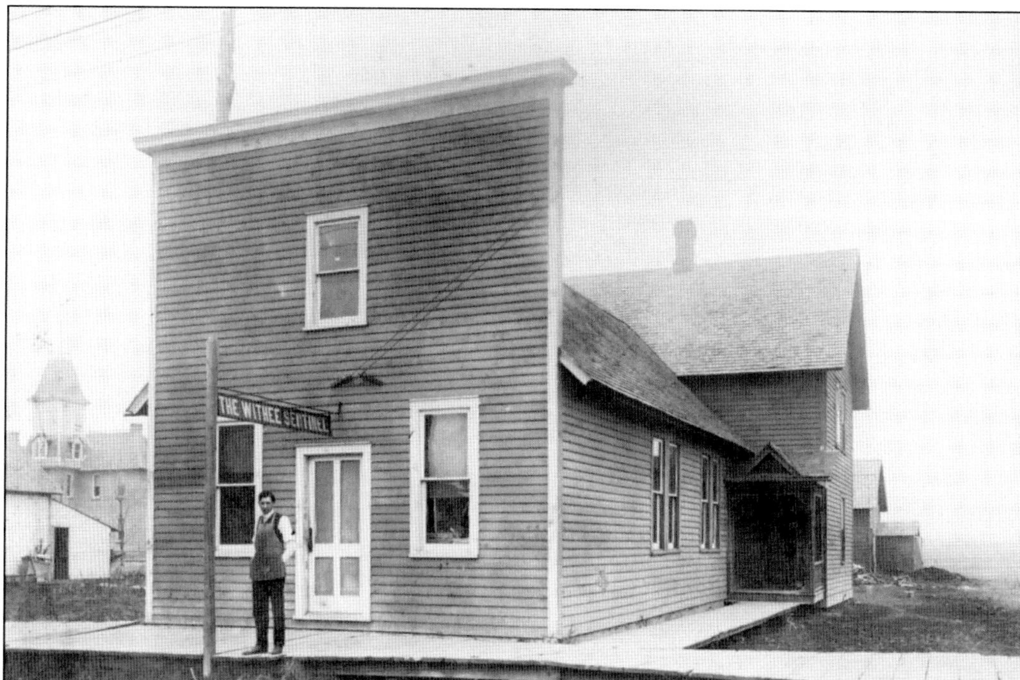

In 1902, James Barager founded the *Withee Sentinel*, which he ran with his wife, Anne, until his death a year later. Anne Barager then took over as publisher and editor. With the help of her three sons, Vernon, Miles, and Irving, she ran the newspaper until 1912, when she sold it to new owners and bought the *Owen Enterprise* together with Vernon.

Three

Government, Education, and Churches

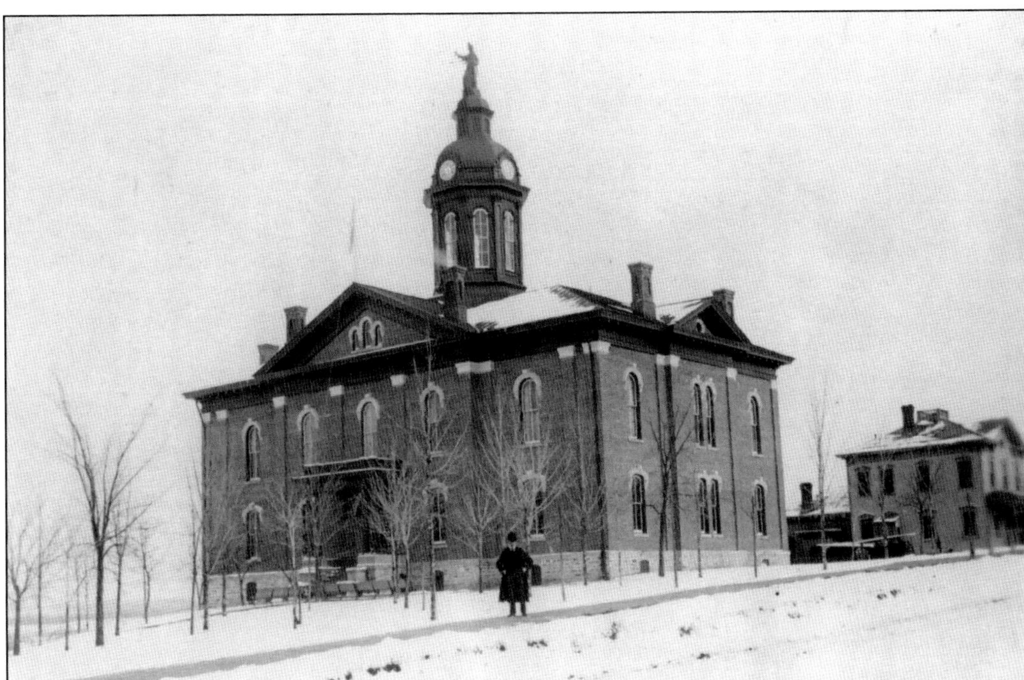

Clark County's second courthouse was built in 1876 at a cost of $35,000. Standing on top of the courthouse dome is Lady Justice. This dignified and inspiring figure was originally carved out of wood, but once it deteriorated, a replacement metal figure was made. The house on the right was the sheriff's residence, with the county jail directly behind it.

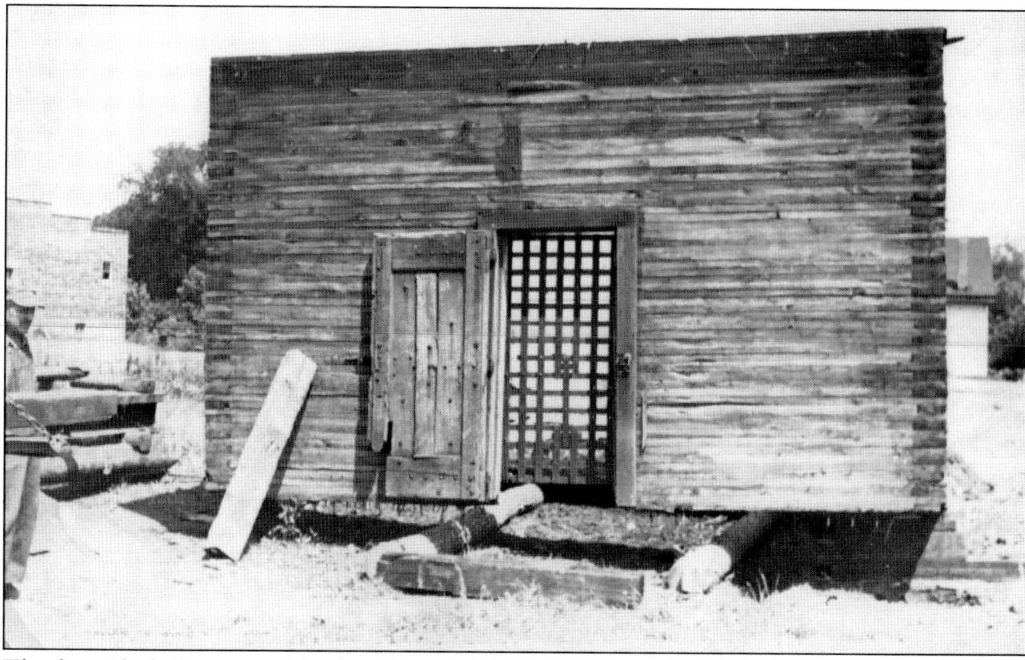

The first Clark County jail, built in 1866, was an unusual structure made of wooden planks and heavily studded with sharp spikes. The one door opened into a single large room with several small cells in it. In 1882, the county sold the jail to the City of Neillsville, and it was moved to city hall. Seen here is what was left of the old jail in the 1950s.

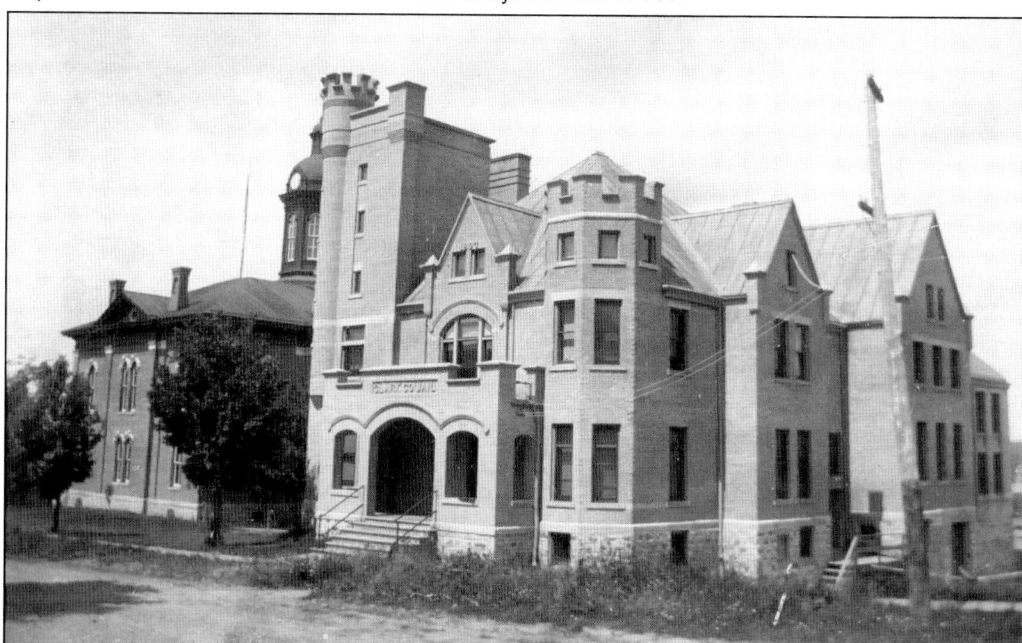

In 1897, Clark County completed the construction of its third jail and sheriff's residence, on the southeast corner of the courthouse square. Seen here, the new structure was built just east of the courthouse. The path between the courthouse and the jail was sometimes called the Path of Sighs. It is easy to image prisoners sighing to themselves after their day in court.

The 1897 county jail had modern amenities like heat, lights, and a sewage system. It was also built to be as fireproof as possible, with brick walls, a stone foundation, and steel and iron. The brick exterior work was done by the local stonemasons seen here. Seated from left to right are John "William" Ketel, August Ketel, and Herman Ketel. The four men standing are unidentified.

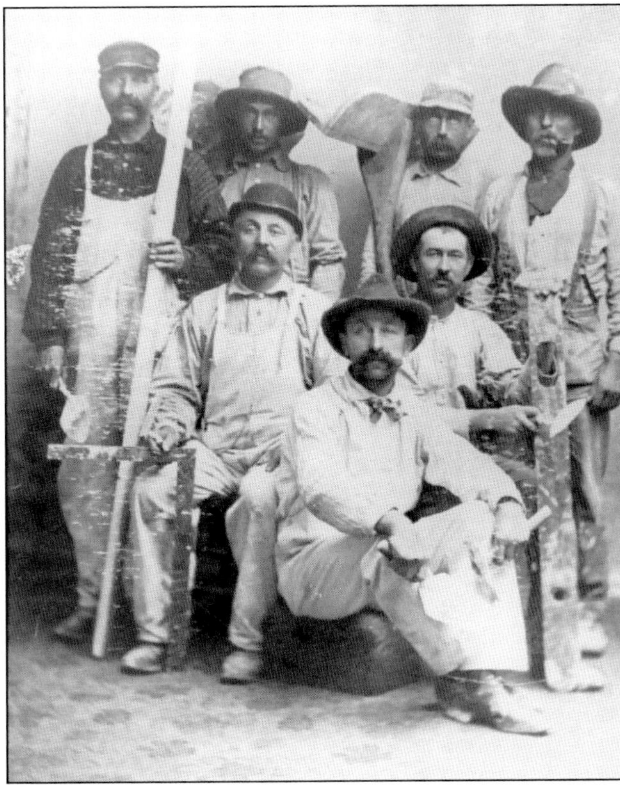

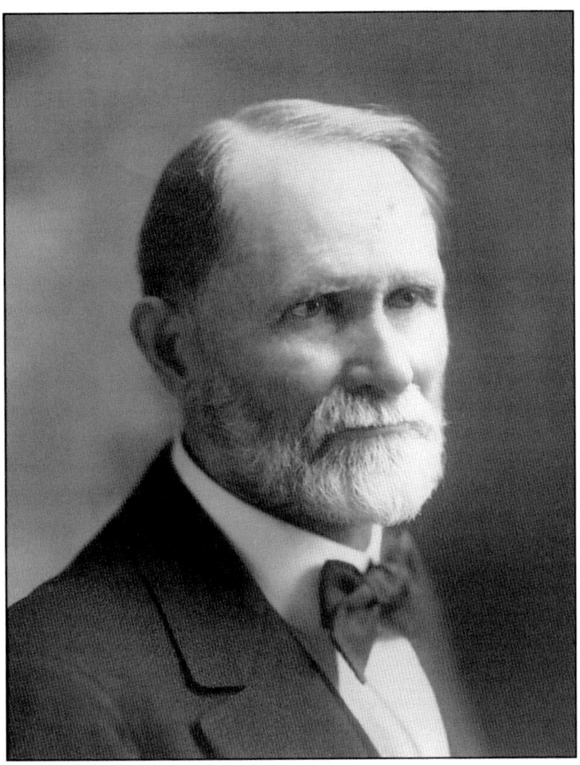

Hon. James O'Neill, born in New York in 1847, came to Clark County in 1873 at the urging of his uncle, Neillsville's founder, also named James O'Neill. A graduate of Cornell University and Albany Law School, Judge O'Neill was the 17th District Circuit Court judge from 1898 to 1921, a state legislator, and a civic leader. He married Marian Robinson and they had two children, Ernest and Marian.

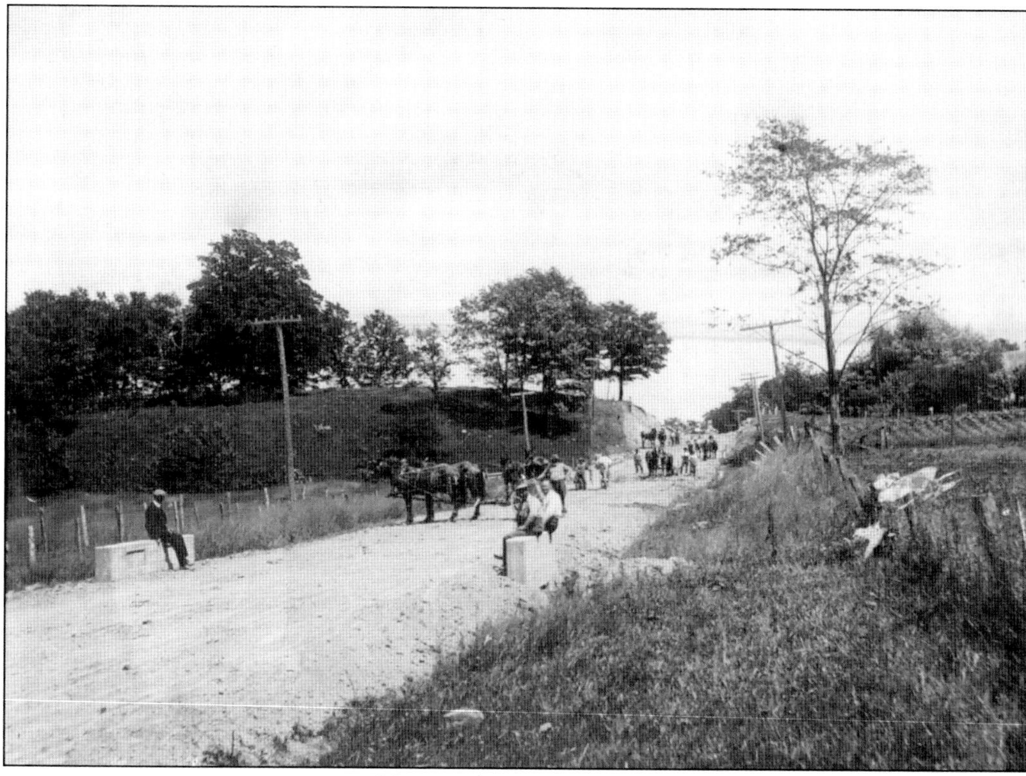

New roads were cut from the brush and woods as more settlers arrived, and as citizens needed better access to the road system. In November 1911, the Clark County board adopted a multiyear plan of road construction that included the grading and surfacing of roads and the building of culverts and bridges, to begin in 1912. These men were making improvements to Highway 18 (now Highway 10) between Granton and Lynn.

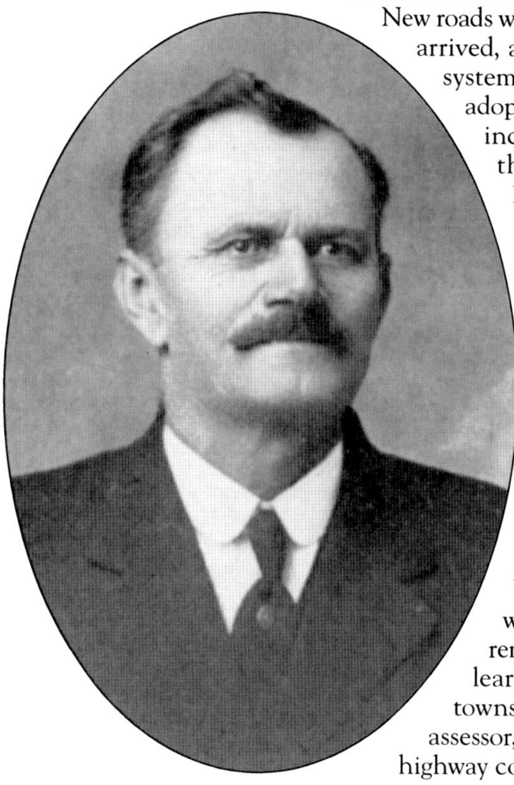

Born in 1860, William C. Thoma was raised by his widowed mother in Jefferson County, Wisconsin. In 1892, he came to Clark County, where he lived with his wife and five children the remainder of his life. He was a very good farmer who learned modern farming methods and held many township offices. In his later years, he was the county assessor, the enumerator (census taker), and the county highway commissioner.

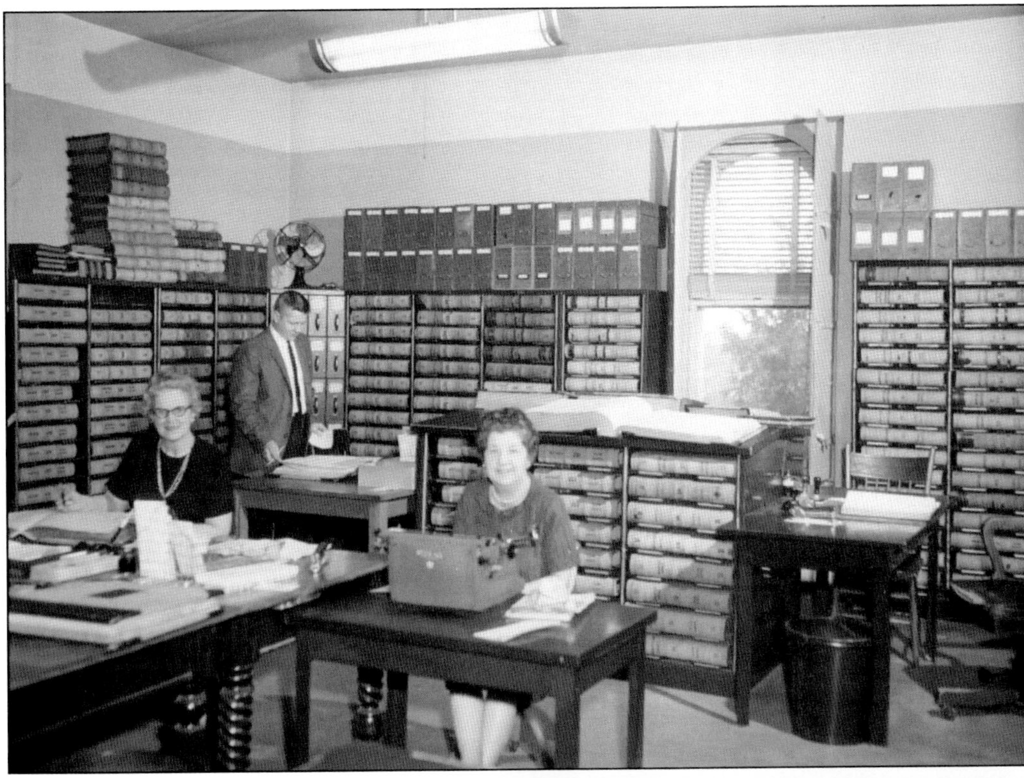

Before the world of computers, or even electric typewriters, the staff of the Clark County Register of Deeds office completed their work very efficiently. In 1965, the staff included, from left to right, Evelyn Walk, deputy; Vern Hansen, register of deeds; and Irene Tibbett, clerk. The large bound record books held information on county land ownership and transfers, as well as marriages, births, and deaths. (Courtesy of the Clark County clerk's office.)

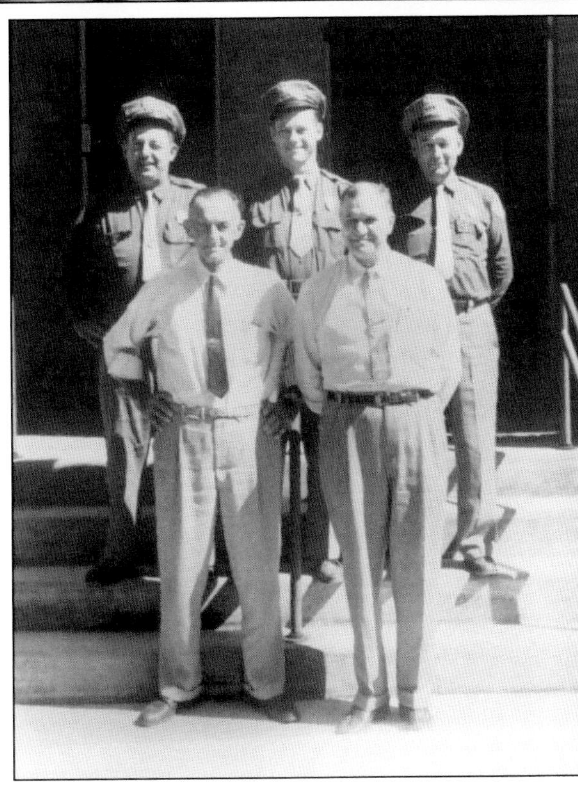

Seen here are, from left to right, (first row) Frank Dobes, under sheriff; and Raymond Kutsche, sheriff; (second row) Duane "Gabby" Schultz, David Bertz, and Harry "Boney" Frantz, traffic officers. From 1943 to 1964, Kutsche and Dobes were elected sheriff a combined total of six times. For those 16 years, they ran the sheriff's department while their wives, who were sisters, took care of the residence and cooked the meals for all the prisoners.

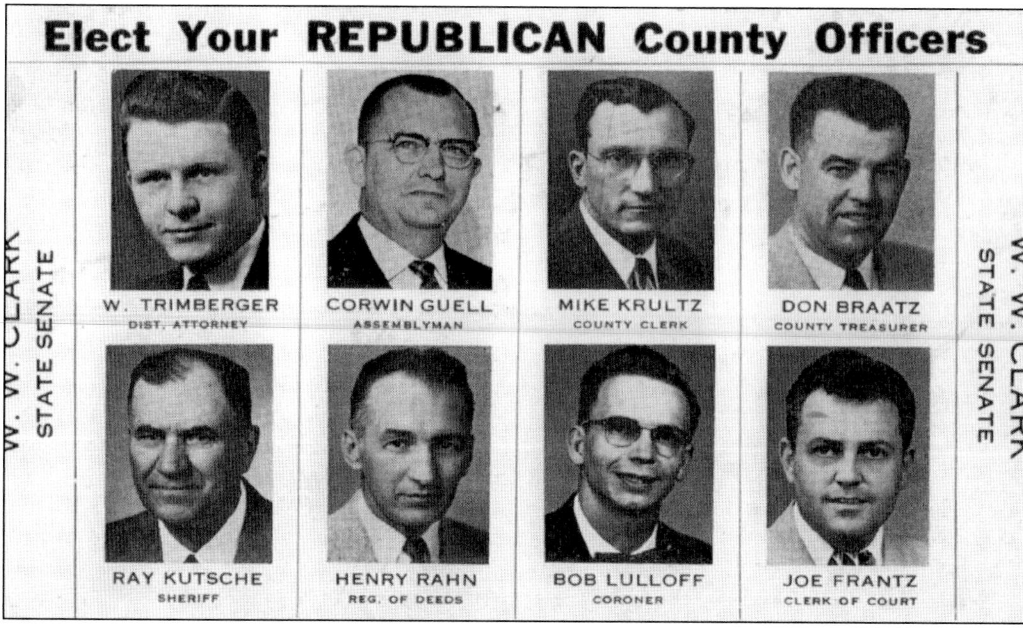

The Republican Party of Clark County distributed postcards in the 1950s with their slate of candidates for the upcoming election. The candidates included, from left to right, (top row) Wayne Trimberger, Corwin Guell, Mike Krultz, and Don Braatz (bottom row) Ray Kutsche, Henry Rahn, Bob Lulloff, and Joe Frantz.

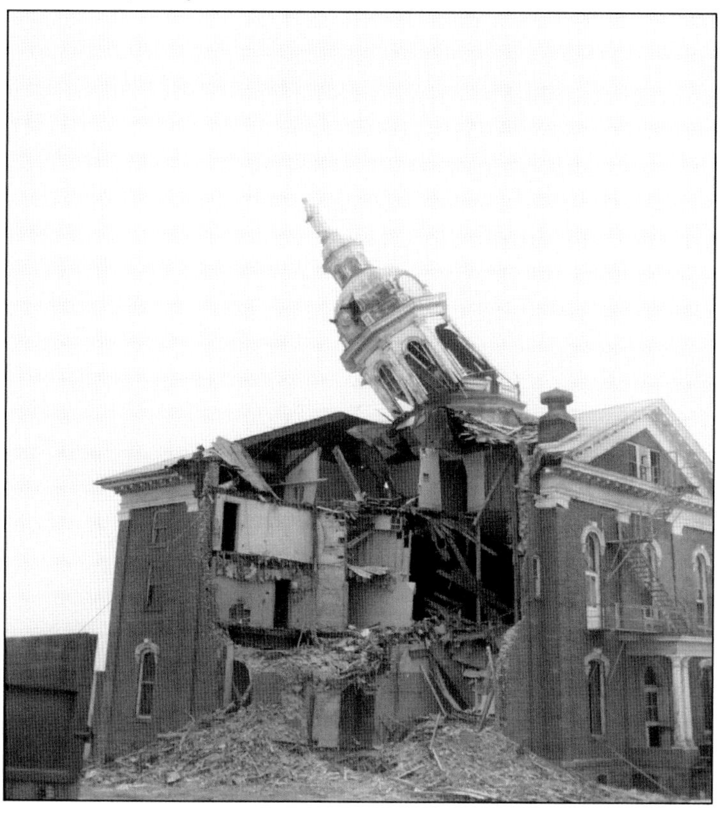

In 1965, the old courthouse was demolished, making room for a parking lot between the new courthouse and the county jail. The plan was to have the dome of the old courthouse, along with Lady Justice, fall to the east, with the hope of salvaging the historic figure. Unfortunately, the plan did not work, and the dome fell onto the newly constructed courthouse, breaking Lady Justice into pieces. (Courtesy of the Clark County clerk's office.)

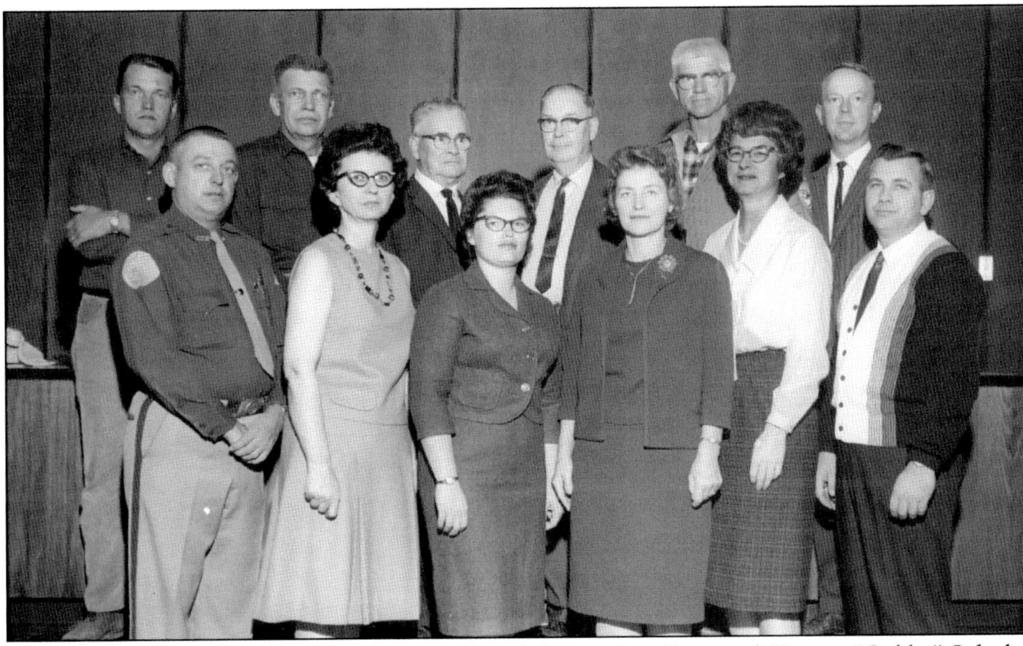

In 1965, the Clark County officials were, from left to right, (first row) Duane "Gabby" Schultz, traffic head; Mildred Lawson, register in probate; Ann Filitz and Lois Guest, nurses; Brooks Rector, home economist; and Ed Bauer, engineer; (second row) Marvin Hemp, highway commissioner; Warren Hemp, police radio operator; Peter Ludovic, veteran service officer; Harold Trewartha, director of welfare; Arnold Rasmussen, head of forestry; and Donald Johnson, family court commissioner. (Courtesy of the Clark County clerk's office.)

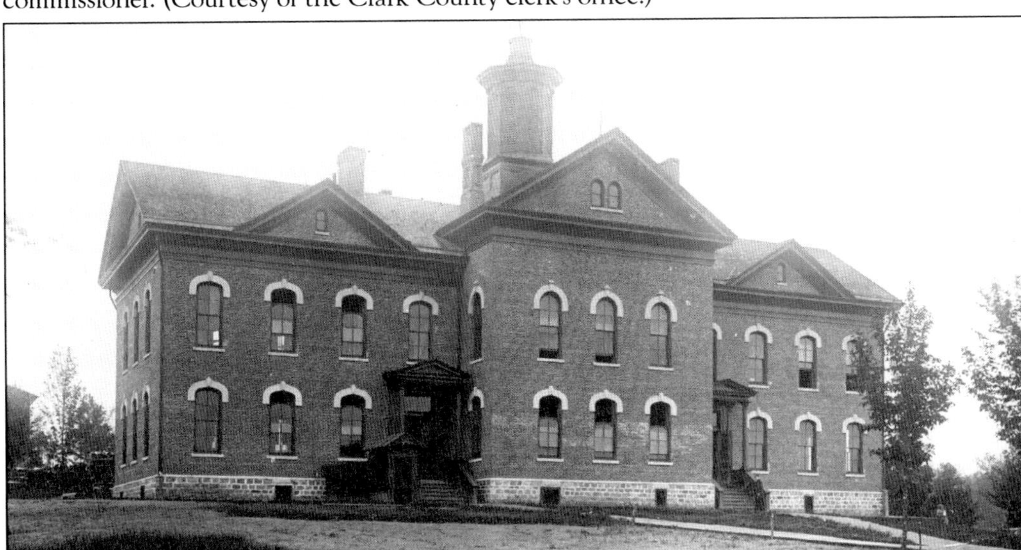

In 1874, all students in Neillsville were taught in this building. The first graduating class from Neillsville High School received their diplomas in 1875. As the number of students continued to increase, a second school, Northside Elementary School, was built in 1885, near Twelfth Street. By 1906, a new high school was needed, and this original school became Southside Elementary School.

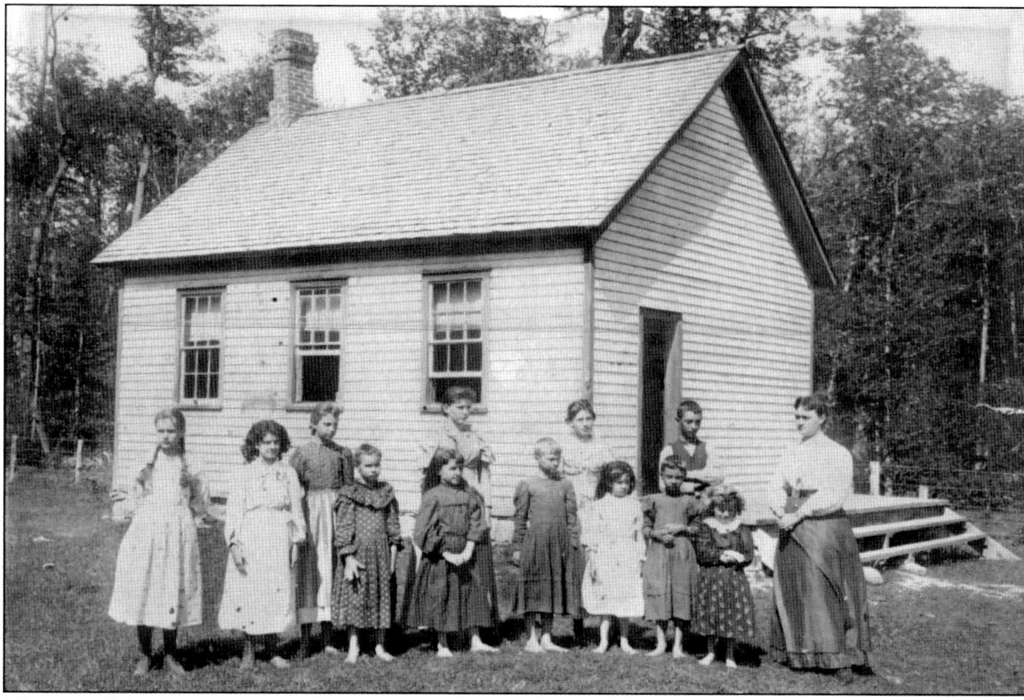

This wood-framed school, known as the Garbisch school and later called the Romadka, served the town of York, District No. 4, from 1887 to 1906. In this early 1890s photograph the teacher was Ethie Kemery, and her students were, in no particular order, Abe Carpenter, Flora Pierlie, Edith Harding, Allie Canfield, Bertha Tische, Effie Breese, ? Harding, ? Harding, Theron Harding, and ? Pierlie. Two students were not identified at all.

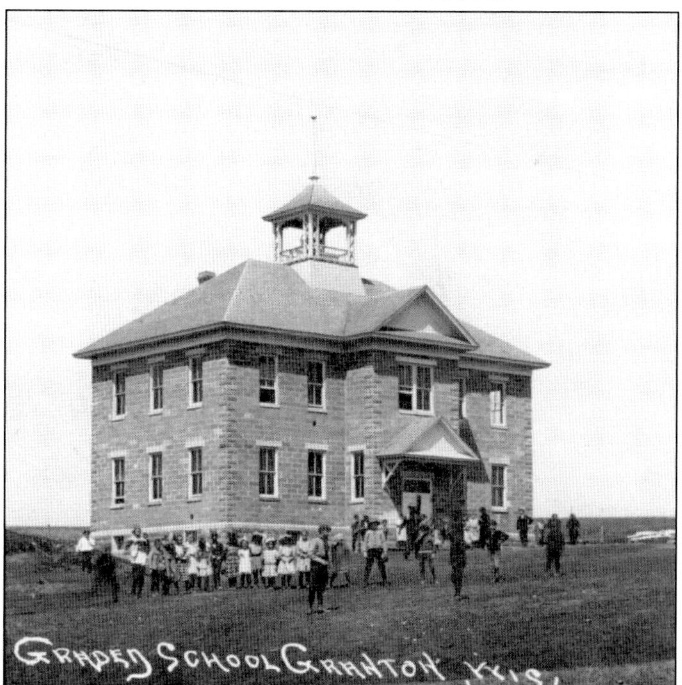

In 1905, the village of Granton voted to build a four-room schoolhouse at a cost of $6,000. Built on two acres of land just north of the village, the first classes were held there in 1907. Because it was a graded school, graduates had the equivalent of three years of high school. If a student wanted a high school diploma, they attended their fourth year elsewhere, usually in Neillsville.

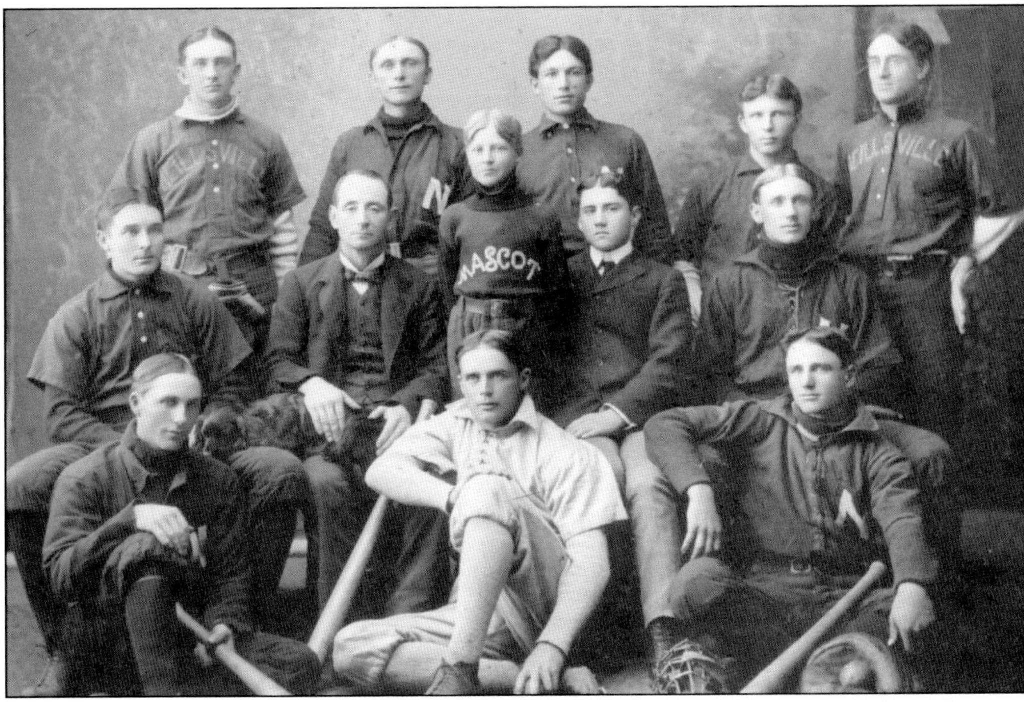

The 1897 Neillsville baseball team included, from left to right, (first row) Hans Carlson, shortstop and pitcher; Chas Cook, pitcher; and Harry Bearwald, catcher; (second row) Emil Ketel, first base; Bob Bullion, manager; Freddie Stowell, mascot; Billie Dickinsen, scorer; and Bill Campbell, third base; (third row) Ben Hart, left field; Frank Burnett, second base; Pat McIntyre, center field; unidentified; and Walt Cattanach, center field.

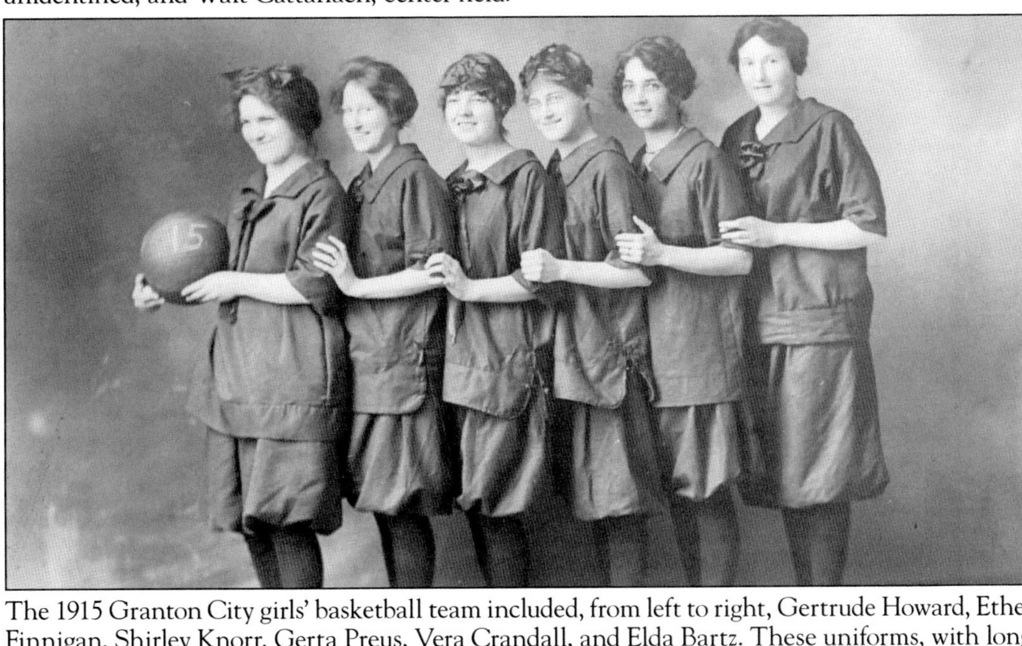

The 1915 Granton City girls' basketball team included, from left to right, Gertrude Howard, Ethel Finnigan, Shirley Knorr, Gerta Preus, Vera Crandall, and Elda Bartz. These uniforms, with long blouses and pantaloons, were quite fashionable at the time. Several of the ladies used scarves to keep their hair back while playing.

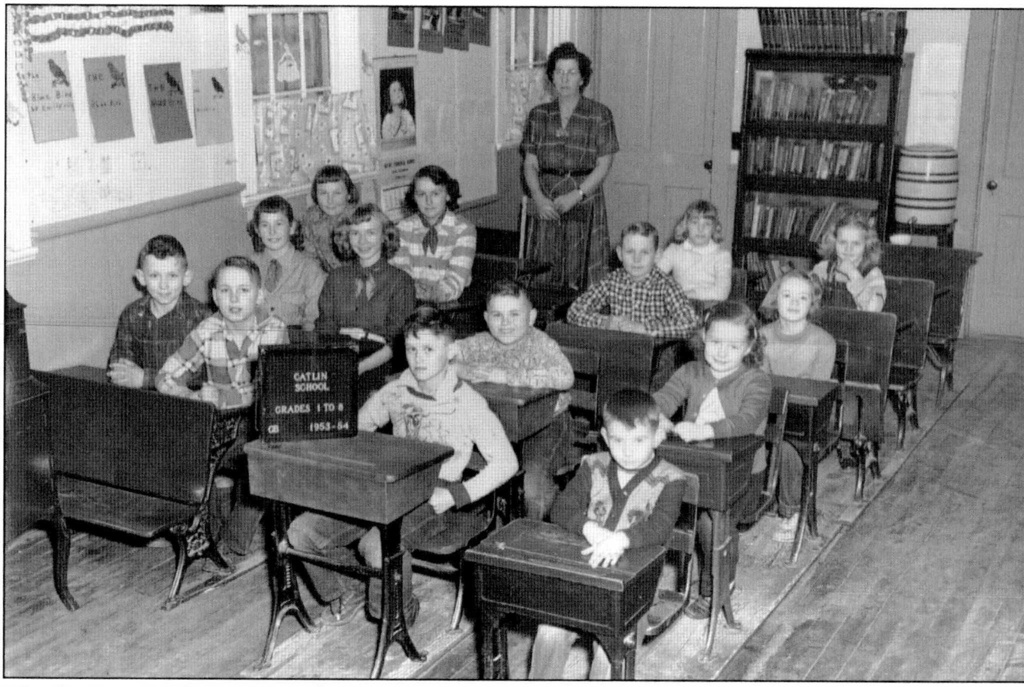

The Catlin school, a rural grade school in Sherman Township, had 15 students in 1953. They were, from left to right, (front row) Jimmy Rudoll, Karen Haslow, Dale Teter, and Dicky Wehymiller; (second row) unidentified, Patsy Pagelsdorf, Dale Rothamer, and Barbara Lempke; (third row) Caroline Pagelsdorf, Kathleen Stevens, Billy Pagelsdorf, and Karen Liske; (fourth row) teacher Ruth Kline, Ellen Haslow, and Beatrice Heinz.

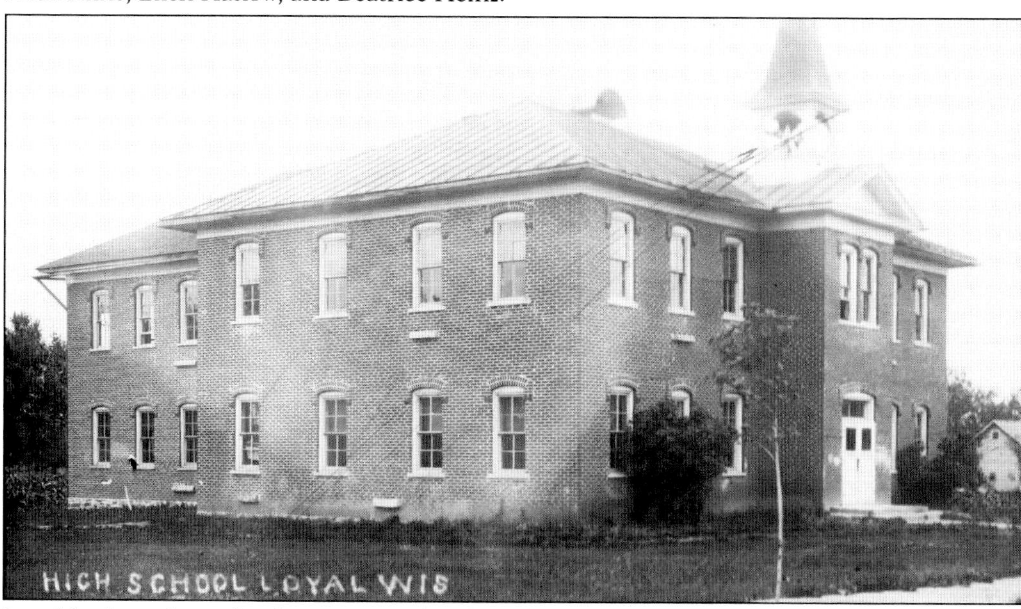

Loyal built its first school in 1882, and enlarged it in the 1890s and again in 1903. In Loyal's graduating class of 1897, there were four women and one man. Until the early 1900s, it was common for young men to leave school after eighth grade, as there was work to be done at home and parents felt that they had received enough education. (Courtesy of the Loyal Area Historical Society.)

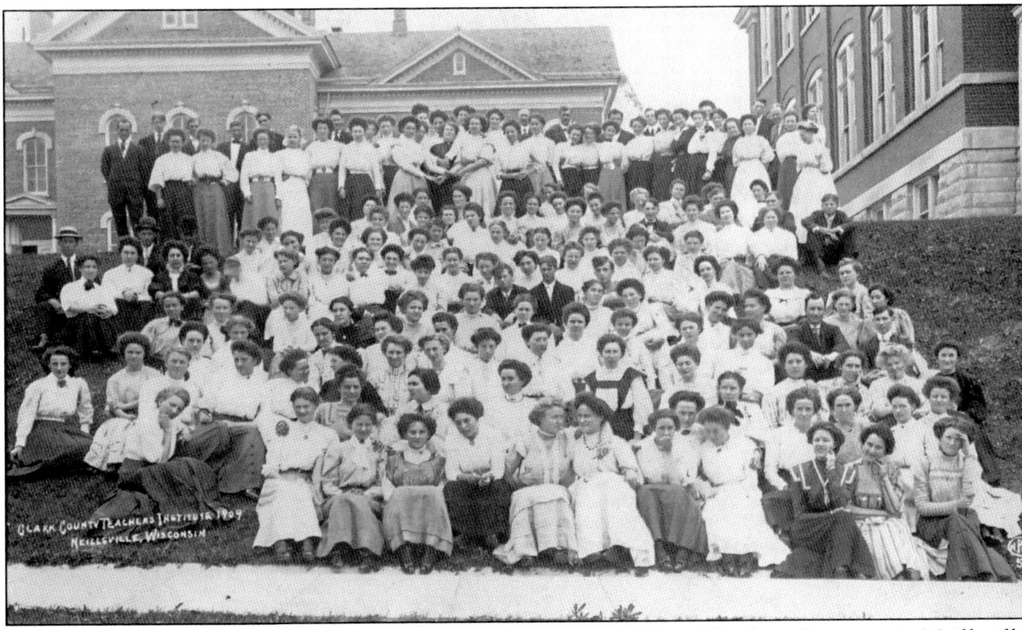

This photograph was taken of the class of 1909 at the Clark County Teachers Institute, in Neillsville. These teaching institutions were called normal schools in later years. The graduates gathered in front of Southside Elementary School to capture this memorable event. Many graduates were able to secure teaching positions in the Clark County school system upon graduation.

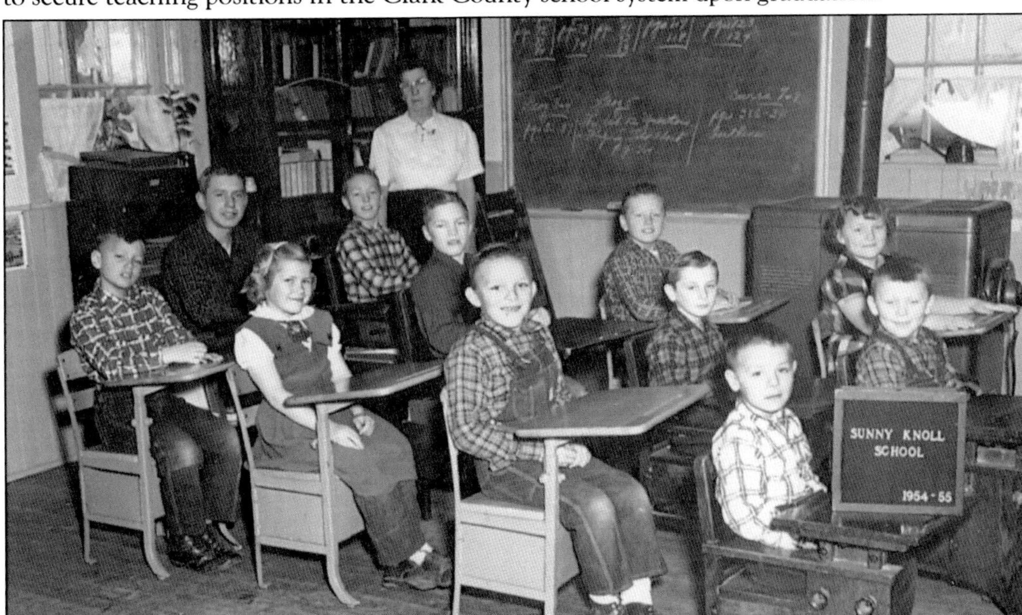

These students at the Sunny Knoll school, near Loyal, pose during the 1954–1955 school year. They are, from left to right, (first row) Bryan McNeely, second grade; Nancy Haslow, second grade; Raymond Gardner, third grade; and Marvin Miller, first grade; (second row) Noel Olson, eighth grade; Billy Haslow, fifth grade; Allen Miller, second grade; and Bobby Gardner, second grade; (third row) Donald Olson, fourth grade; teacher Ruth Kline; Dennis Olson, fourth grade; and Nancy Gardner, fourth grade.

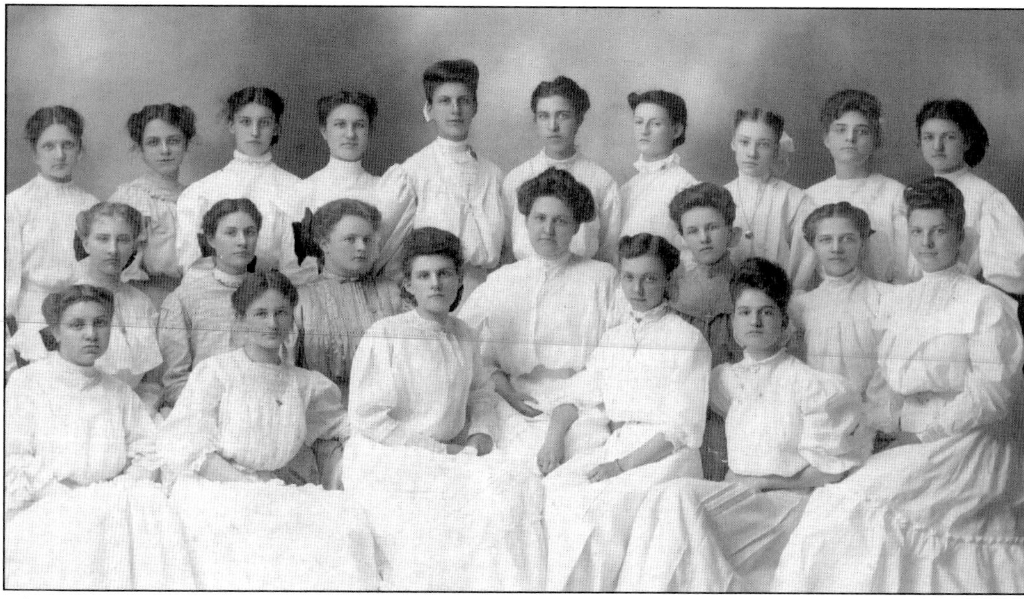

The 1906 Neillsville High School glee club included, from left to right, (first row) Clara Ketel, Jess Snyder, Hazel Lee, Sadie Campbell, and Theresea Schwentkofske; (second row) Vivian Brooks, Lola Neff, Maude Bruley, music teacher Miss Whiting, Alice Neverman, Olga Knoop, and Emma Ruege; (third row) Ethel Stowell, Clarabelle "Kit" Marsh, Clarice Dodte, Elsie Jahr, Francis Lippert, Blanche Morris, Blanche Heaslett, Helen Hemp, Louise Dangers, and Marian Myers.

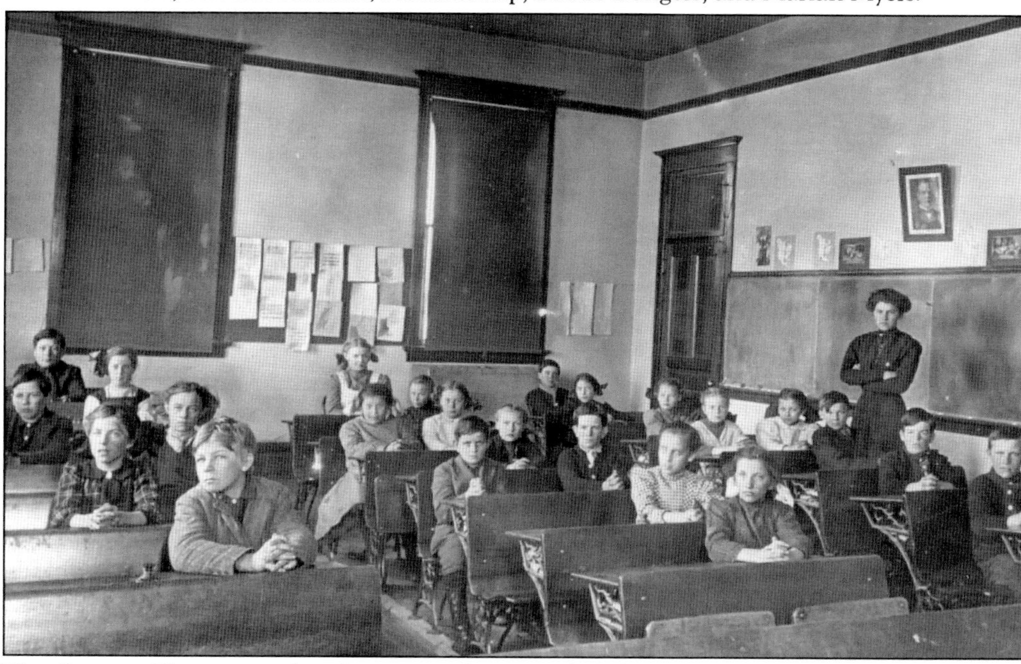

The Granton Elementary class from around 1912 included, from front to back, (left row) Clifton Paulson, unidentified, Myrtle Lawson, unidentified, Mabel William, and Roy Hart; (center row) Lydia Krause, Amy Marsh, Roderick Rausch, Tim King, Lydia Neinas, Alva Rose, two unidentified, and Florence Davis; (right row) unidentified, Ted Smith, Maynard Cole, unidentified, Beulah Lee, Leone Beaver, Anita Beaver, unidentified, and teacher Hallie Eberhardt.

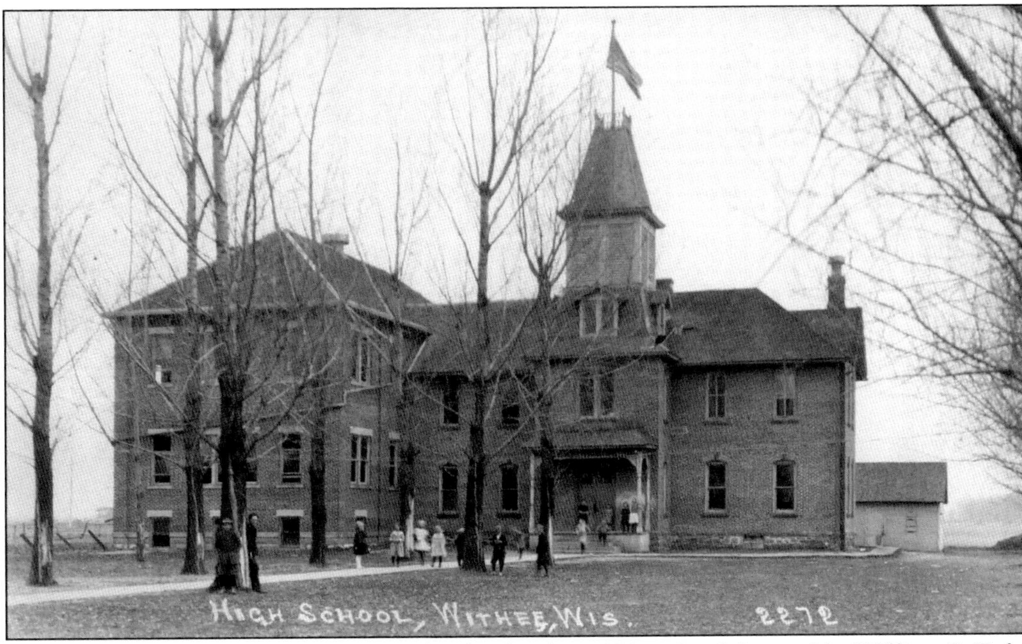

The village of Withee built a two-story brick school in 1890 on land donated by William S. Tufts. As the local population grew, a new wing was added in 1911. Initially, both elementary and high school classes were taught in this building; later, it was strictly a high school. After 1955, after consolidating with Owen, this building became the Owen-Withee Junior High School.

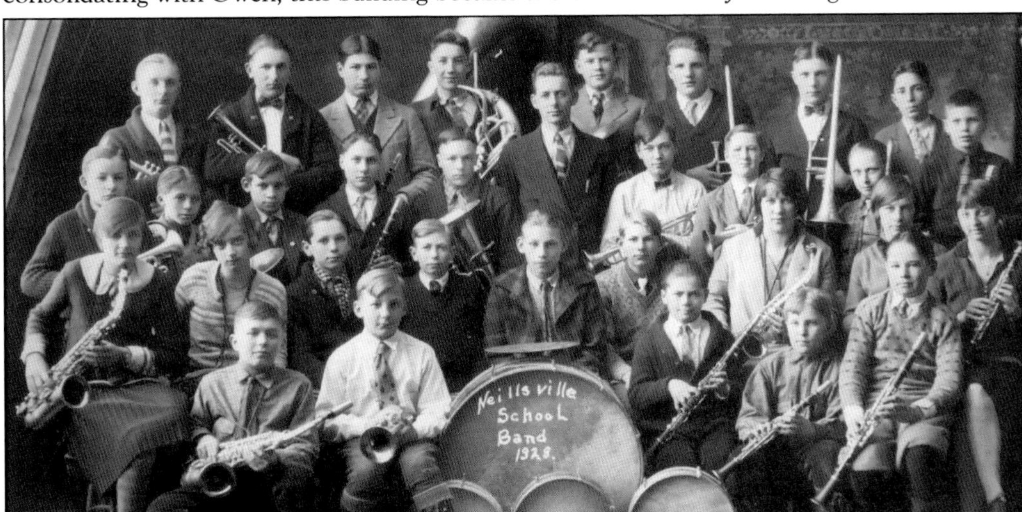

The 1928 Neillsville High School band included, from left to right, (first row) Walter "Buster" Brown, Lowell Schoengarth, Bob Schiller, Bob Unger, and Welton Brooks; (second row) Mary Neverman, Virginia Kleckner, Chet Wagner, Vernon Scholtz, Ed Krantz, Bud West, Marie Walk, G. Walk, and Marian Huntley; (third row) Oran Welch, C. Schweinler, H. Frantz, Bill Gallagher, Herb Kurth, Ralph O'Neill, C. Gangler, H. Hauser, L. Zaeske, and W. Hemp; (fourth row) Herb Borde, Art Gress, Herb Keller, Walt Weaver, Fred Anderson, Irv Gerhart, Owen Higgins, and Dale Schweinler.

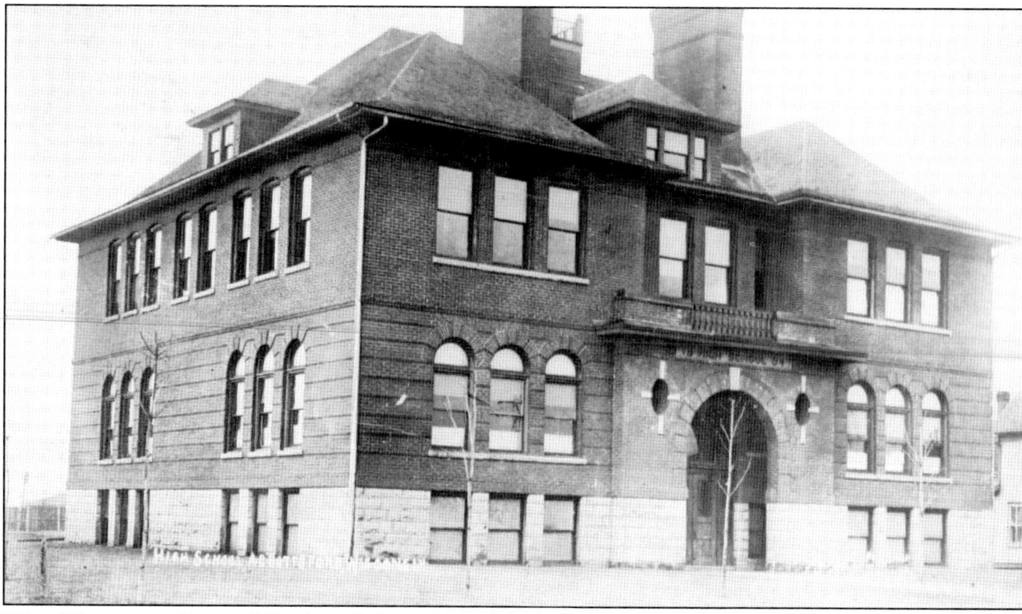

The Wisconsin Central Railroad Company decided to move its division headquarters in both Chippewa Falls and Stevens Point to Abbotsford. With its village population then almost doubled, the Abbotsford schools could hardly keep up with the increasing student population. In 1904, Abbotsford High School was built. It served the community well until 1966, when it was torn down to make way for an addition to the elementary school.

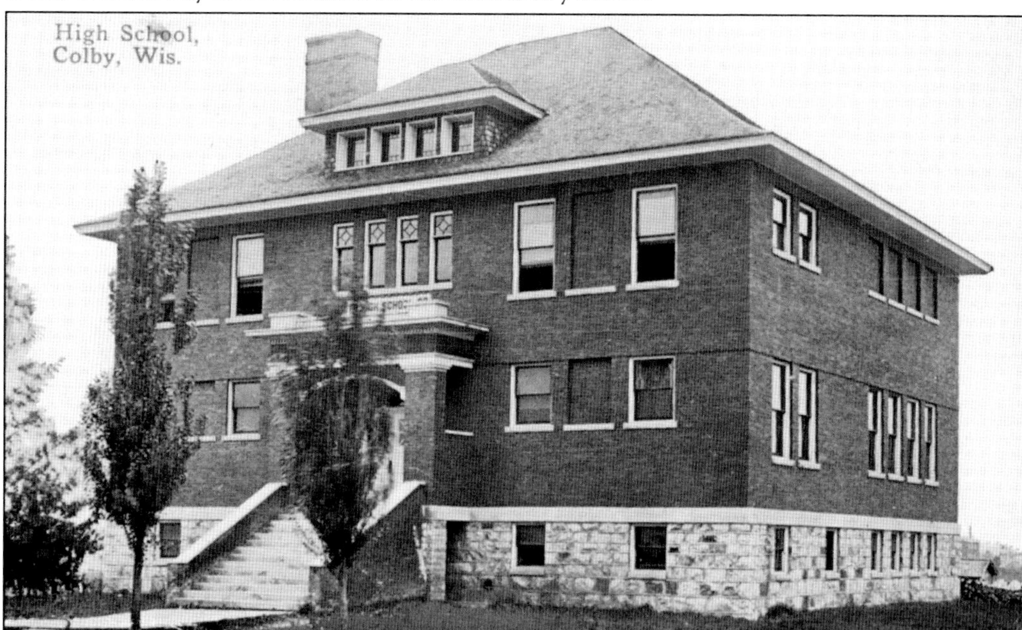

In January 1907, the townships of Hull, in Marathon County, and Colby, in Clark County, and the city of Colby dedicated a new high school. At the time, it was one of the first significant public buildings to be built in the city, and it had every modern convenience imaginable. While country schools had woodstoves and little else, this new building had electricity, steam heat, a gymnasium, a laboratory, and well-equipped classrooms.

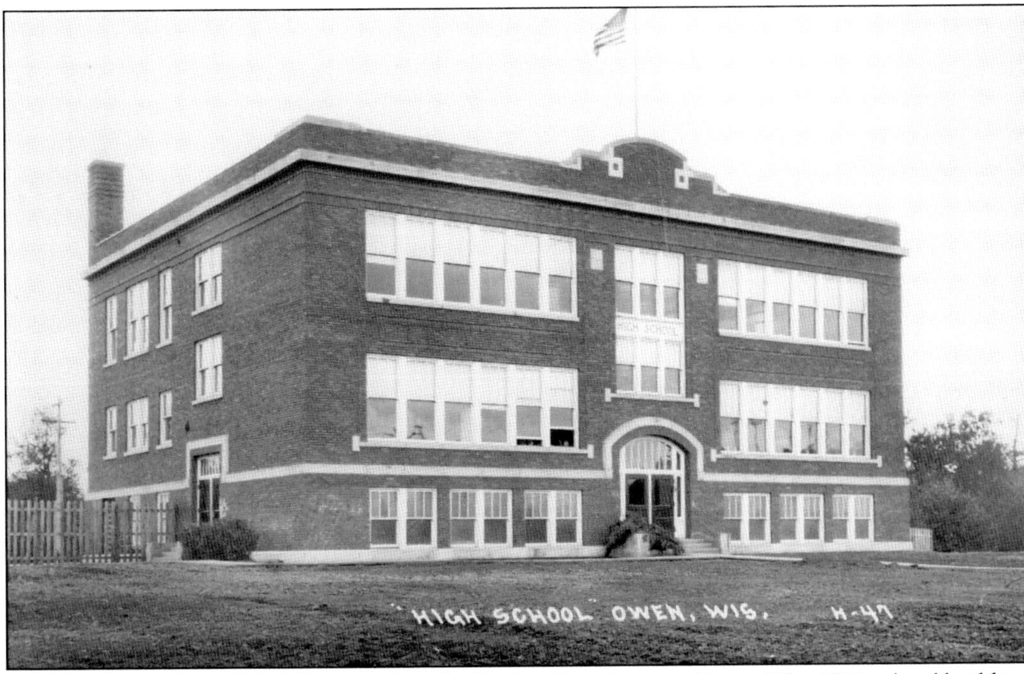

In 1921, with increased enrollment, a new high school was built in Owen. The 1907 school building, which had housed all grades 1–12, became the Owen Grade School. In 1955, when the Owen school district combined with the Withee district, Owen High School became the high school for the combined district. This building is now owned by the Friends of the Old School Museum.

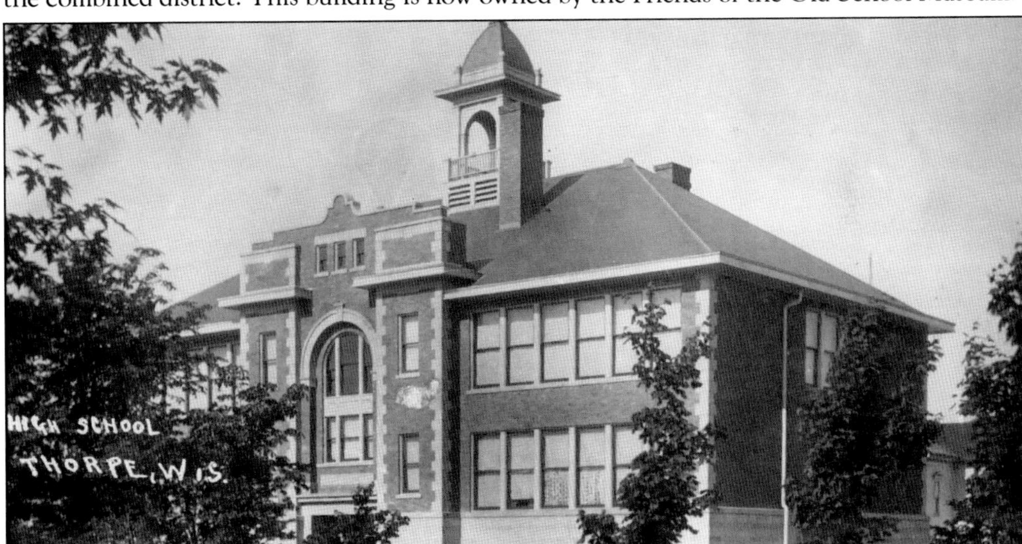

Thorp(e) High School, seen here in 1910, was built in 1890. At the time, it was one of the finest schools in northern Wisconsin, with the best equipment, furnishings, and teachers possible. Considering that just 20 years before it was built, there were no settlers in Thorp, it was a remarkable accomplishment to have such a fine school.

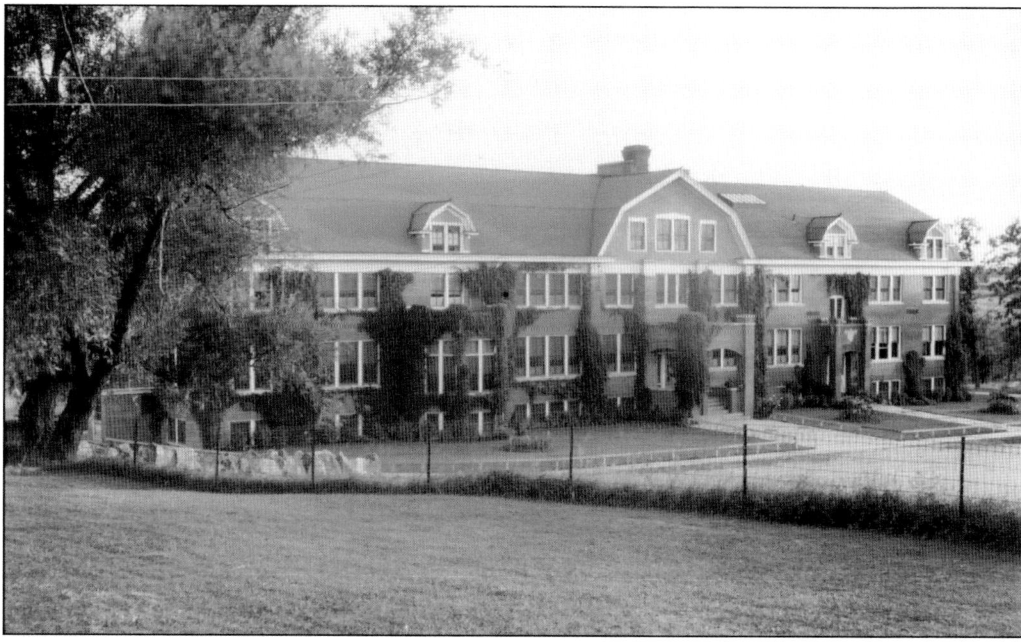

The Winnebago Indian School was built in 1920 on 33 acres along the Black River in Neillsville. A continuation of the missionary work begun by Rev. Jacob Hauser and Rev. Jacob Stucki, this school was run for 42 years by Rev. Ben Stucki and his wife, Ella. Young boys and girls from local Winnebago Indian families lived and studied here during the school year.

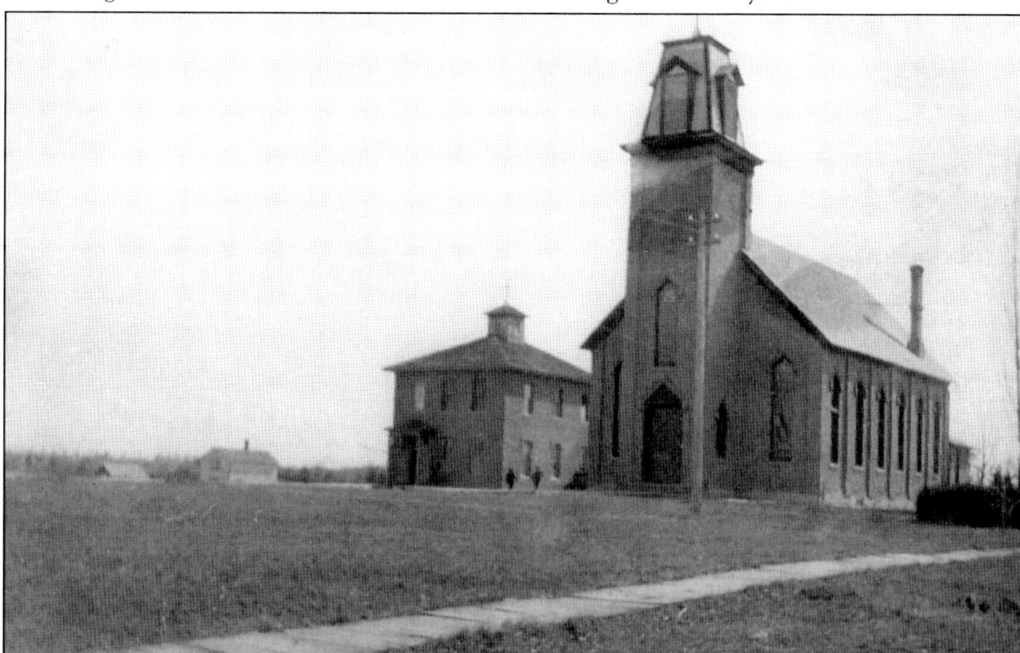

The first St. Mary's Catholic Church building in Neillsville (right) was built in 1878, and the school (left) was built in 1887. This church served the congregation well, until June 24, 1923, when a massive bolt of lightning struck the church steeple, causing a fire and the complete loss of the church. However, a new church was soon built, and it was in use by the end of 1924.

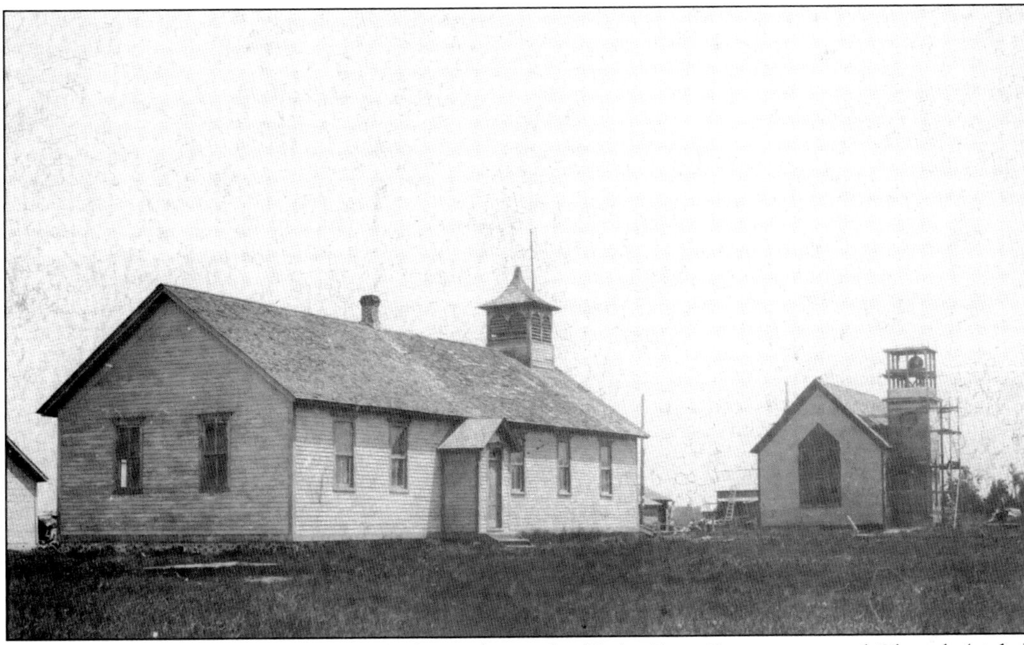

In 1895, early settlers in Curtiss worked together to build the First Congregational Church (right). Members worshipped together until 1905, when several German Lutheran members supported the decision to build a new Lutheran church, thereby leaving the Congregational Church. The building on the left has not been identified, but it appears to be a wood-frame school building or town hall.

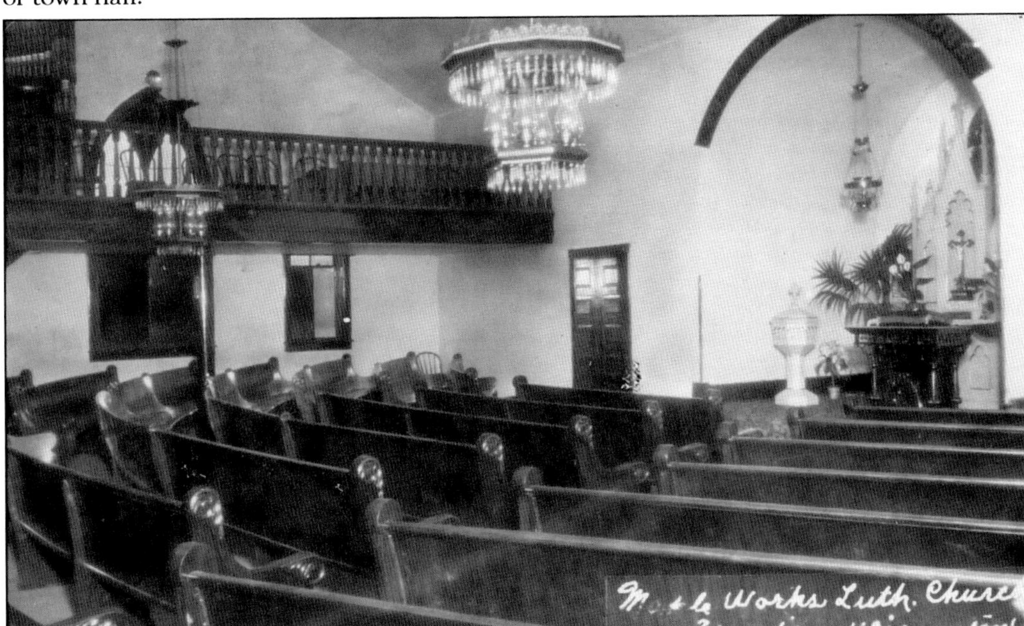

Zion Evangelical German Lutheran Church in Granton, also known as Maple Works, was first organized in 1883. Services were held in the little white frame church until 1905, when a new brick church was built a short distance away. In 1907, the new kerosene chandelier lamps were mounted in the sanctuary of the church, as seen here.

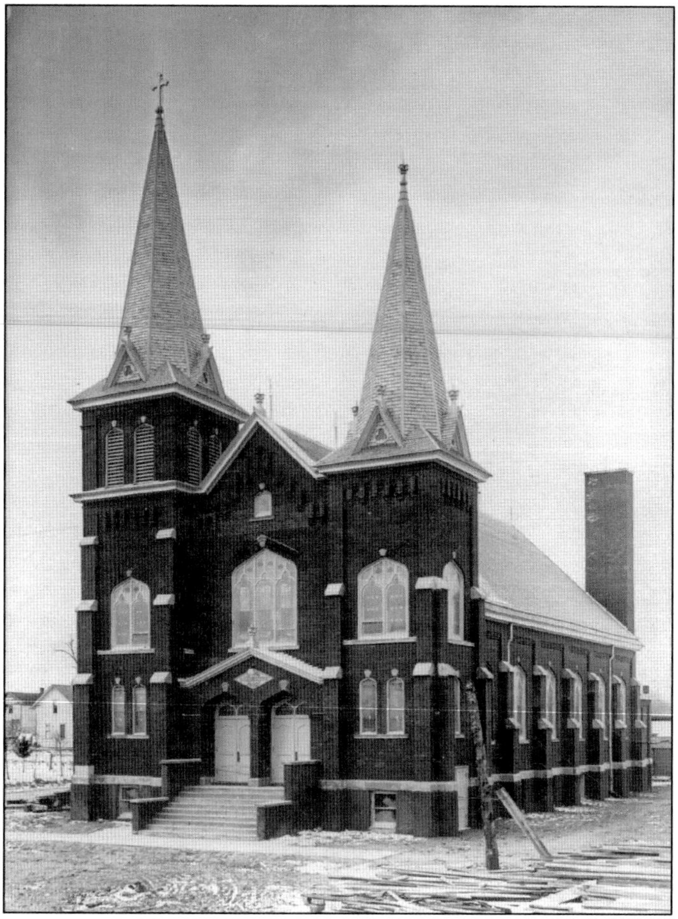

The second Trinity Lutheran Church in Loyal is seen here in the 1930s. This beautiful church was built with two steeples and two sets of double front doors. The first church was severely damaged by lightning in 1913. (Courtesy of the Loyal Area Historical Society, Bertz Collection.)

The Methodist church in Thorp sits on the same parcel of land that the first parishioners purchased in 1884 for $100. From 1881 to 1887, the Methodist congregation used the First Baptist Church's building to hold their church services, until their new church home was completed. In the 1950s, church members raised thousands of dollars to complete needed repairs and improvements.

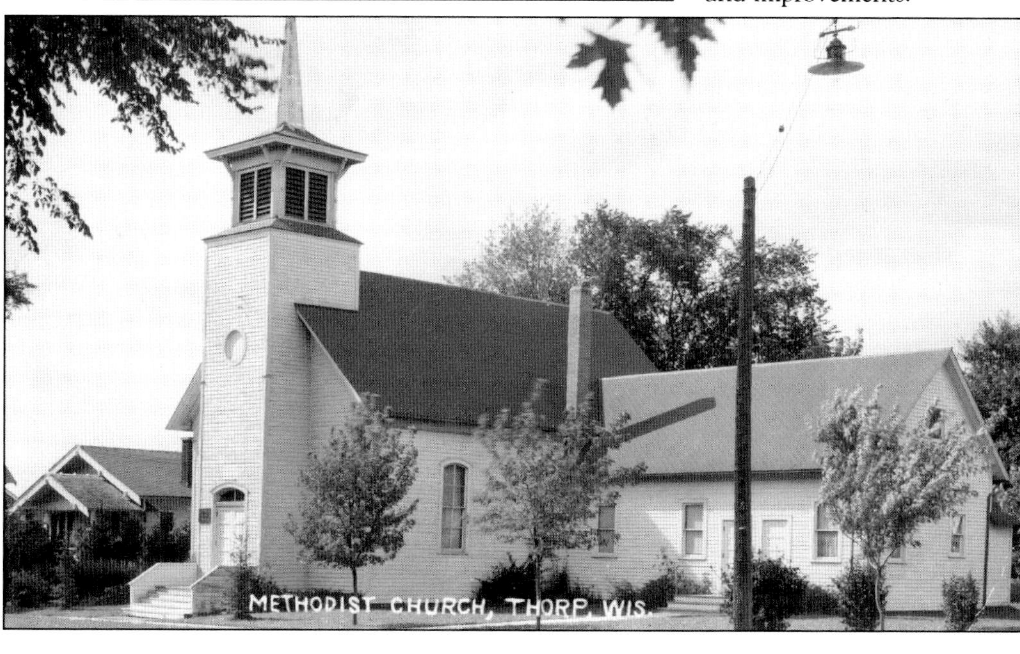

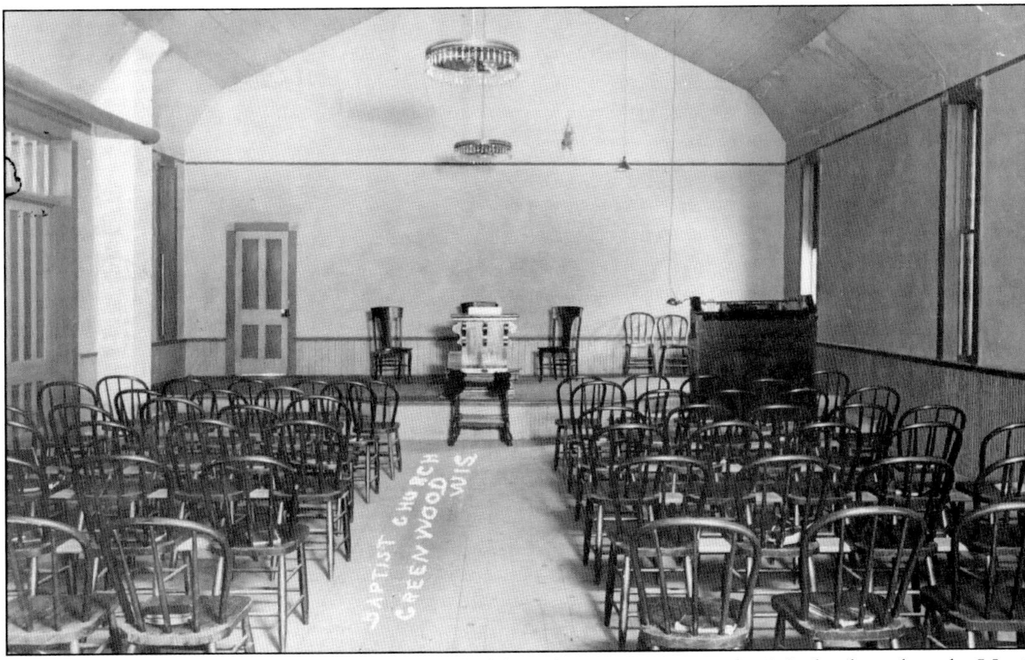

In 1888, the Greenwood Baptist Church held its first services in the Methodist church. Until 1896, they worshipped in the Methodist church, in a hall owned by John Shanks, and, at times, in members' homes. Their new church was built and dedicated in 1897. The sparse furnishings of the church are seen here around 1900.

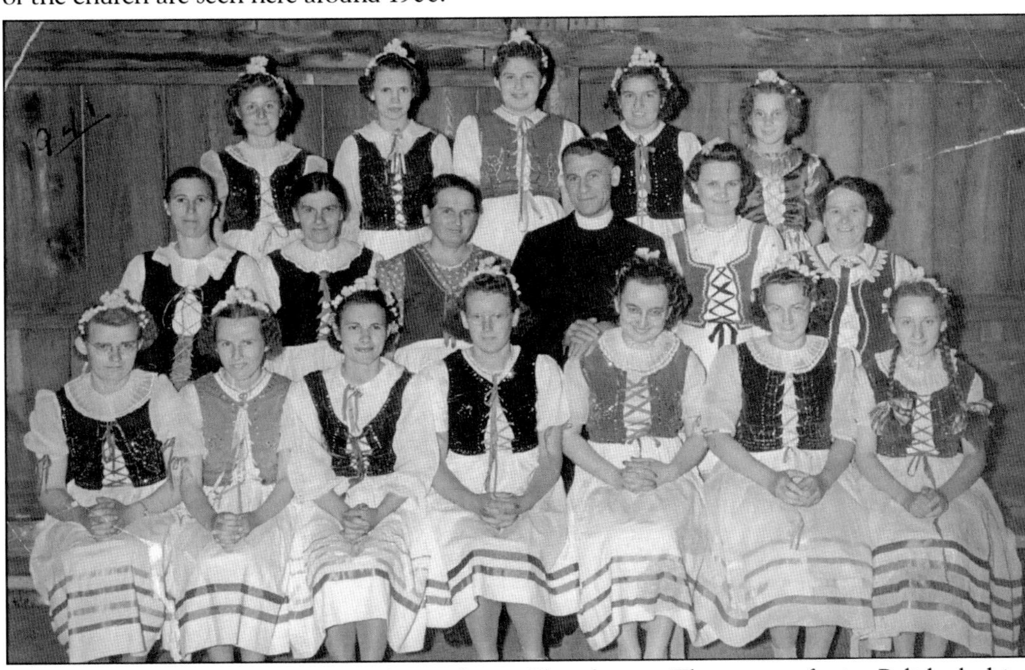

These young ladies from St. Mary's Czestochowa Church, near Thorp, wear festive Polish clothing and bands of flowers in their hair in the 1940s. Sitting in front of the Stanley Auditorium, the young ladies have just served food at the church's annual Swienconka, or chicken and polish sausage dinner. (Courtesy of the Stanley Area Historical Society.)

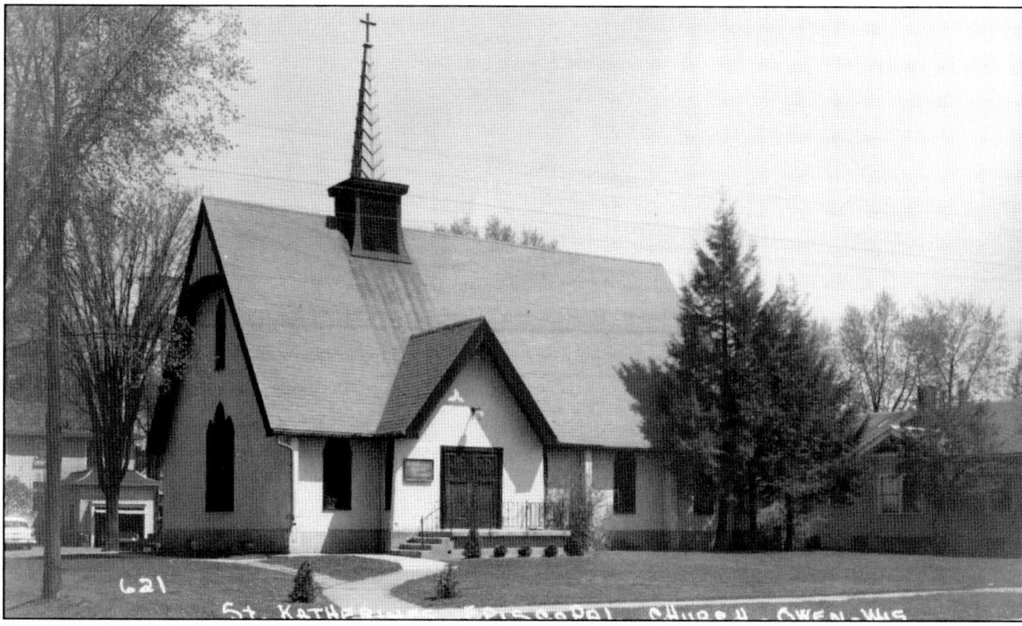

In 1914, the Episcopal church in Owen had its first services at a member's home. Rev. Phillip Linley of Eau Claire traveled to Owen every week to conduct services. In 1917, the congregation bought the Eau Claire church building, dismantled it, and shipped it to Owen by railcar. St. Katherine's Episcopal Church then reassembled the church in Owen, holding its first service in 1917. (Courtesy of the David Jankoski collection.)

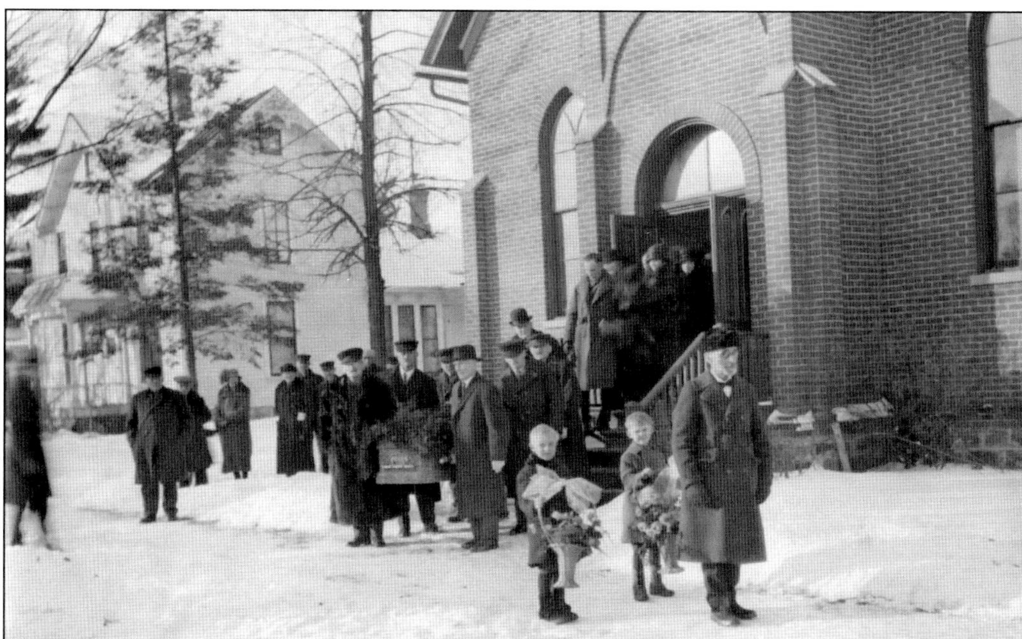

On January 15, 1925, the community mourned the death of Adolph F. Radke. An honest and respected man, he owned the hardware store in Neillsville. The funeral procession from St. John's Lutheran Church, at Fifth and Clay Streets, was led by Rev. H. Brandt. These two small boys carry flowers ahead of the casket and pallbearers.

Four

Businesses of Clark County

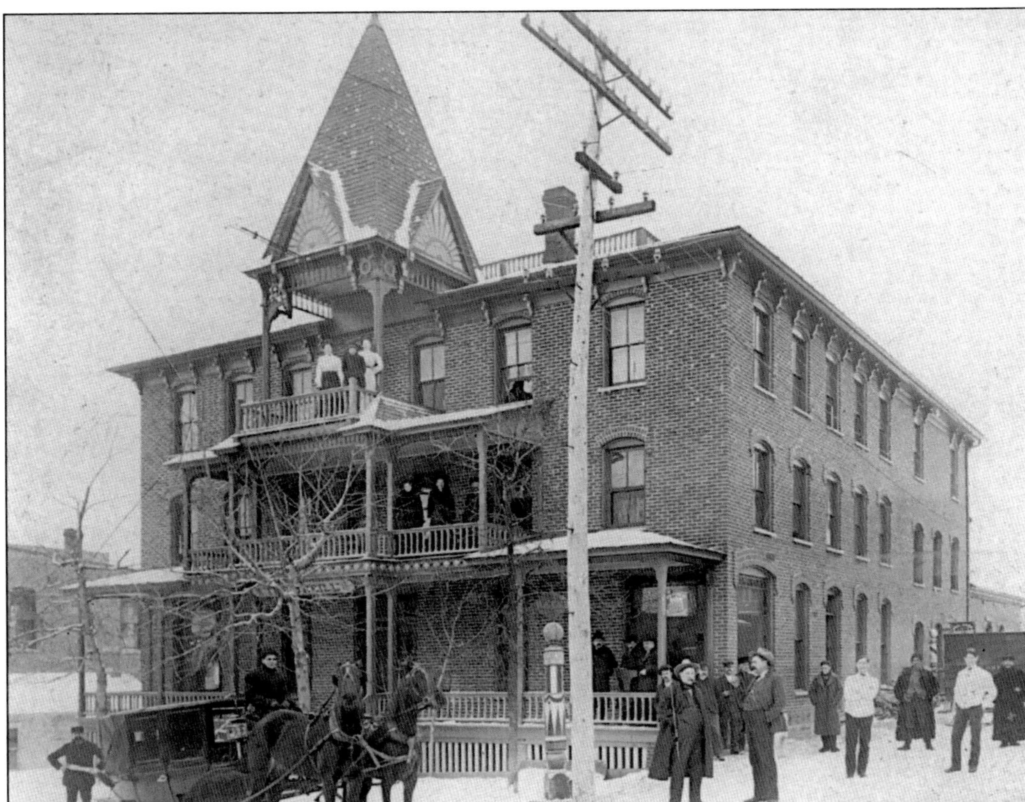

In 1860, James O'Neill began construction on the O'Neill House hotel and restaurant on the corner of Sixth and Hewett Streets. A third floor was added years later, along with a brick veneer. At the time, the O'Neill House was considered one of the finest hotels in central Wisconsin. Destroyed by fire in 1906, the lot sat vacant until the late 1930s, when Neillsville built a new post office there.

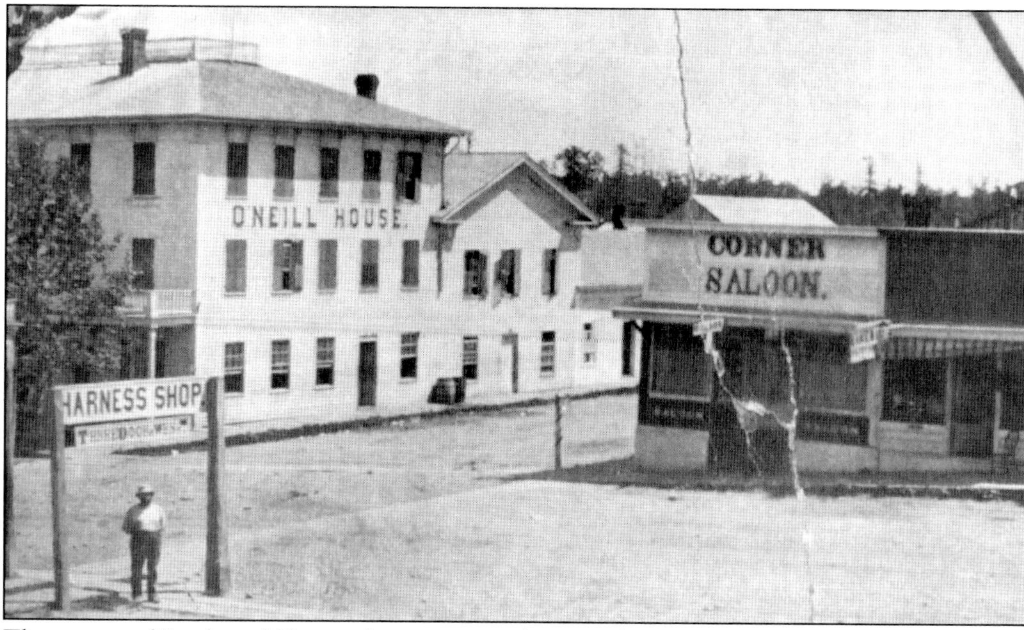

The corner of Sixth and Hewett Streets is seen here in the late 1880s. The prominent O'Neill House burned in 1906. The Corner Saloon was replaced in 1903 by the Kapellen building, which included R.T. Boullion's Palace Buffet and Math Kapellen's shoe store. The harness shop became Tourigny & Vaughan's Hardware Store.

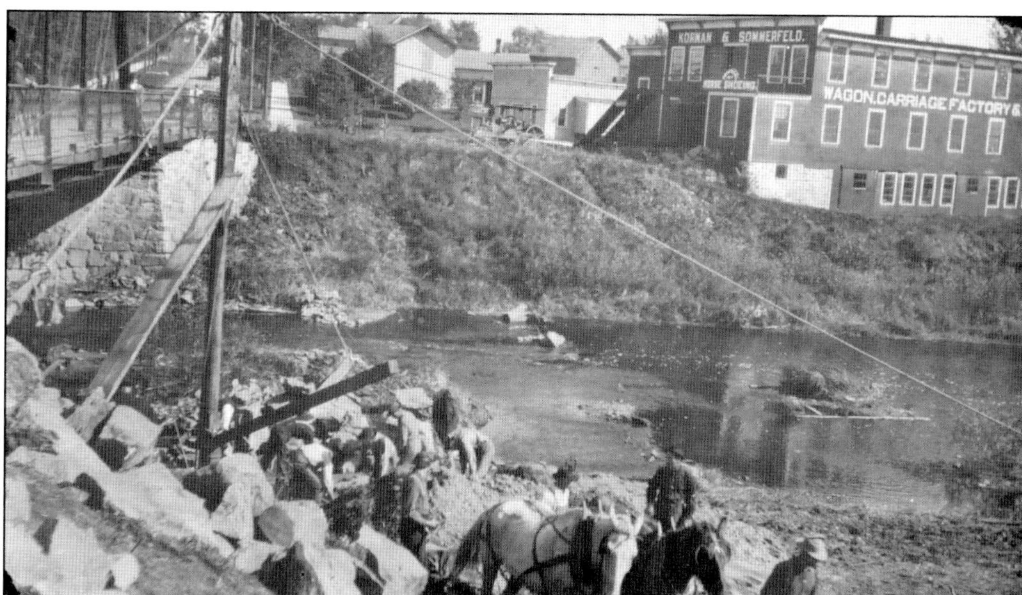

In 1911, a rock-and-concrete dam was constructed across O'Neill Creek. The dam was 130 feet long and 16 feet high, with a base of 12 feet at the bottom and 3 feet at the top. The construction of the dam began on September 5 and was completed 58 days later, on November 3, 1911. During construction, the men were hampered by five floods and the cold fall waters.

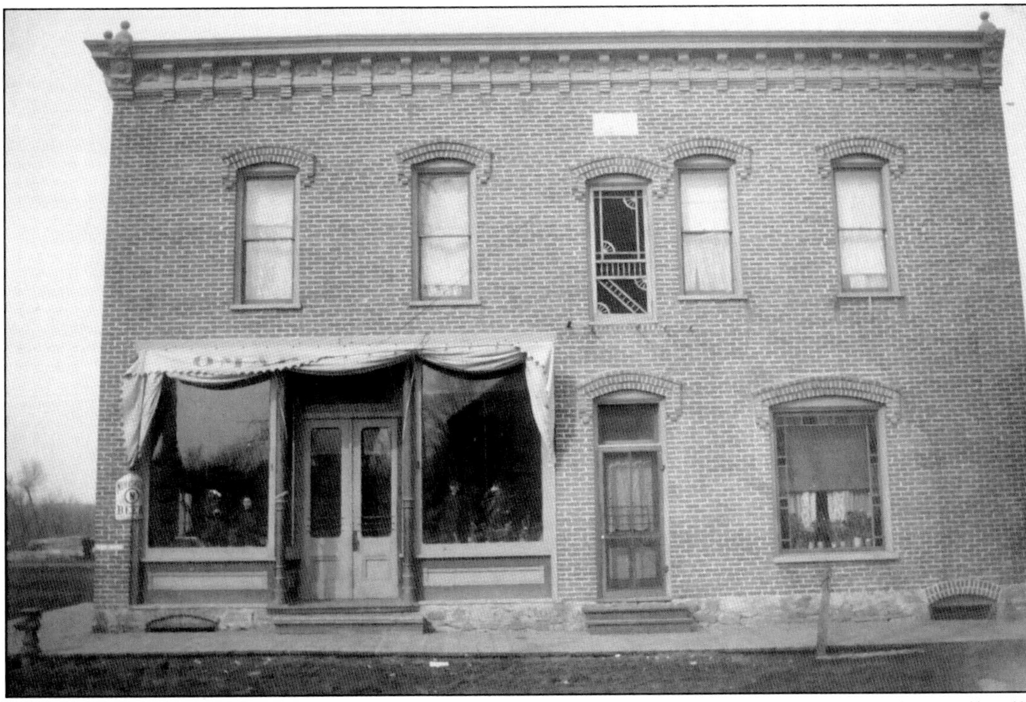

The Omaha House was built in the early 1880s. It was located a short half-block from the Neillsville depot, offering travelers a convenient night's stay. It was later sold to James and Janie Paulus, who renamed it after themselves. It was then sold in 1915 and renamed the Hamilton House. It has since been the location of several businesses and is currently undergoing restoration.

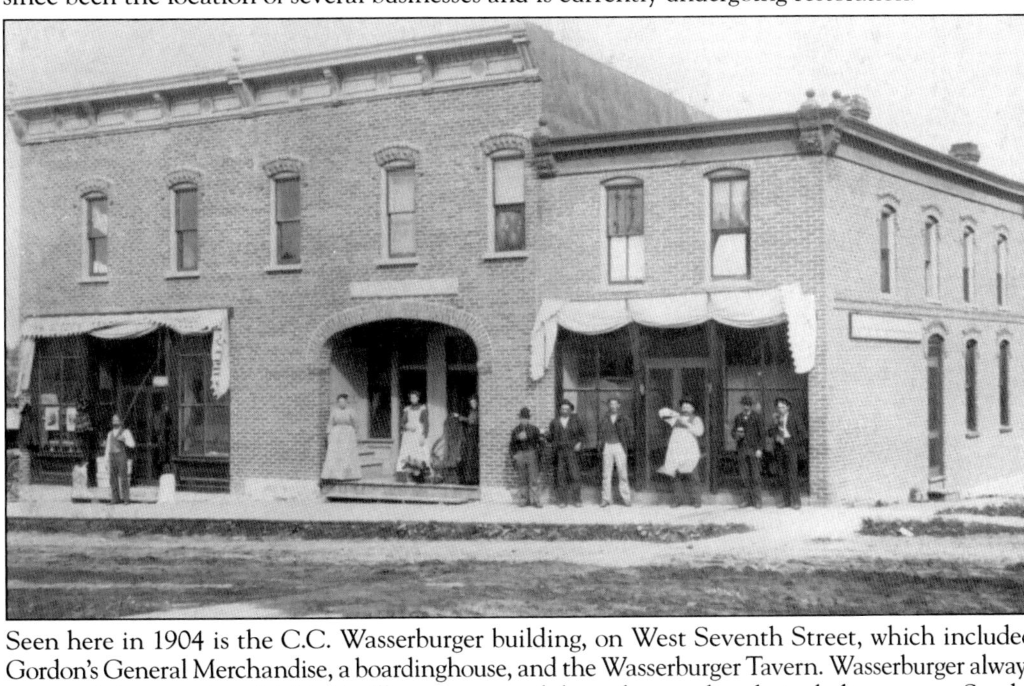

Seen here in 1904 is the C.C. Wasserburger building, on West Seventh Street, which included Gordon's General Merchandise, a boardinghouse, and the Wasserburger Tavern. Wasserburger always managed the store, but this Neillsville tavern passed through many hands, including owners Sparky Helwig, Merle Lindow, Buck Demert, Jim Skroch, and Roger and Sharon Christopherson.

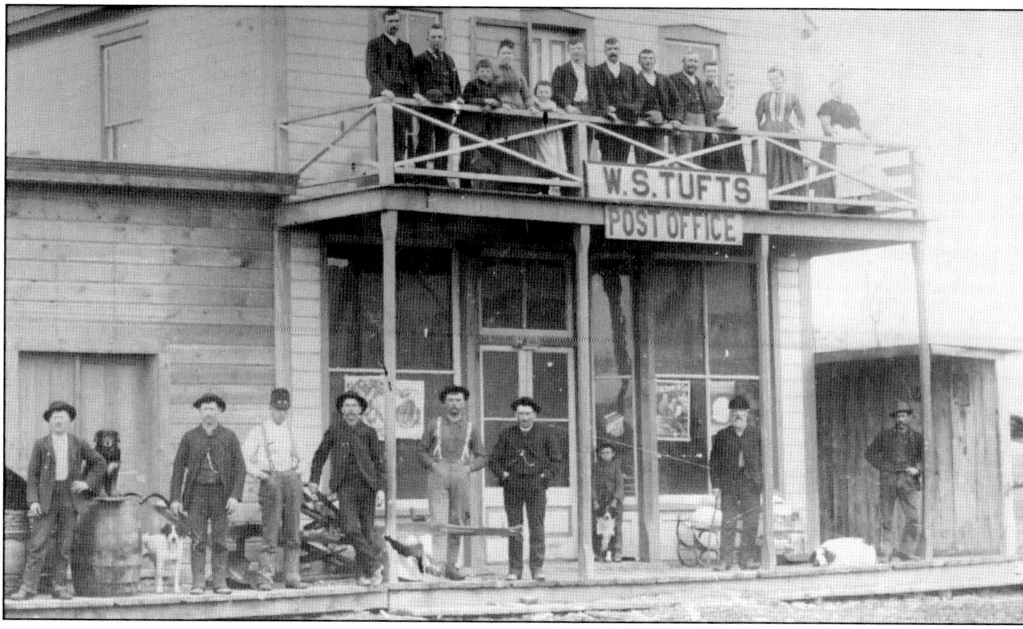

William S. Tufts was an early settler and business entrepreneur in the Withee area who had a general store and ran the local post office. His store grew with the population of Withee until it was the largest business in town. Tufts also owned the Withee Hotel, lumber acreage, and other business interests. He served as the Withee postmaster, was on the township board, and was Clark County's sheriff in 1899.

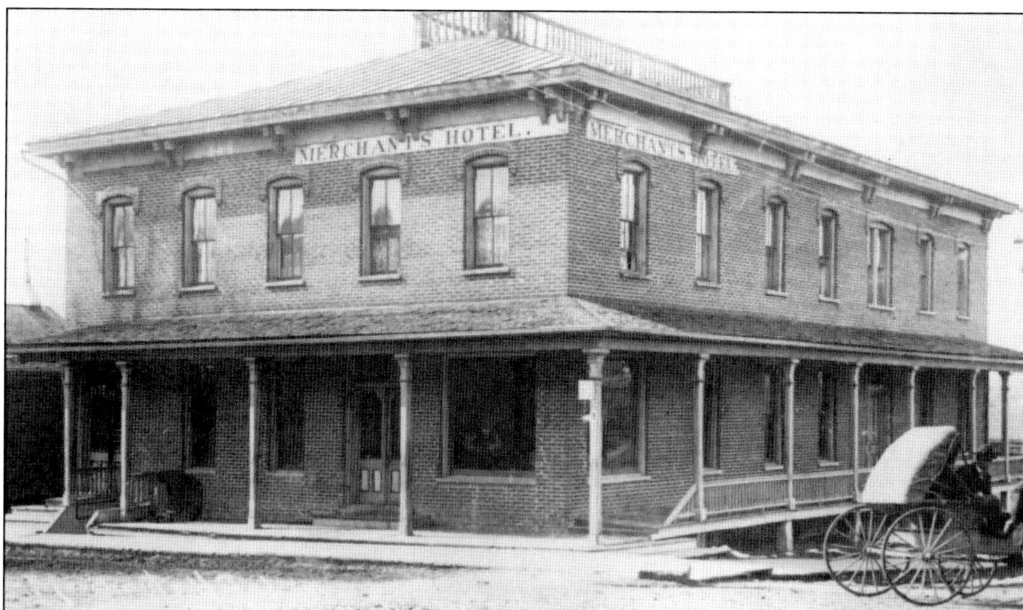

Originally built as the Northside Hotel, this building was later moved across O'Neill Creek to its present location. Once on the south side of the creek, owner George Huntzicker renamed it the Merchant's Hotel. Later additions enlarged the building to its present size. The additions housed many businesses over the years, most notably the Neillsville clinic. After passing through many hands over the years, the old hotel is now used as apartments.

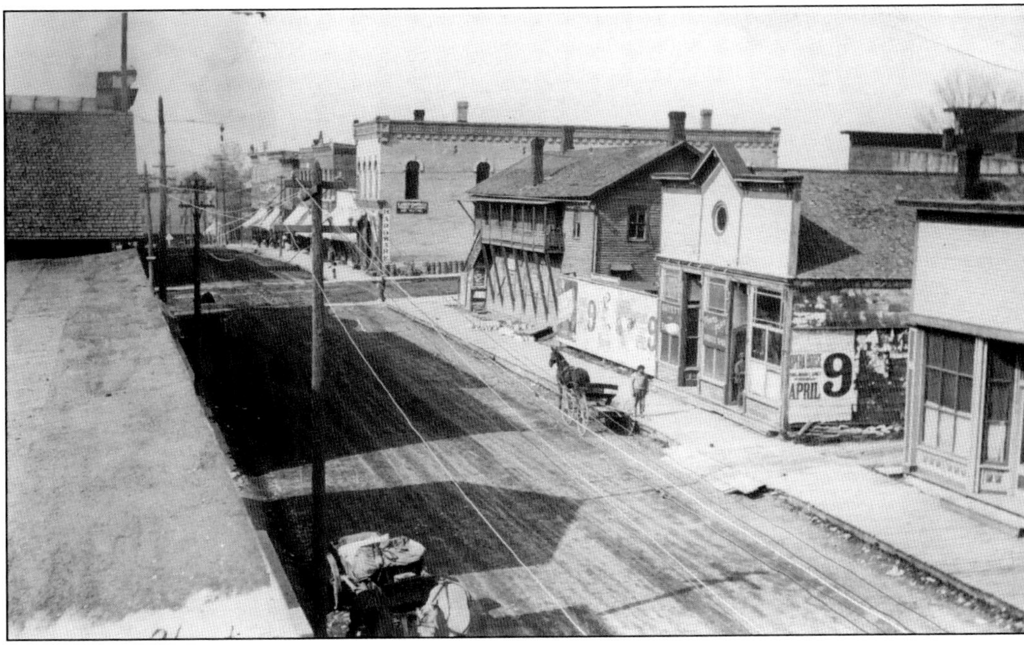

J.W. "Tom" Hommel's theater and Frank Hemp's grocery are seen above on the right side of Hewett Street. The theater was home to traveling entertainers and early motion pictures, while the grocery faced onto Fifth Street and had apartments on the second floor. The buildings were either used or replaced over the years by various businesses. A gazebo and sitting benches now grace this downtown Neillsville area. Below, Phil Zimmer stands to the left, next to the buggy, in front of the theater. In later years, Robert Dwyer had an electrical shop in the front, and Badger State Telephone used the rear of the building as a warehouse.

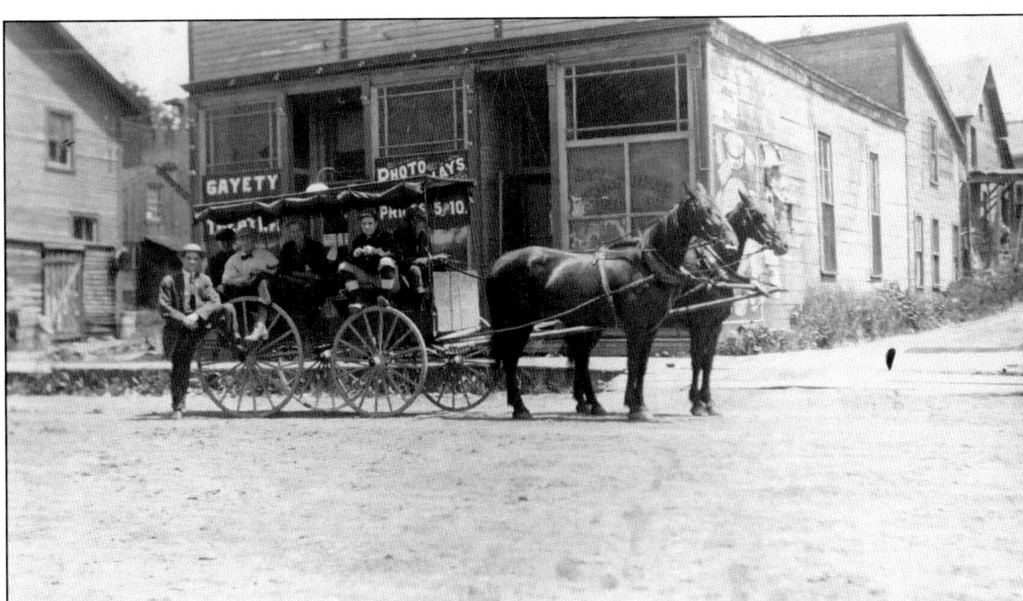

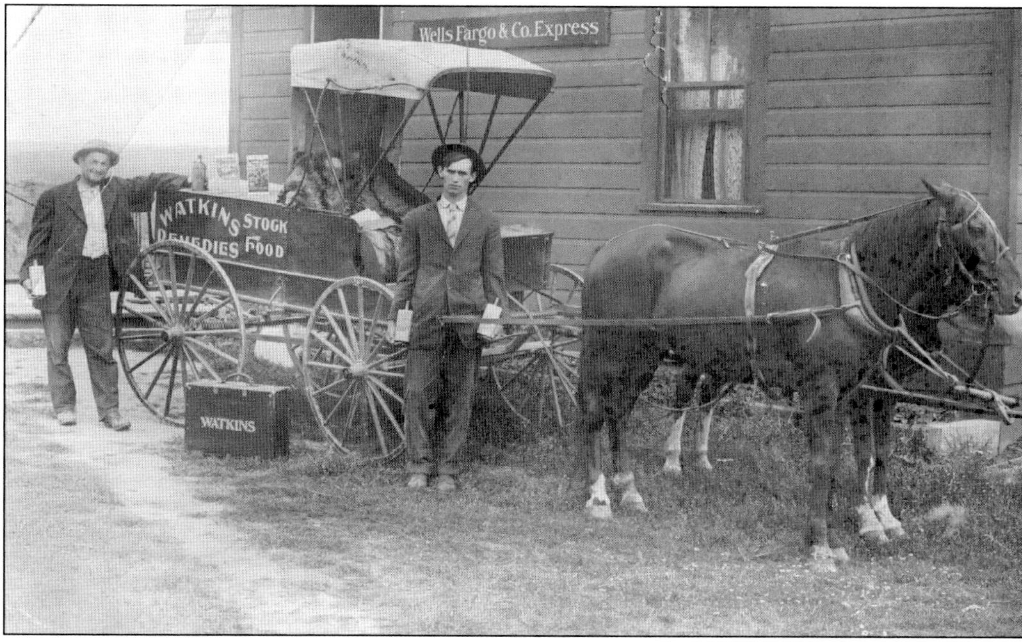

Max Neverman (left) and Blucher Paulus (right), known as the Watkins Peddlers, are seen here by their wagon, ready for a day's work around 1910. Neverman was also a carpenter, and was very adept with a lathe as a shingler. Paulus became a rural mail carrier before entering the service in 1918, returning after the war to help his father, James, in the bottling business.

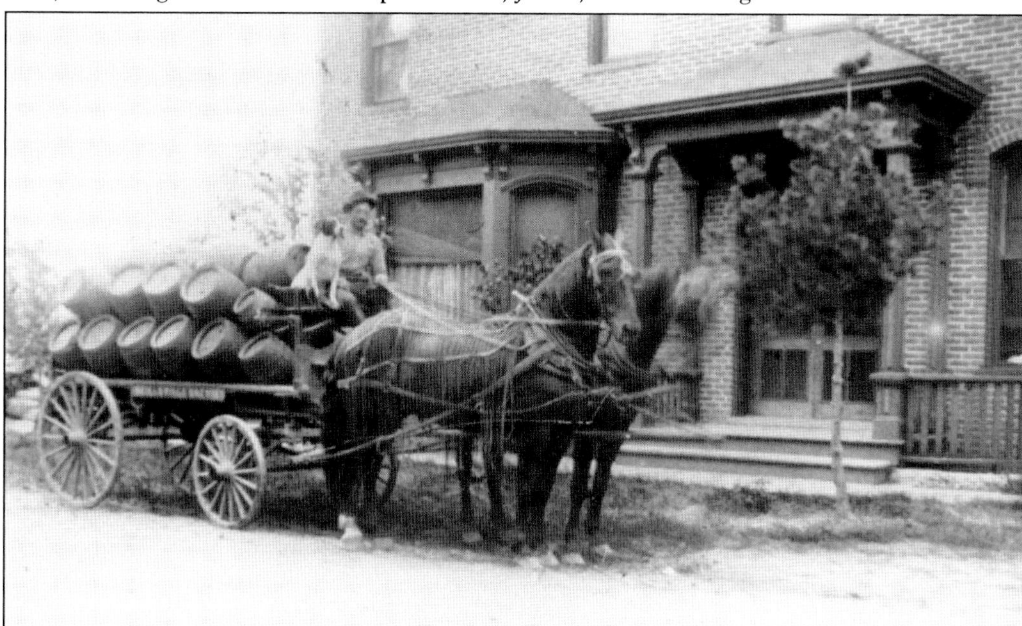

A load of Neillsville Beer sits in front of the old brewery on East Sixth Street. Opened in 1869 by William Neverman and later owned by Louis Sontag, Herman Schuster, Ernest Eilert, and Kurt Listeman, the brewery operated until the beginning of Prohibition, in 1920. Listeman sold the building in 1925 and it was converted into a canning company, and later, into a local bowling alley, which burned in 1959.

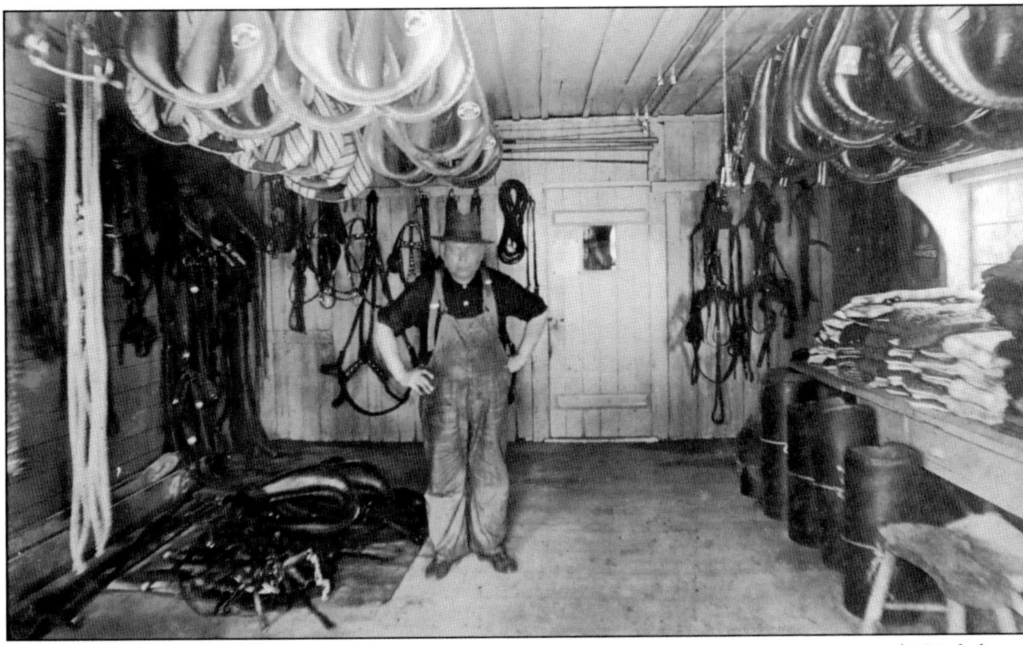

Pickrun's harness shop, pictured here in 1910, was a thriving business in Greenwood. With horse collars, harnesses hung for sale, and leather stock yet to be fashioned into goods, the aroma of leather wafted from inside the building, catching the senses of passersby. The ample supply of readymade goods allowed the store to quickly meet the needs of any customer's horse.

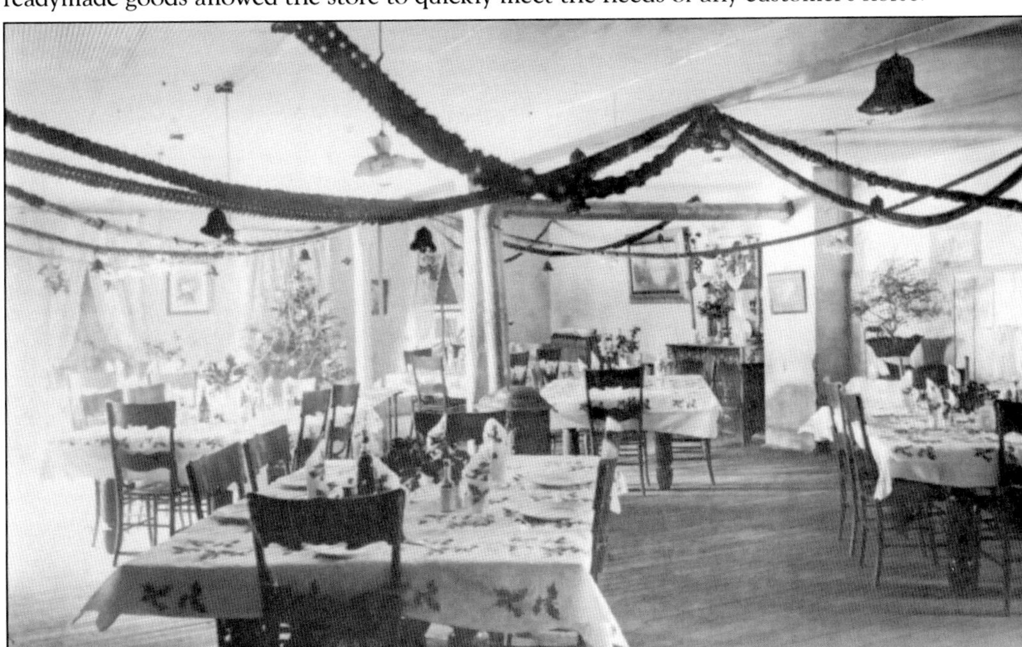

The dining area at the O'Neill House is all decorated for the holidays around 1900. With decorations hung from the ceiling and linens adorning the tables, a central fireplace greeted guests as they arrived for fine dining and evening festivities. A Christmas tree is on the left in the background.

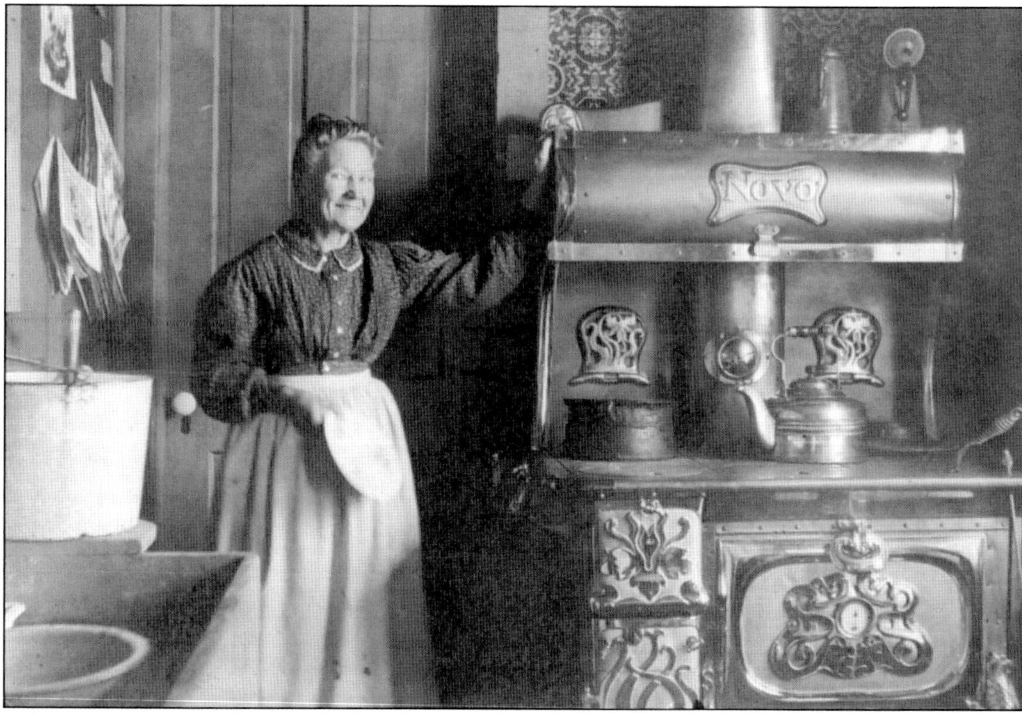

After the death of her husband, Maribah Stafford, formerly of the Stafford Hotel, opened a boardinghouse at 137 East Fifth Street in Neillsville. She married James Redden in 1873, and the boardinghouse became the Redden House. In 1917, Knorr & Rausch of Granton built a Ford garage on the former Redden lot. The Ford dealership remained under various owners until 1982. Today, this site is home to a rental business.

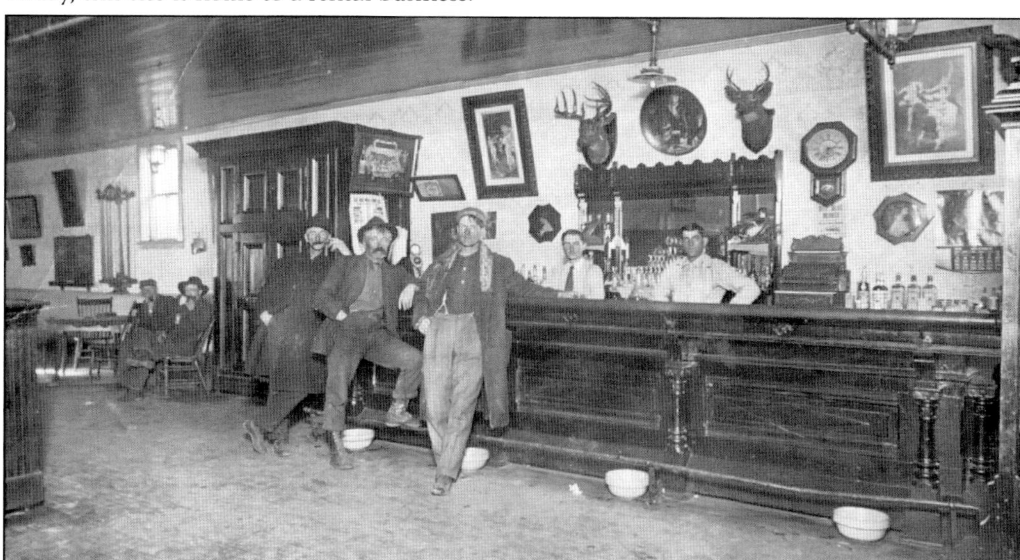

The Al Cowles Saloon was a Neillsville business in the early 1900s. Standing behind the bar are bartenders Al Cowles (left) and Frank Lange (right). Seward Way, the man in the middle of the three standing at the bar, is the only other person identified in the photograph. Way left Neillsville in 1916 to go west. Frank Lange later became the owner of the tavern.

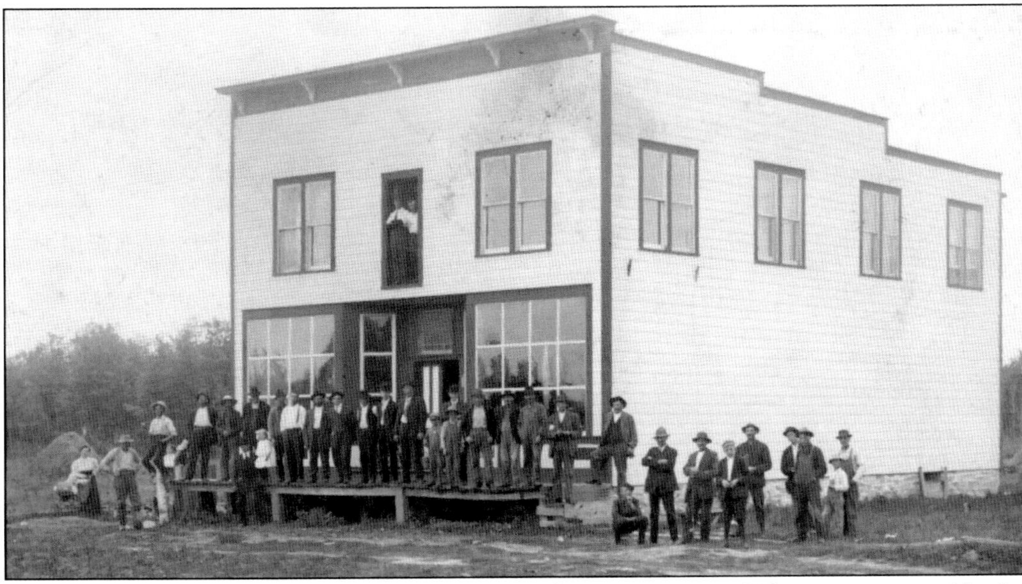

This store was built by Steve Sandburg in Willard. From 1911 to 1915, it was operated by Joe Justin, Steve Legate, and then George Kocancic. In 1916, Ignatz Cesnik ran a land office and hotel in it, while Steve Plautz's family operated a store. In 1926, the building was purchased by Joseph Lunka, who ran a general store and feed store there for more than 30 years. (Courtesy of the Willard Historical Society.)

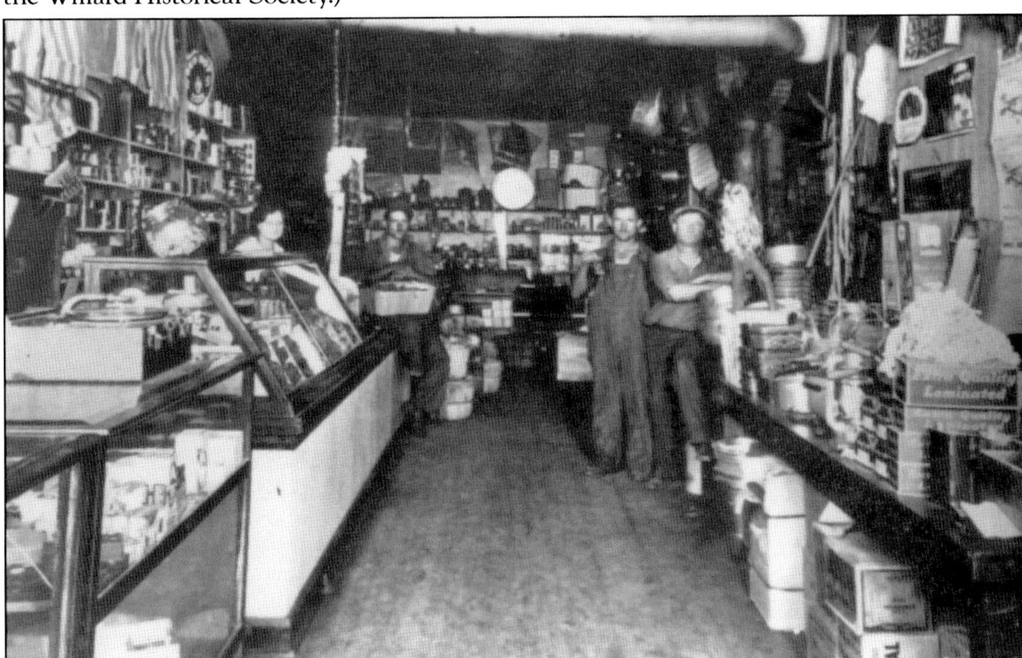

This is an interior view of the Joseph Lunka general merchandise and feed store, which Lunka operated with his wife, Lucille, from 1926 to 1957. Seen from left to right are Anne (Lunka) Ulesich, John Zallar, Martin Kokaly, and Joseph Lunka. In 1957, Lunka's daughter Avis and her husband, Stanley Suda, took over operation of the store, which they ran until 1984. (Courtesy of the Willard Historical Society.)

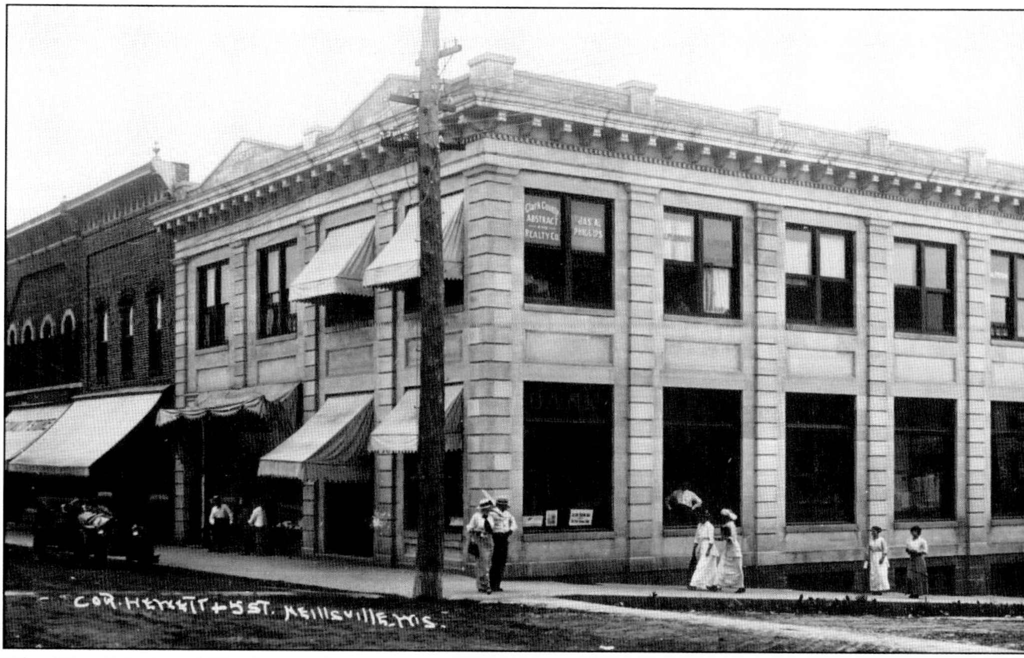

The First National Bank, on the corner of Hewett and Fifth Streets, was built in 1909. On the bank's corner was a large clock, which was hit several times as tractor-trailers made the tight turn onto Highway 10. In the 1970s, the bank expanded into its neighbor to the south. The bank later merged with Marshall & Islley Bank, and a new building was constructed on Division Street.

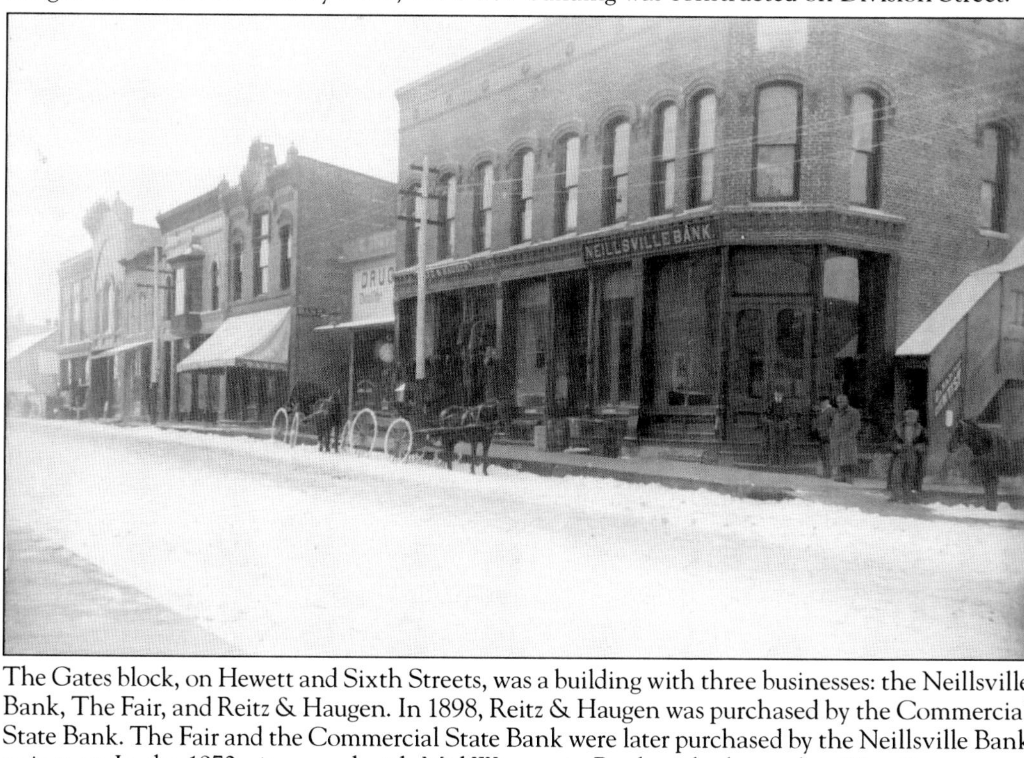

The Gates block, on Hewett and Sixth Streets, was a building with three businesses: the Neillsville Bank, The Fair, and Reitz & Haugen. In 1898, Reitz & Haugen was purchased by the Commercial State Bank. The Fair and the Commercial State Bank were later purchased by the Neillsville Bank as it grew. In the 1970s, it merged with Mid-Wisconsin Bank and relocated to West Street.

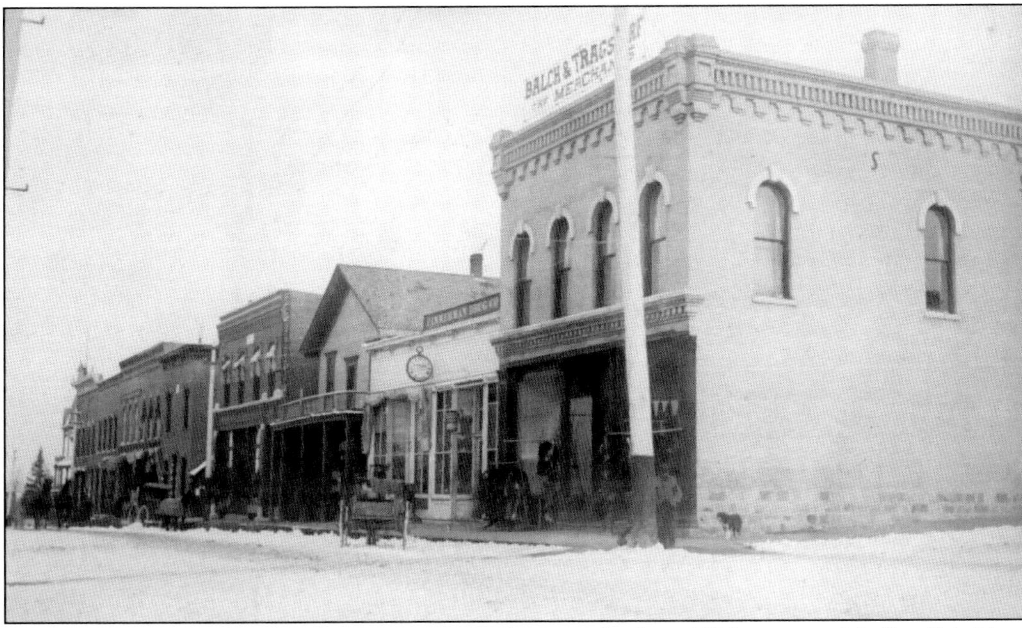

The Balch & Tragsdorf hardware store, seen here in the late 1890s, was in Neillsville's Lloyd building, on the northwest corner of Hewett and Fifth Streets. In 1910, it was sold to the Cash Hardware Company. In 1933, Schultz Brothers Variety came to the location. In the 1950s, Schultz Brothers purchased the Zimmerman Drug property next door and local contractor Art Carl built a modern store where the two had previously stood.

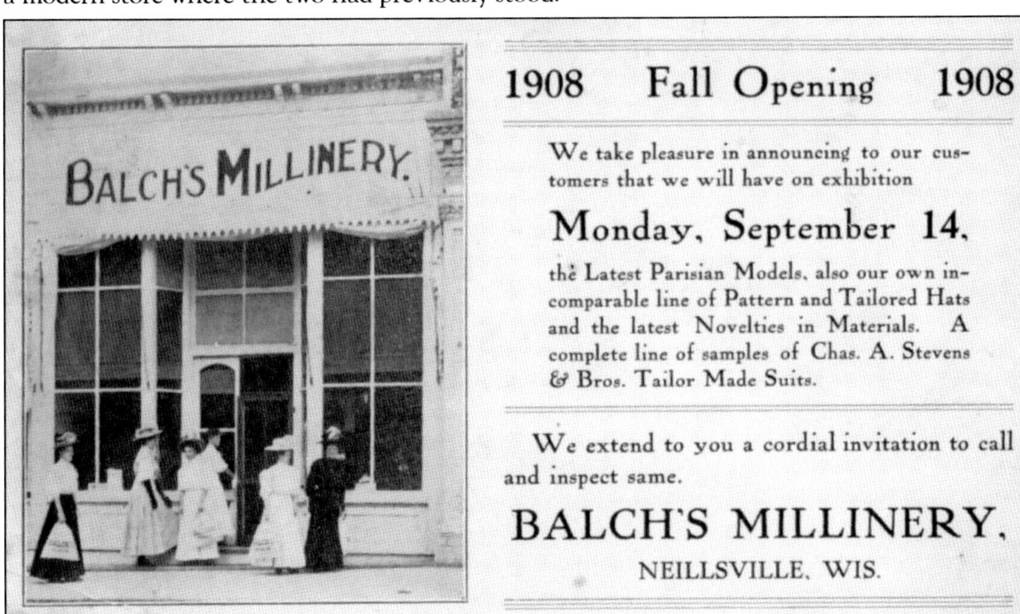

Balch's Millinery was next to the hardware stores above. This postcard was an advertisement for the store mailed in 1908. The store operated here until 1910, when the Balches moved to Milwaukee, running a successful millinery business there until 1920. After returning to Neillsville, Grace Balch opened a new millinery store north of the former location and on the opposite side of Hewett Street.

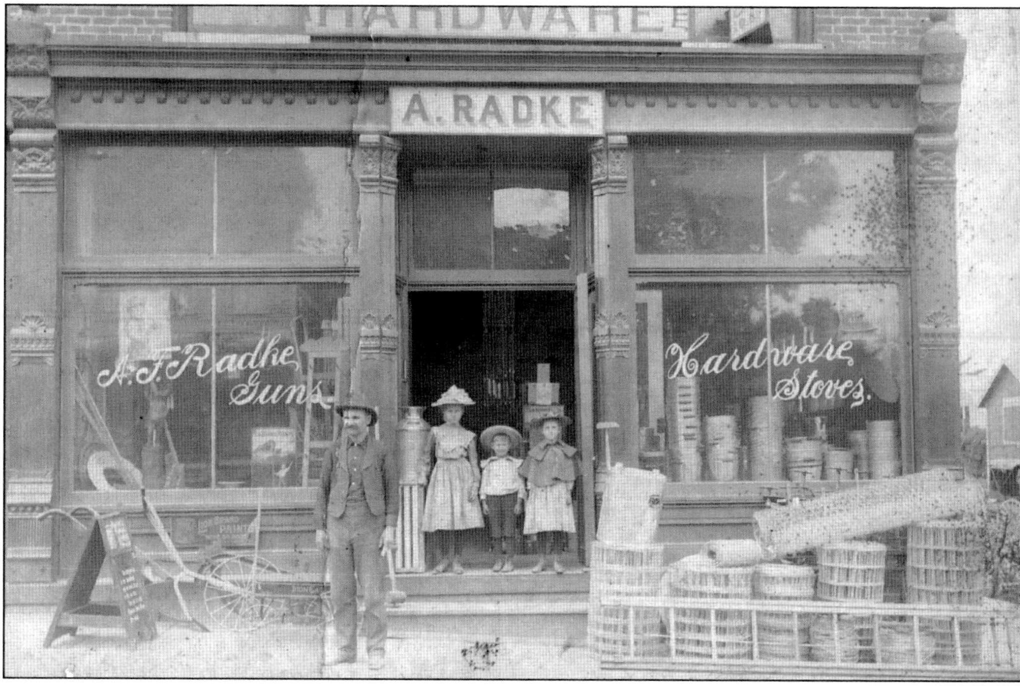

The A.F. Radke hardware store was located on the corner of Fifth and West Streets. Radke also owned a warehouse on West Street. Seen here are, from left to right, Adoph, Elsie, Herbert "Tubby," and Freida Radke. In the late 1950s, WCCN Radio had its studio here. Today, it is the home of O'Reilly Auto Parts.

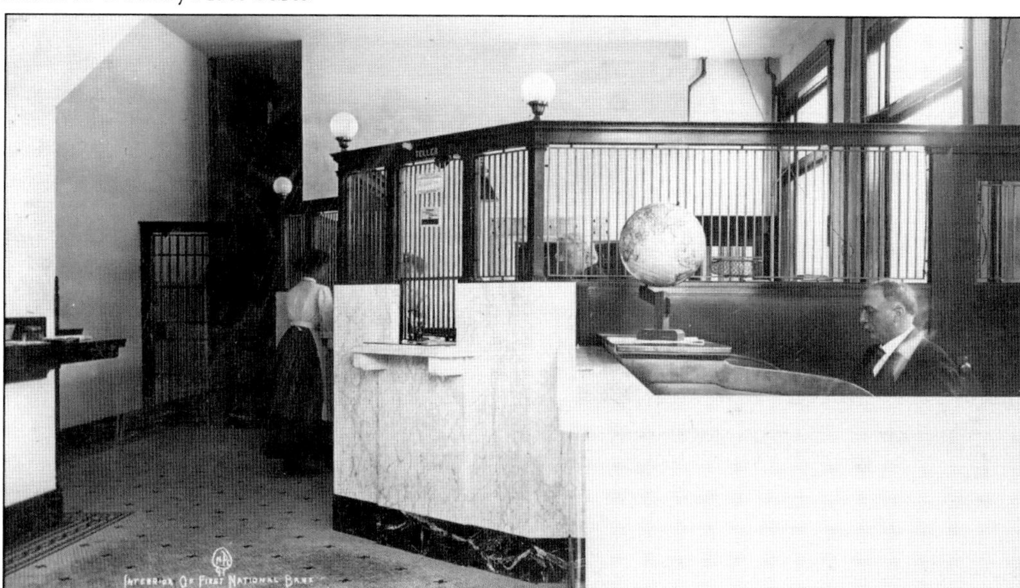

Charles Cornelius, seen here at his desk at the First National Bank in Neillsville, was a banking pioneer. In 1904, he was the vice president of the Commercial State Bank in Neillsville, and by 1909, he had built and opened the First National Bank. He was instrumental in establishing several other banks in Clark County, and was influential in the growth of many Neillsville businesses.

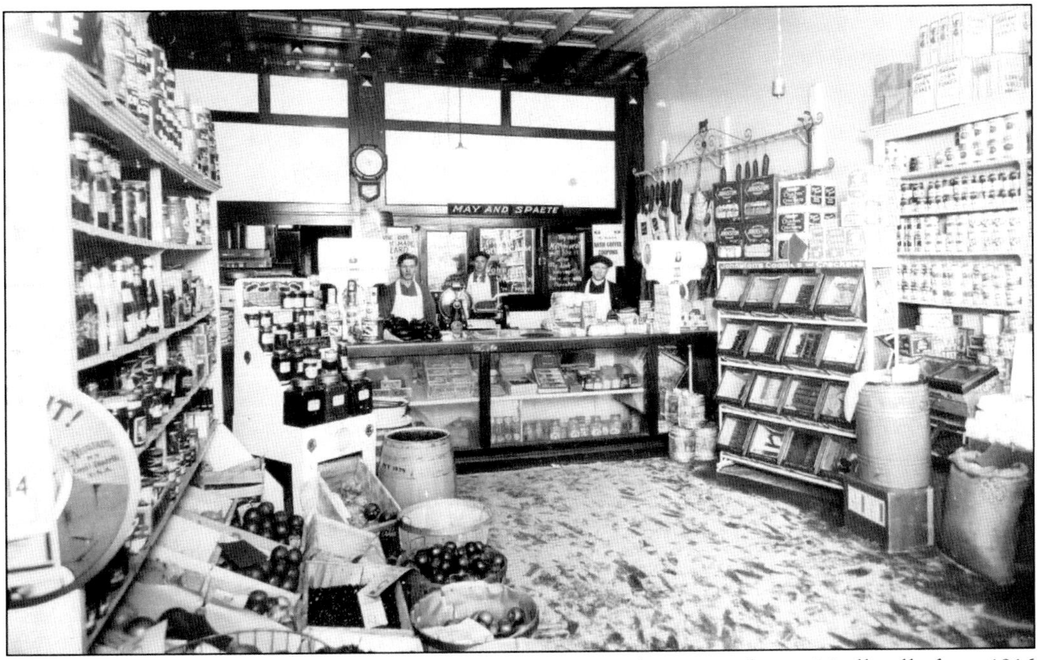

George May and Alfred Spaete operated a grocery store and meat market in Neillsville from 1916 to 1930. This 1926 photograph of the interior of their store shows all of the groceries, canned goods, and fresh fruits they had for sale. Spaete later moved to Granton, purchasing the Granton Meat Market, which he ran until 1946, along with his cold storage locker business.

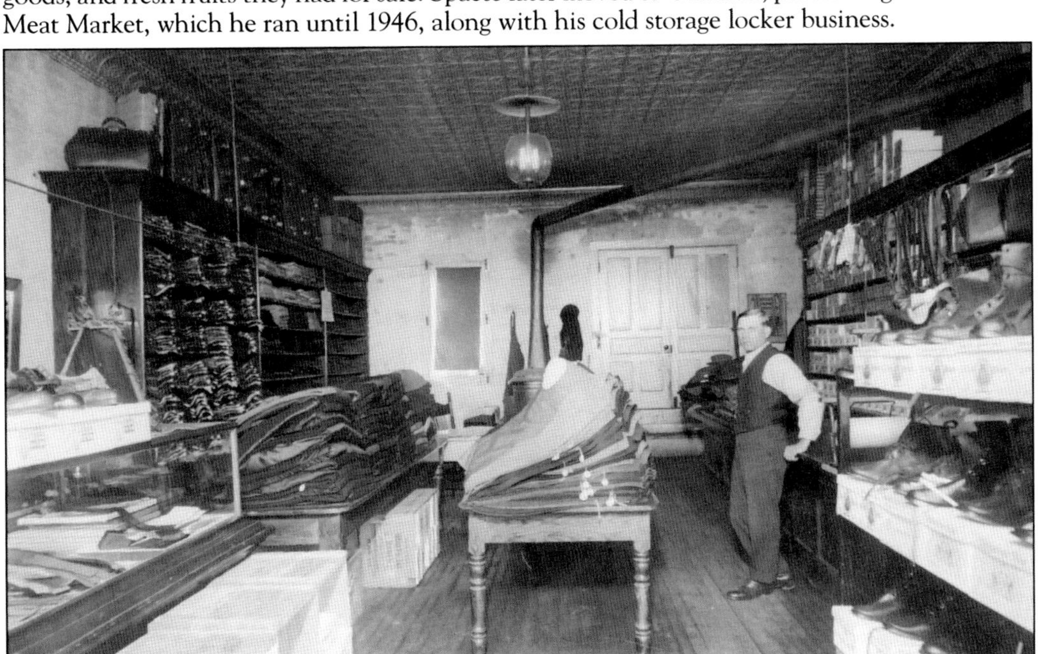

Gustave Deutsch was the manager of August Snyder's Granton Clothing Store in the early 1900s. He taught school and clerked in many stores in addition to operating the general merchandise store. He later returned to Neillsville, where he operated the Northside Store for 18 years. He also served as Neillsville's poor commissioner and cemetery commissioner for 25 years.

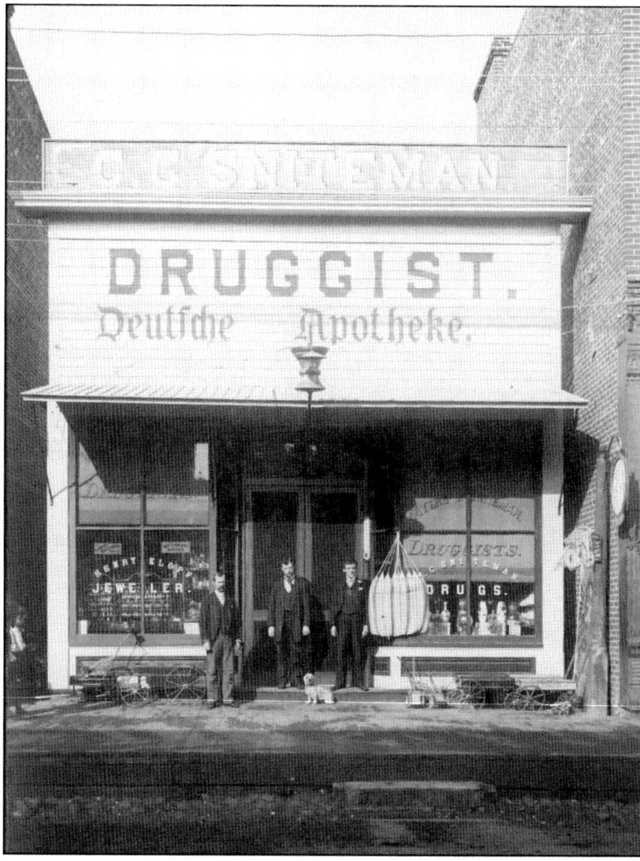

C.C. Sniteman managed the Myer brothers' drugstore when he first arrived in Neillsville, later buying out both Isaiah and Henry Myer. Seen here around 1880 are, from left to right, Henry Klopf, who ran his jewelry shop in the store; Isaiah Myer; and C.C. Sniteman. Shortly after this photograph was taken, the store was enlarged and a brick veneer exterior was added.

This is an interior view of Sniteman's drugstore around 1940. From left to right are Agnes Meinholdt, George Sontag, Dave Parry, and Marge Hauri, who staffed the business at the time. Sontag was a protégé of Sniteman's, who encouraged local youth to pursue their education. All three men were civic-minded supporters of the Neillsville business community.

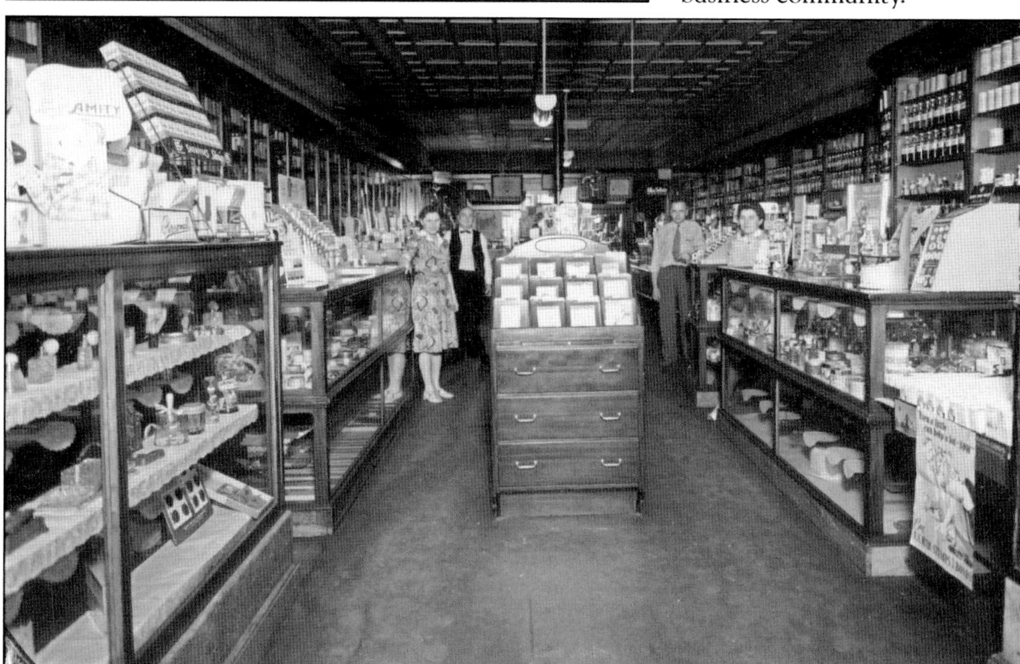

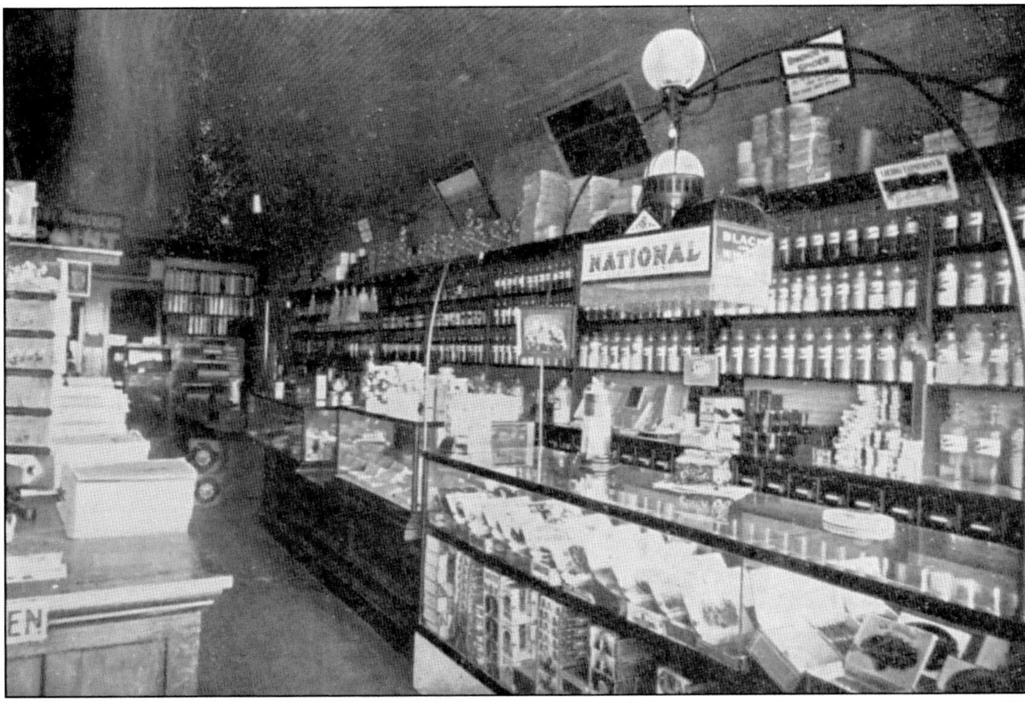

This is an interior view of the Frank Wing drugstore in Abbotsford. The store opened in 1901 on Main Street and Highway 29. In the early 1900s, pharmacists had to measure, weigh, and mix prescriptions for their clients. An apothecary scale, used by Wing, is on display at the 1897 Clark County Jail Museum in Neillsville.

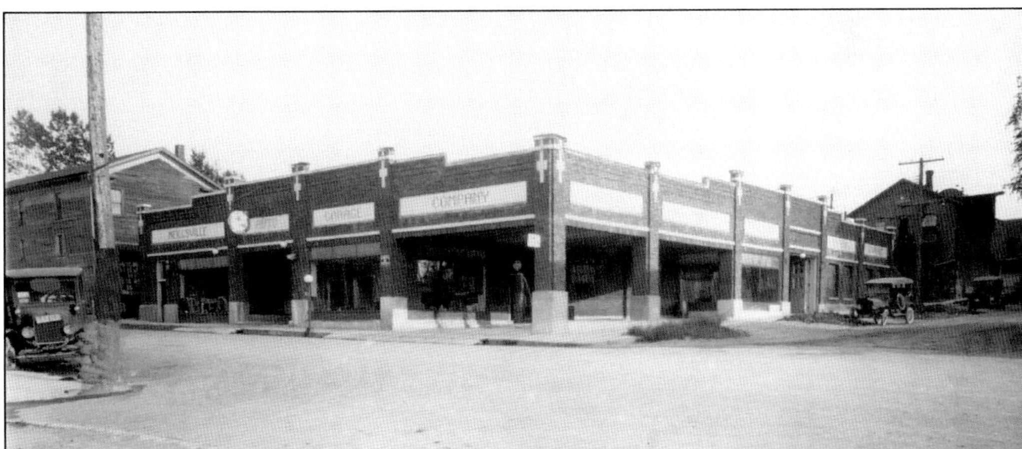

The Neillsville Auto Garage Company was built by the Schultz brothers in the early 1920s. One of its most notable features was the gasoline station that was built into the building's corner. Early on, it sold gasoline- and oil-related products under the Husky brand. In 1965, Pete Smith sold the service station business to Joe and Bob Urban, the owners of a Chrysler and Plymouth Dealership.

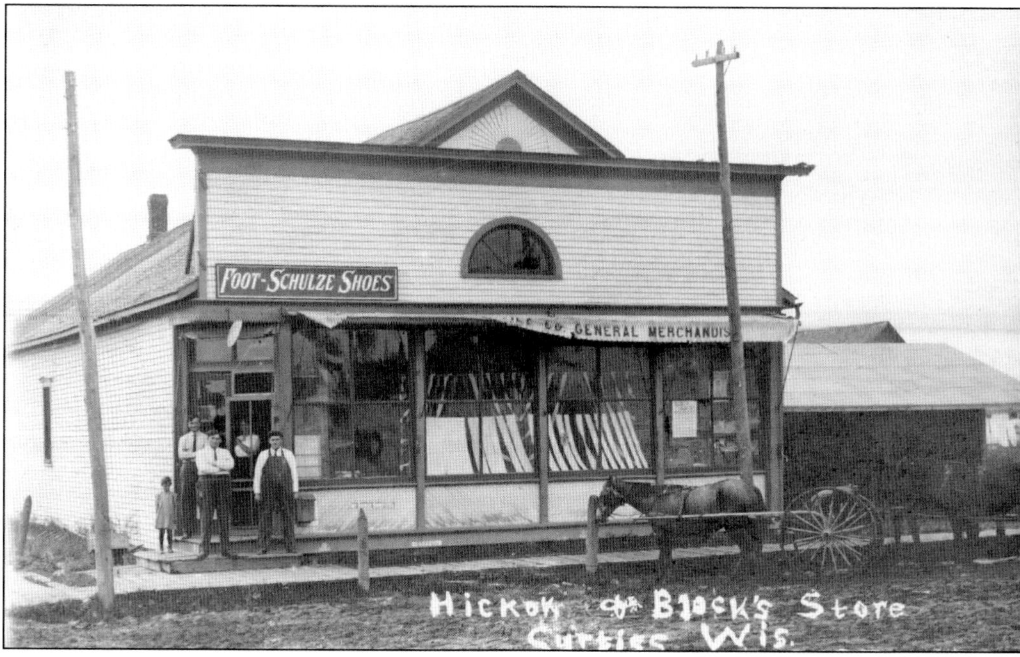

This is the Hickok and Block's store as it appeared in February 1910. Built in 1894, it was a general mercantile store that sold Schulze shoes and other items. In 1910, the Green brothers purchased the store, operating it until New Years Day 1913, when it was destroyed by fire. (Courtesy of the David Jankoski collection.)

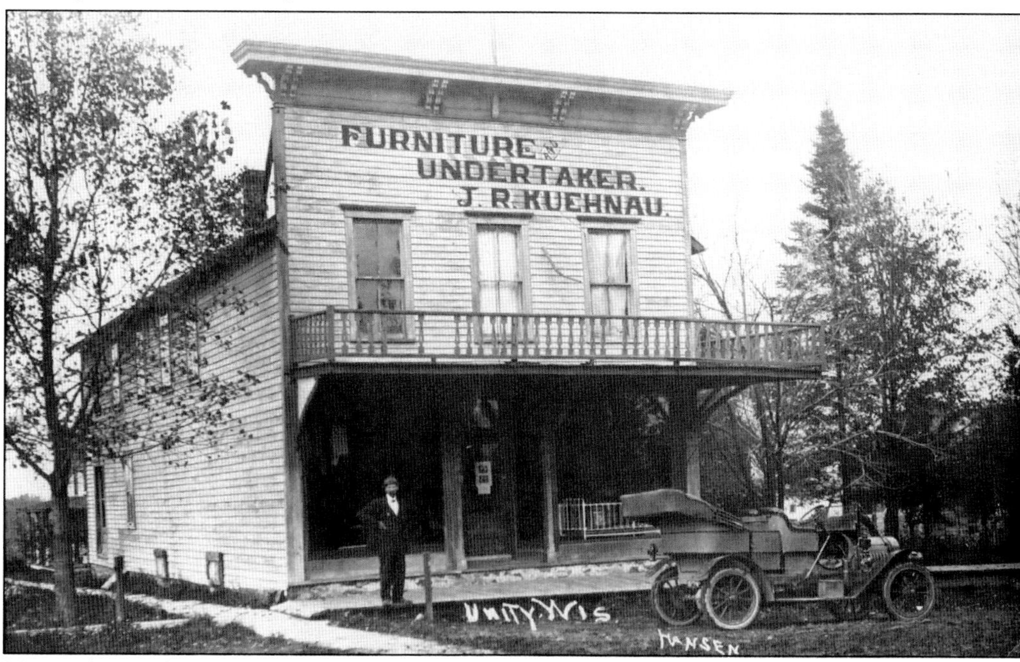

J.R. Kuehnau of Unity had a furniture manufacturing and undertaking business. The combination of those two occupations was common around 1900. In 1905, the post office was located in his business, but as newer stores were built, the post office moved on. (Courtesy of the David Jankoski collection.)

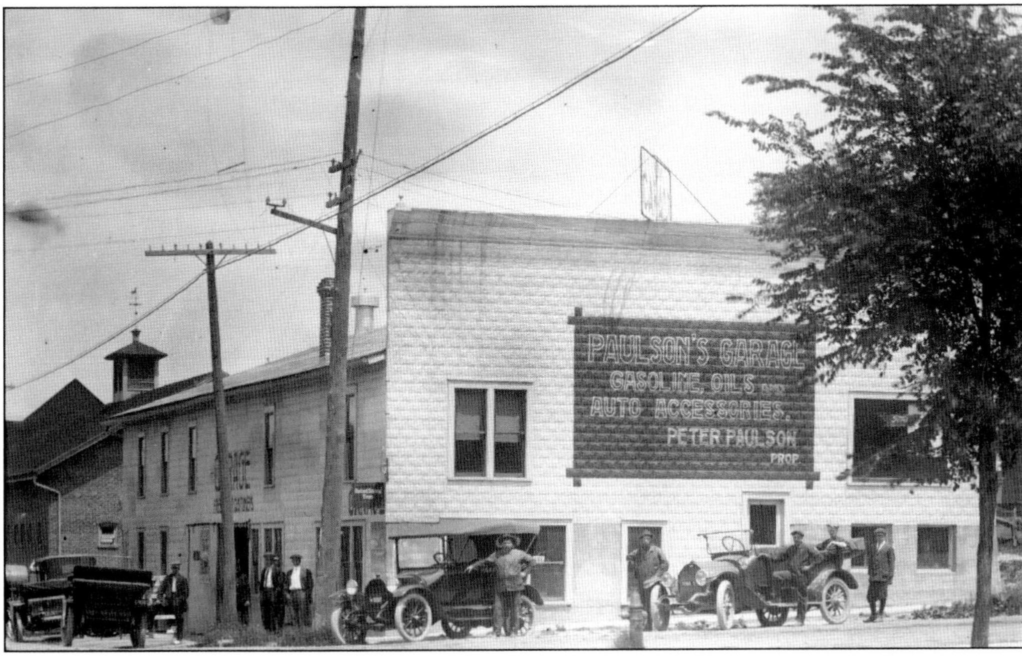

Facing Grand Avenue from the corner of Grand Avenue and Fifth Street was Paulson's Garage. Ford and Dodge cars were sold and repaired in the lower level. The second floor had a large open area that hosted wedding dances, civic events, and Moose and other lodge meetings. Sitting at the base of the easterly rising Fifth Street, the second-story entrance was at ground level.

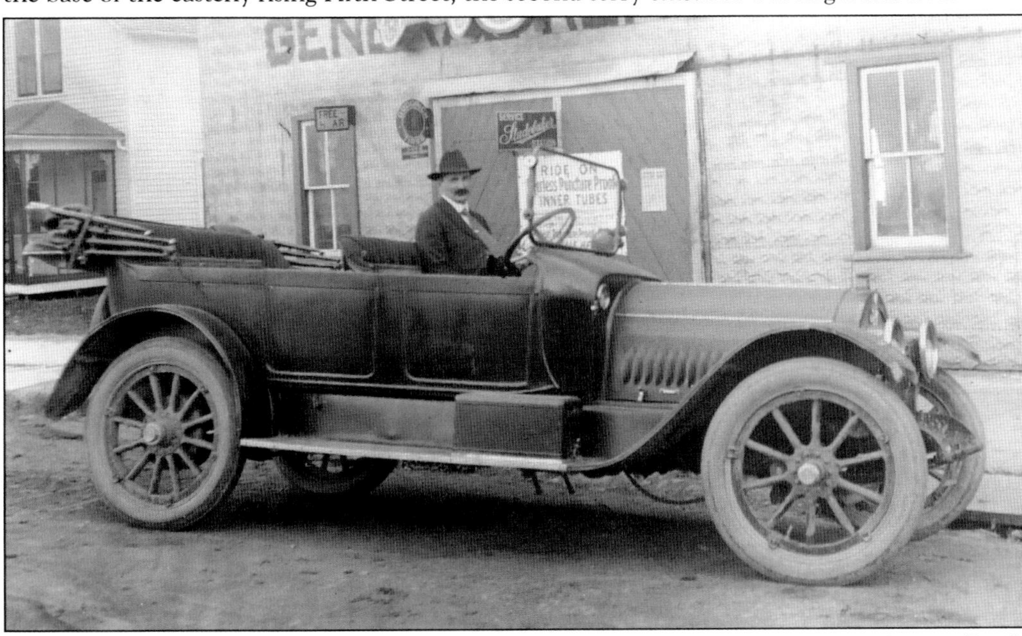

Len Howard is seen here in his Studebaker in front of his tire and radiator shop. This Neillsville business was located on West Street between Fourth and Fifth Streets. The building was razed and replaced by a single-story office complex in the 1950s. In the 1960s and 1970s, it was home to a beauty shop, an abstract business, a gift shop, and the office of John Roberts, a seller of yearbooks and class rings.

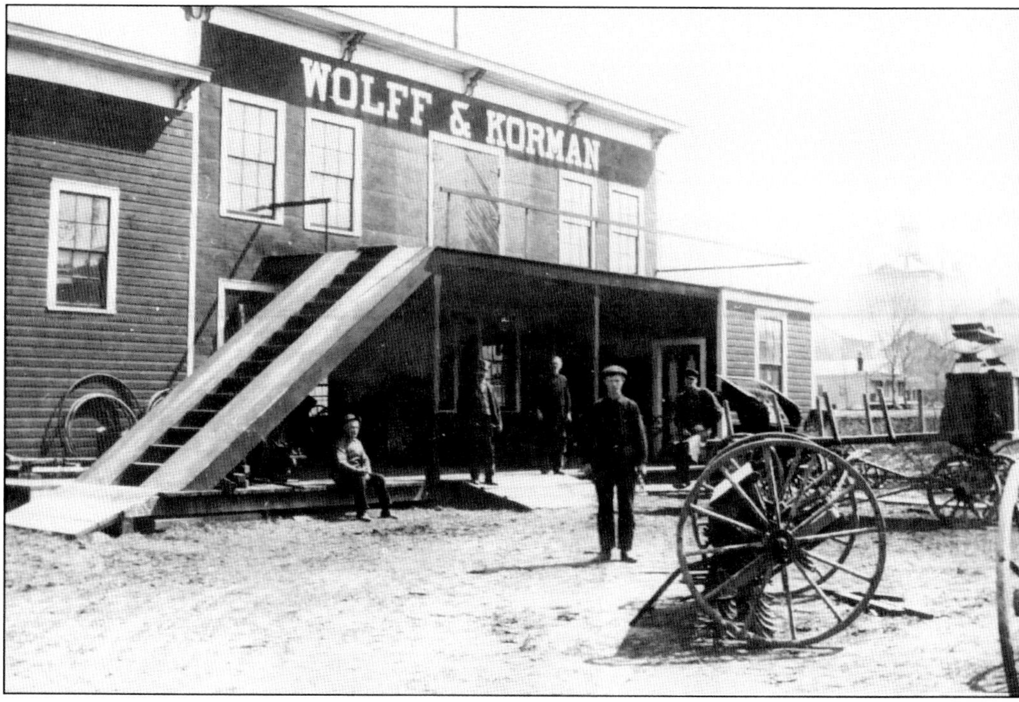

The Wolff & Korman wagon and machine shop was on Hewett Street, along the north bank of O'Neill Creek. Its primary business was the making of wagons, sleighs, and other needs for the logging industry, as well as ornately decorated carriages and sleighs for the general public. The building has been used by different tradesmen in the years since. Presently, it is home to Kwik-Trip Inc.

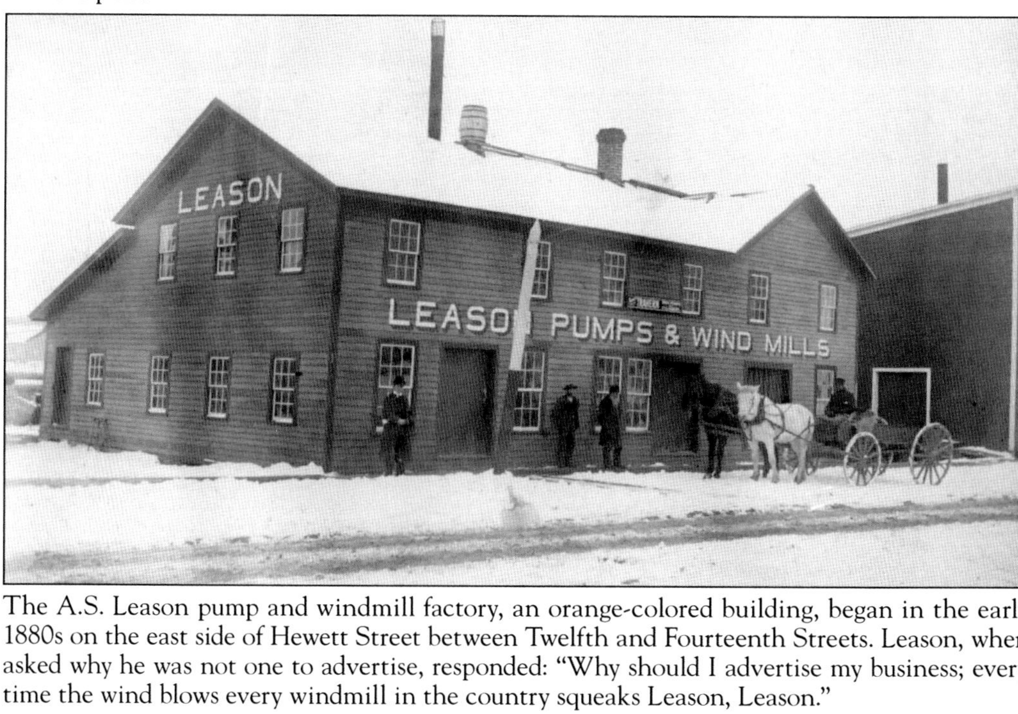

The A.S. Leason pump and windmill factory, an orange-colored building, began in the early 1880s on the east side of Hewett Street between Twelfth and Fourteenth Streets. Leason, when asked why he was not one to advertise, responded: "Why should I advertise my business; every time the wind blows every windmill in the country squeaks Leason, Leason."

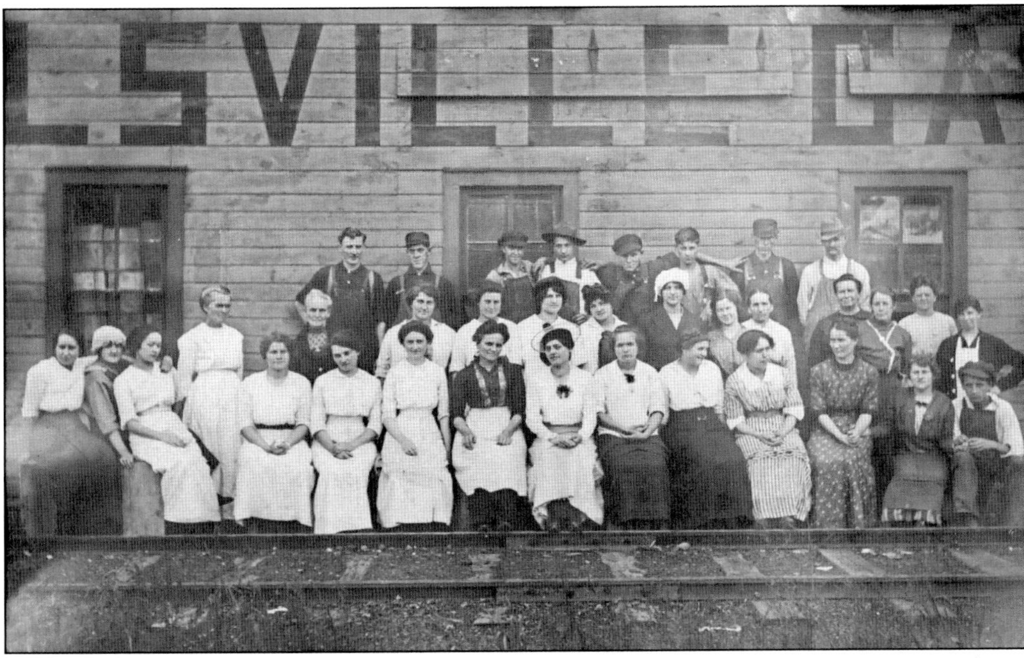

The Neillsville Canning Company was on West Eighth Street. It began in 1917, canning string beans and locally grown corn, and occasionally pumpkin and kraut. Its products were labeled with the Lake Arbutus, Marathon, and Big Farm brands. The canning business passed, and the building has since been the home to Nelson Muffler, Auto Test Inc., and storage and warehousing concerns.

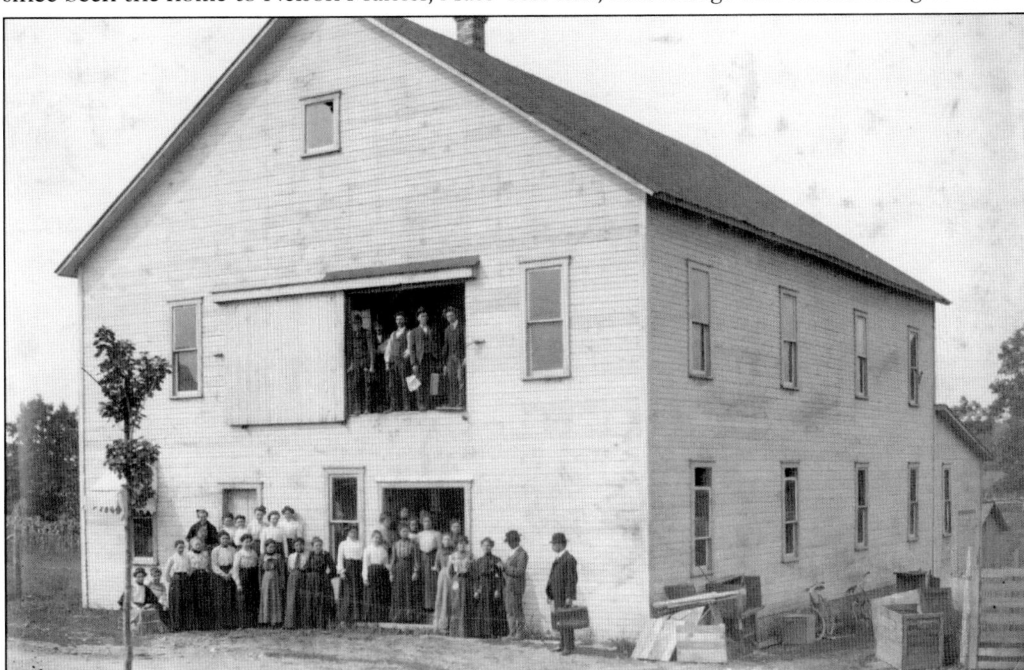

This factory building, seen around 1910, has been identified as being in the 500 block of South Main Street in Greenwood. Two different lumber businesses were located on this lot after this building was removed.

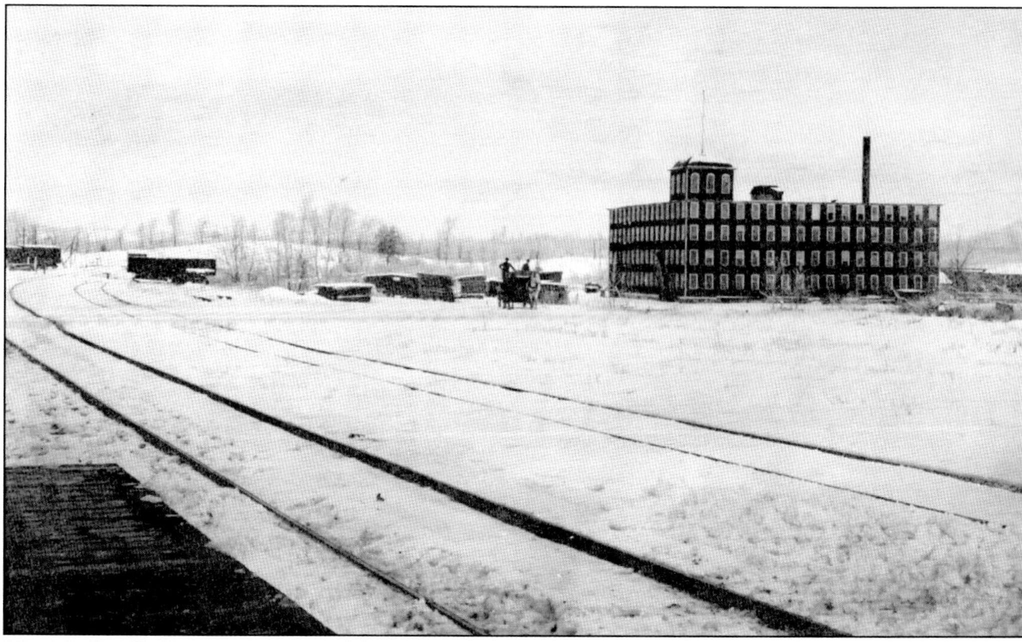

The Neillsville Furniture Factory (above and below) began as a business venture by local businessmen in 1889. Located just past the junction of Oak and Eighth Streets, near the rail lines and the mouth of O'Neill Creek, the factory provided employment for hundreds of people. During the hard times of the Panic of 1893, it was purchased by a furniture company from Baltimore and renamed Neillsville Manufacturing Company. In 1912, a night watchman observed a flickering fire and summoned the volunteer fire department. Consumed in a raging fire, the building was a total loss. The local community approached the parent company in an effort to have the business rebuilt, but the citizenry was not able to secure the needed funds and the business was never rebuilt—a huge economic blow to the community.

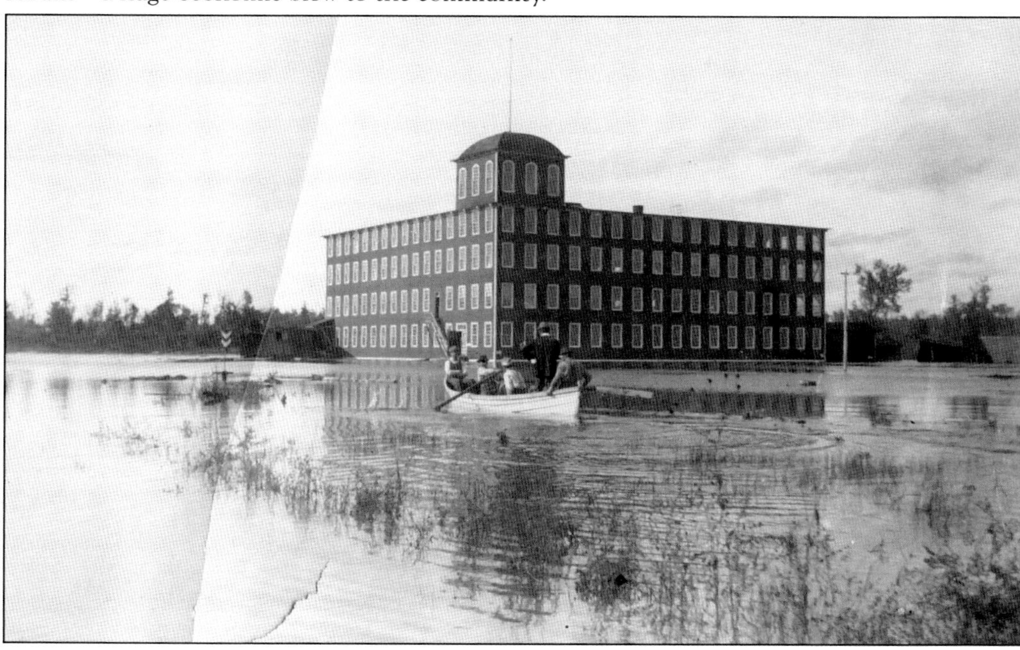

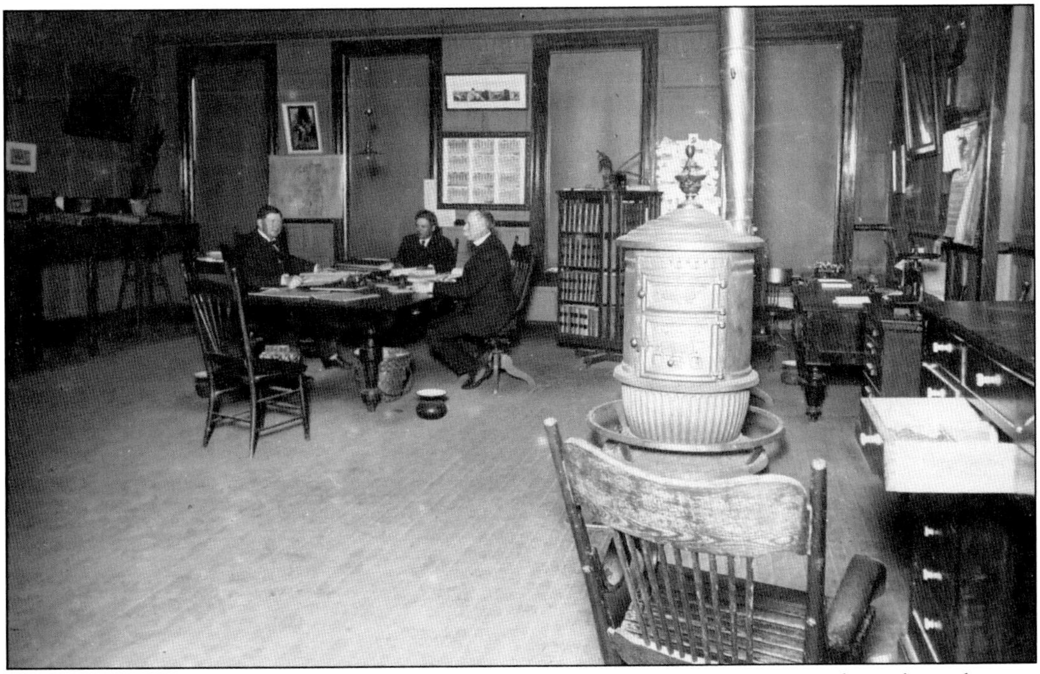

From left to right, Jeff Schuster, William Campman, and Charles Grow work in their abstract and title business above C.C. Sniteman's drugstore. These three were responsible for drawing the new city map after the streets were renamed in August 1889. William Campman served with the corporation for 78 years. At the time of his death, Campman was Wisconsin's last surviving soldier of the Spanish-American War.

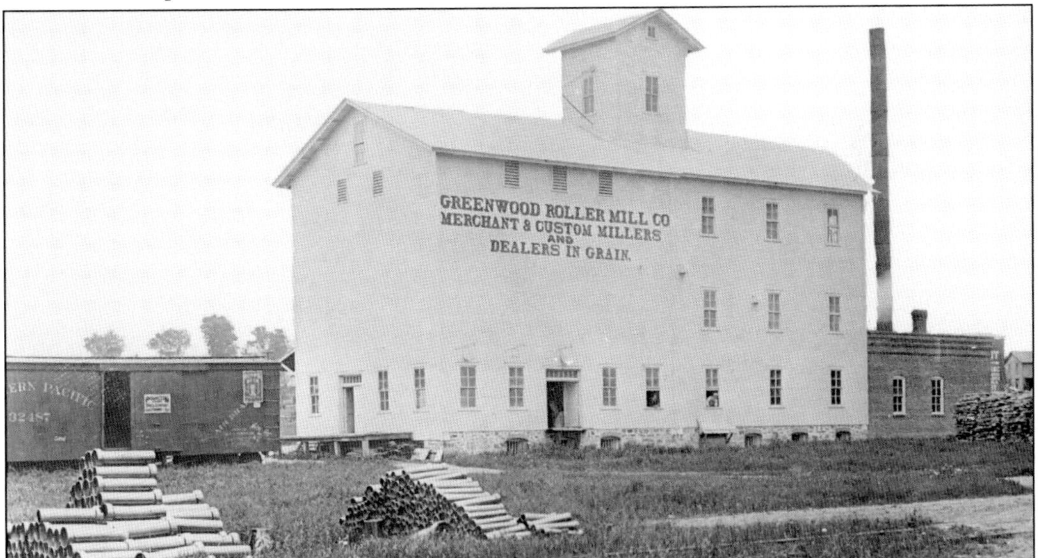

Greenwood Roller Mills was started in 1899 by railroad magnate Nathaniel Caldwell Foster. The mill became operational in the spring of 1900 and was incorporated in 1902 as Greenwood Roller Mills Inc. It specialized in making wheat, buckwheat, rye, and graham flour, and in custom milling. Vast quantities of grains were purchased and shipped by the railroad through its operation. (Courtesy of the David Jankoski Collection.)

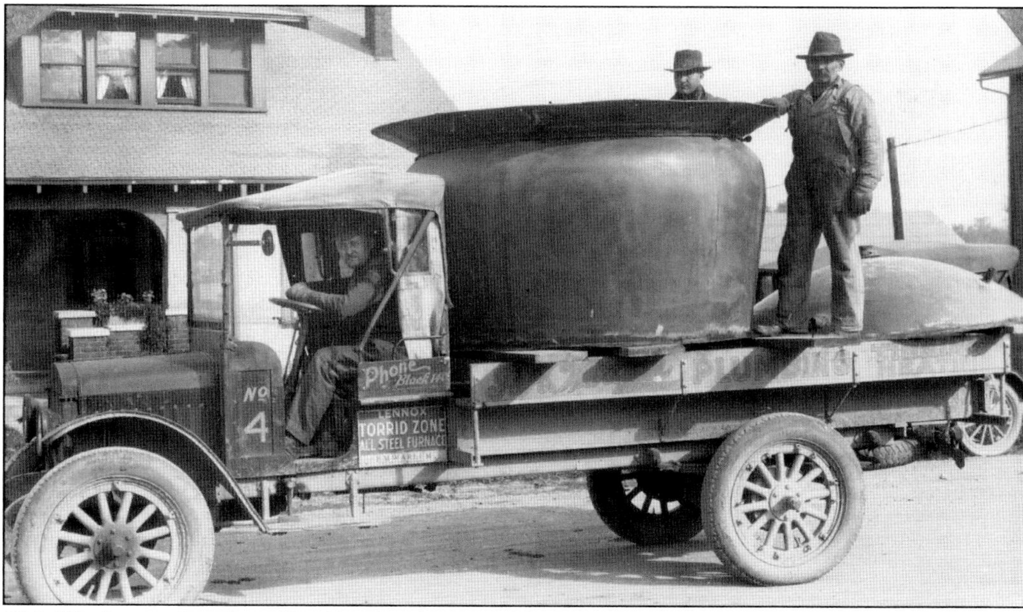

P.N. Warlum, a local Neillsville plumbing and heating contractor, is pictured with his truck and load on East Sixth Street, near the corner of Court Street. It is not known what was on the truck; it could have been a large pot removed from the old brewery or canning factory a block farther east.

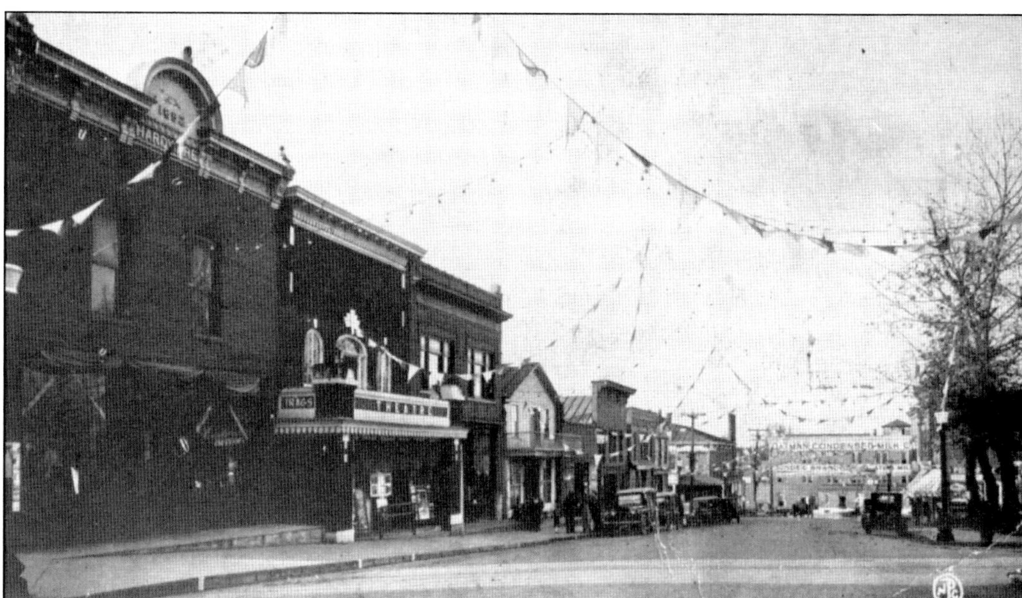

The Trags Theatre was in the 600 block of Hewett Street. William Tragsdorf built it after returning to Neillsville from working on the Panama Canal. Later, Tragsdorf, yearning to return to the Canal Zone, sold it to John Adler of Marshfield. It was managed for many years by William Meier. After Meier's retirement, it served briefly as a video rental store. The building, after falling into disrepair and becoming a hazard, was eventually razed.

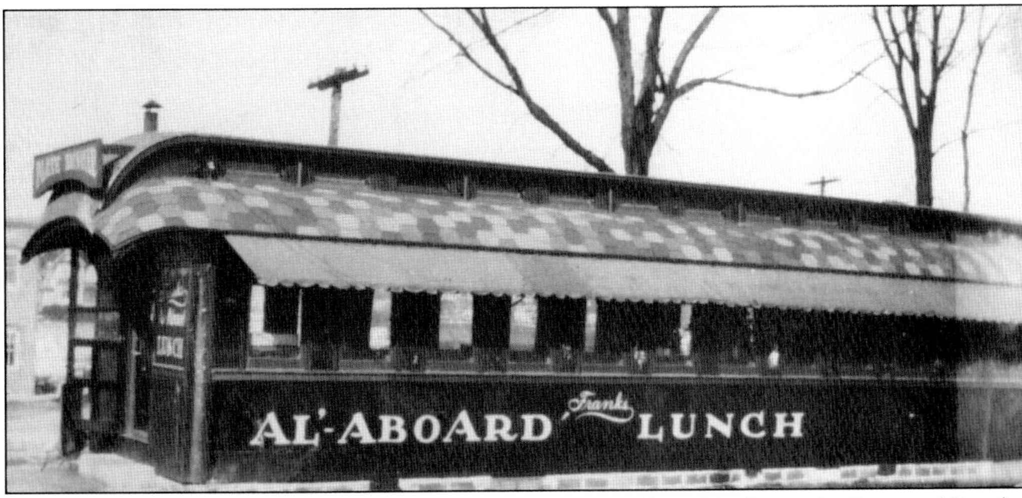

The Al-Aboard Restaurant, a railroad dining car, was purchased by Louis La Bonte of Stanley. Located across from Neillsville's Merchant's Hotel on the property of H.J. Brooks on Hewett Street, it served short order meals from 1930 to 1955, when it was sold and moved. Notable owners included Frank and Harvey Quesnell, Julia Reber, and Nell, Hallie, and Robert Horswill.

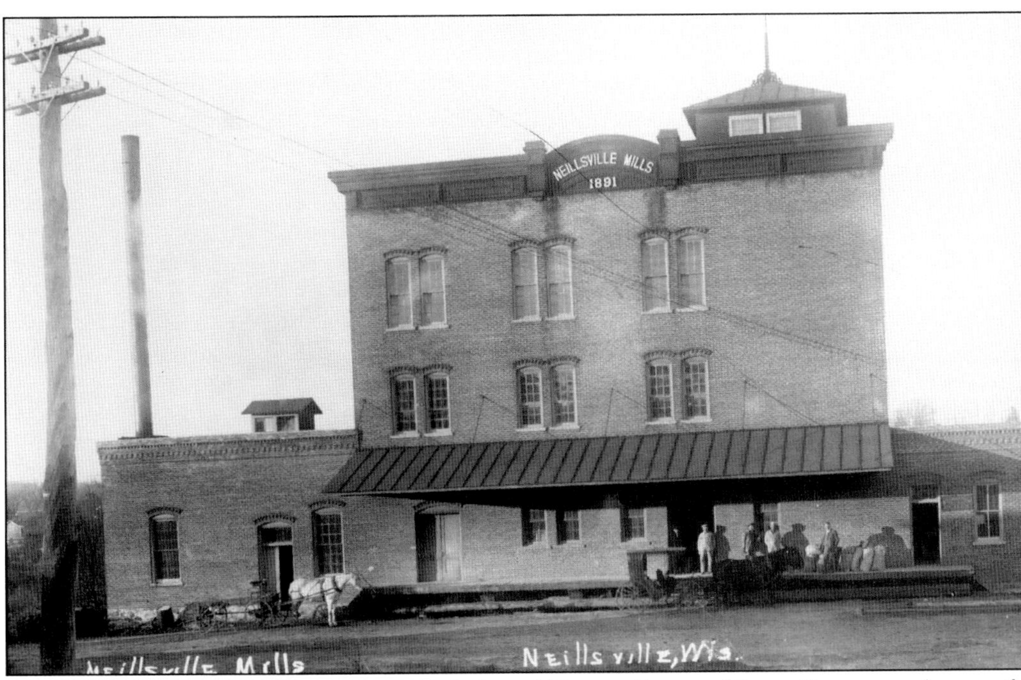

Neillsville Mills was on the corner of Eighth and Hewett Streets. The mill generated steam for the fledgling Neillsville Power and Electric Company's power generation. In 1902, it became the Neillsville Cash Milling Company, and in 1916, it was sold to the Oatman Condensed Milk Company. Later, it was owned by the American Can Company and by Neillsville Milk Products. The building was razed, and the lot is now home to the Neillsville Fire Department.

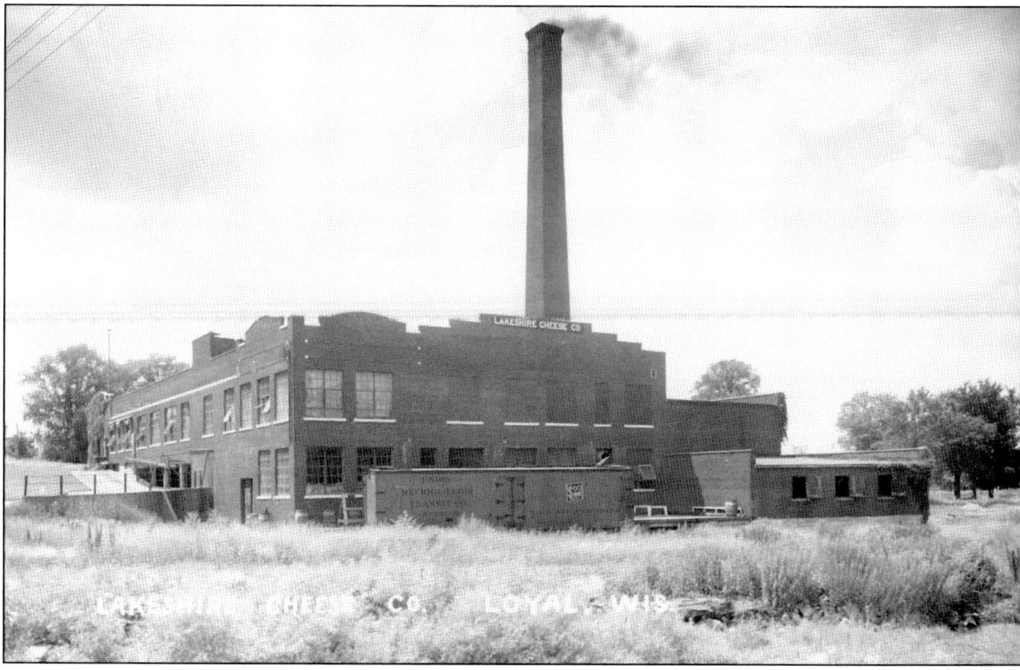

The Lakeshire Cheese Co. of Plymouth announced that its Loyal plant would cease taking milk as of March 31, 1938. No plans were given for its future. It was reported that the lack of an adequate supply of milk was one of the reasons for closure. Built in 1928, it produced cheddar cheese until 1938.

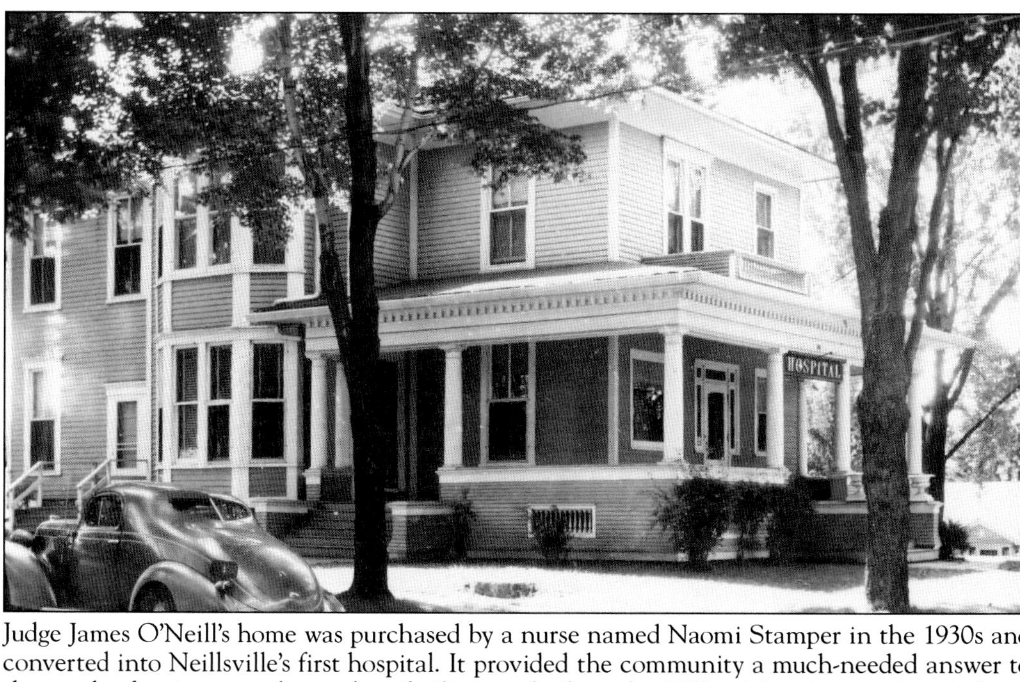

Judge James O'Neill's home was purchased by a nurse named Naomi Stamper in the 1930s and converted into Neillsville's first hospital. It provided the community a much-needed answer to the needs of patients until a modern facility was built in the 1950s. After the new hospital was built, the old one became a nursing home. When a new nursing home was later built next to the new hospital, this building was converted to apartments.

Five

Our Military Contributions

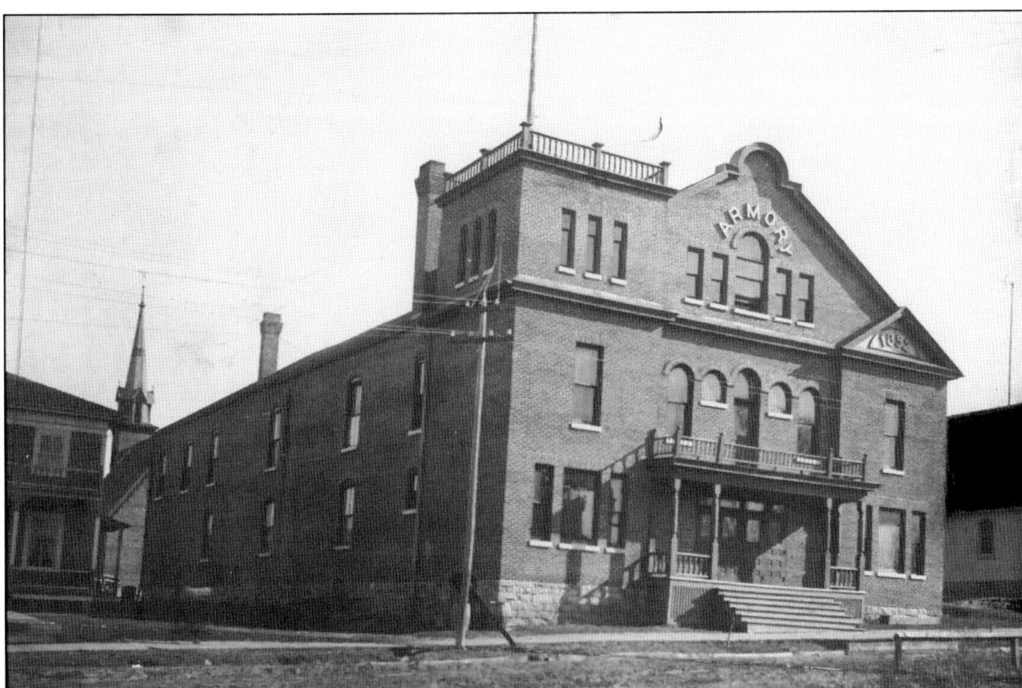

The Neillsville Armory was built in 1892 and quickly became a multipurpose community building. It served as the base for the local guard unit, as the Neillsville Opera House, and as an auditorium for high school plays, dances, basketball games, graduation exercises, and other civic and cultural events. The armory was torn down in the 1990s to make way for improvements to the Neillsville Library.

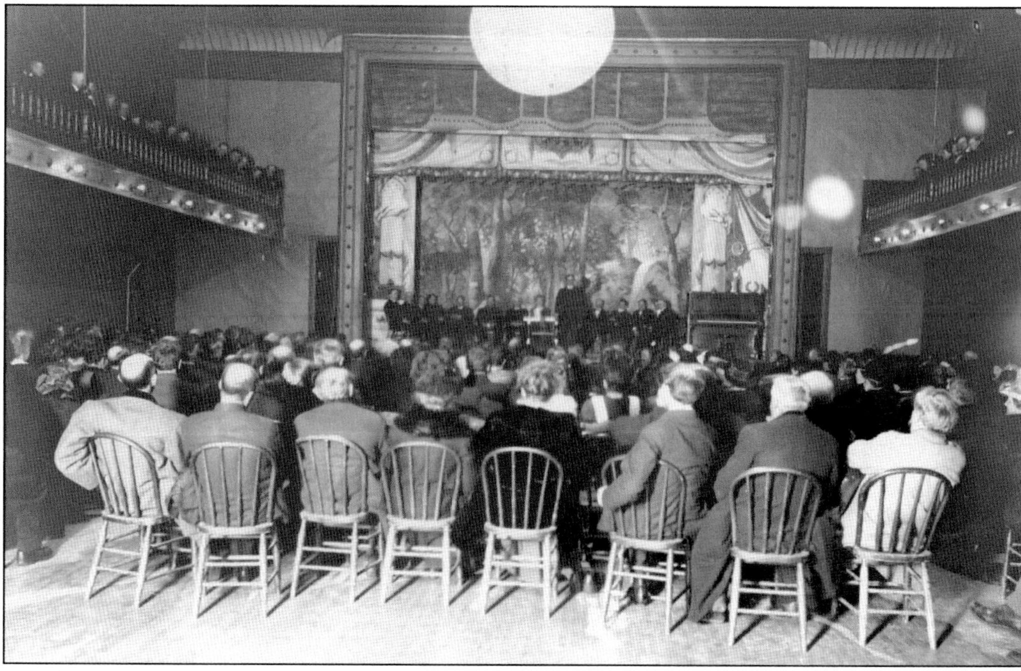

The Neillsville Armory hosted many events over the years, including this gathering, which looks to have been a town meeting of sorts. Perhaps it was a gathering to raise money for war bonds that took place in the armory on December 12, 1917. The featured speaker at that event was C.H. Howell, who had recently returned from fighting in the trenches in France in World War I.

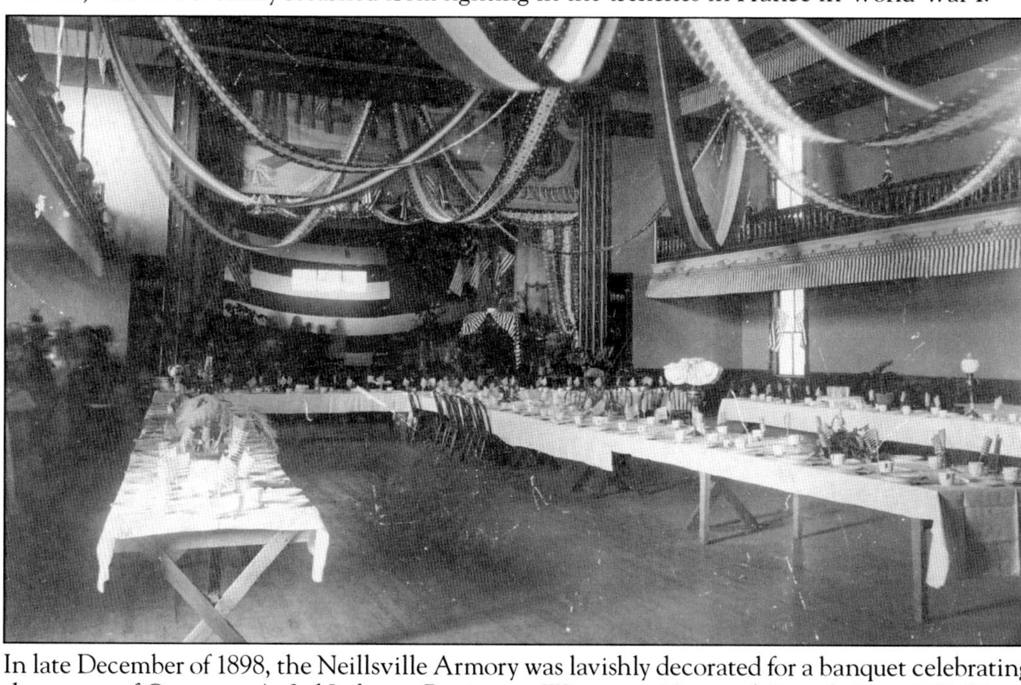

In late December of 1898, the Neillsville Armory was lavishly decorated for a banquet celebrating the return of Company A, 3rd Infantry Regiment, Wisconsin National Guard. Capt. J.W. "Tom" Hommel of Neillsville, the unit's commander, was commissioned to accept the truce for the United States, ending the battle in Puerto Rico during the Spanish-American War.

Gottleib Schlinsog, a young man who wanted to serve in the Civil War, was only 13 years old when he joined Company I, 14th Regiment, of the Wisconsin Volunteers on November 7, 1861. The unit trained at Camp Wood in Fond du Lac in January 1862, and left to join Gen. Ulysses S. Grant in March 1862. Schlinsog was killed on April 7, 1862, at the Battle of Shiloh.

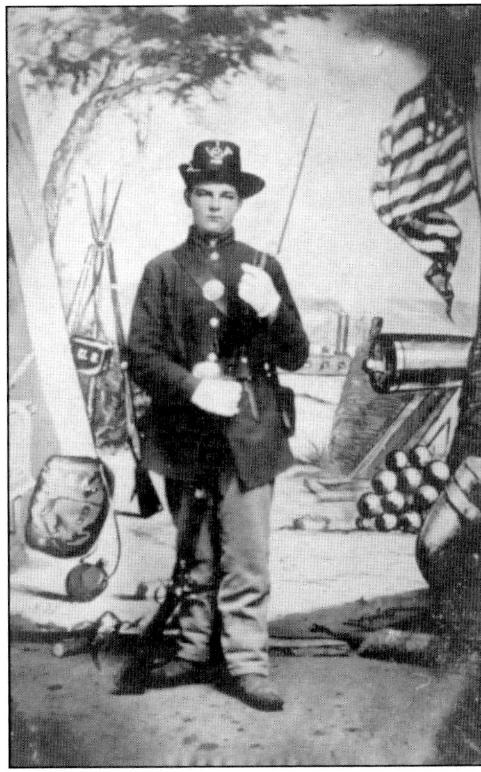

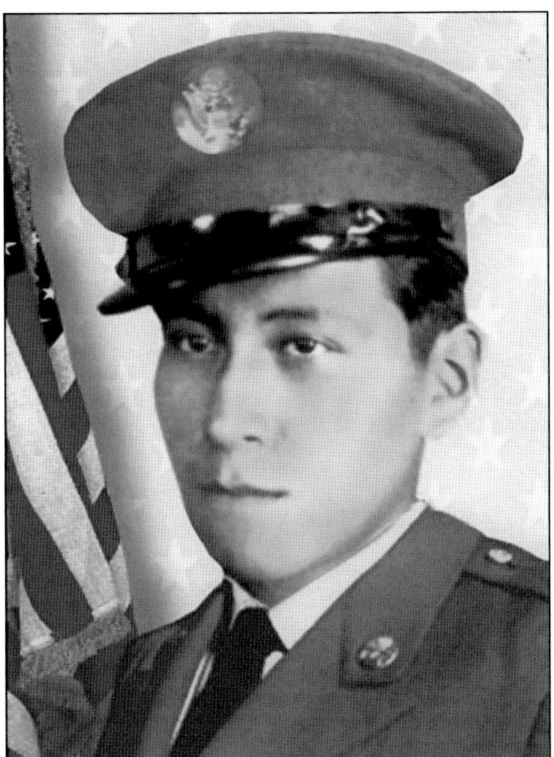

Mitchell Red Cloud Jr. enlisted in the Marine Corps in 1942. After World War II, he transferred to the Army and was then shipped to Korea in 1950. He was posthumously awarded the Congressional Medal of Honor for his courageous actions on November 5, 1950. A Wisconsin historical marker in Black River Falls and a monument in Decorah Cemetery on the Ho-Chunk Indian Reservation were erected honoring him. (Courtesy of the Highground.)

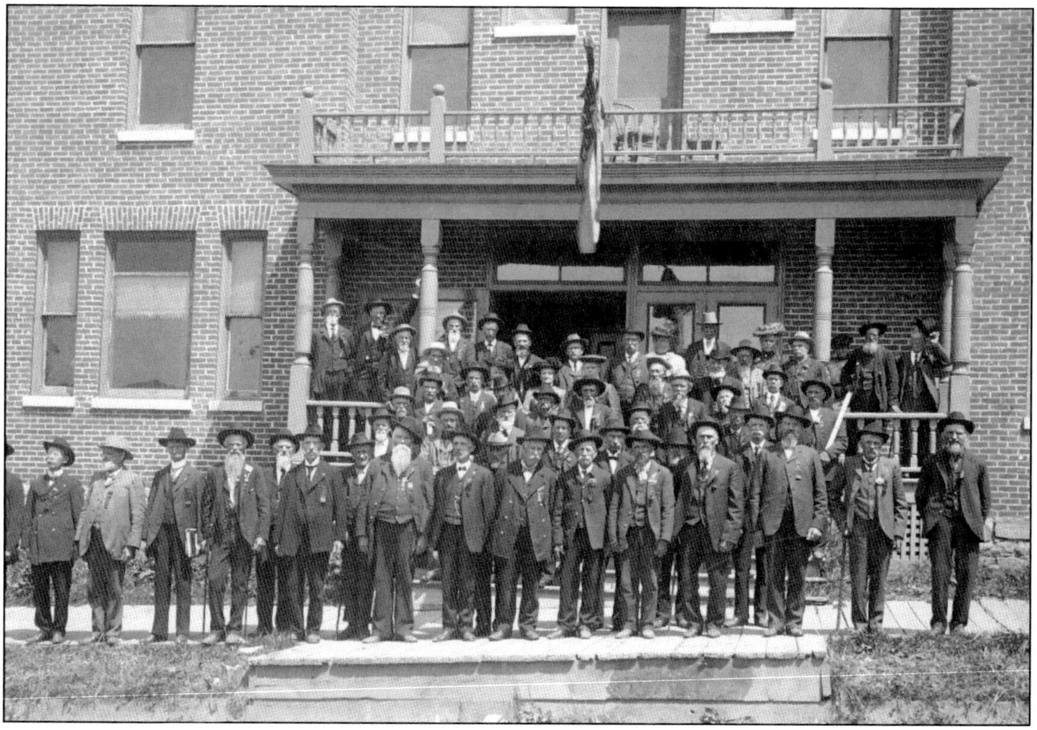

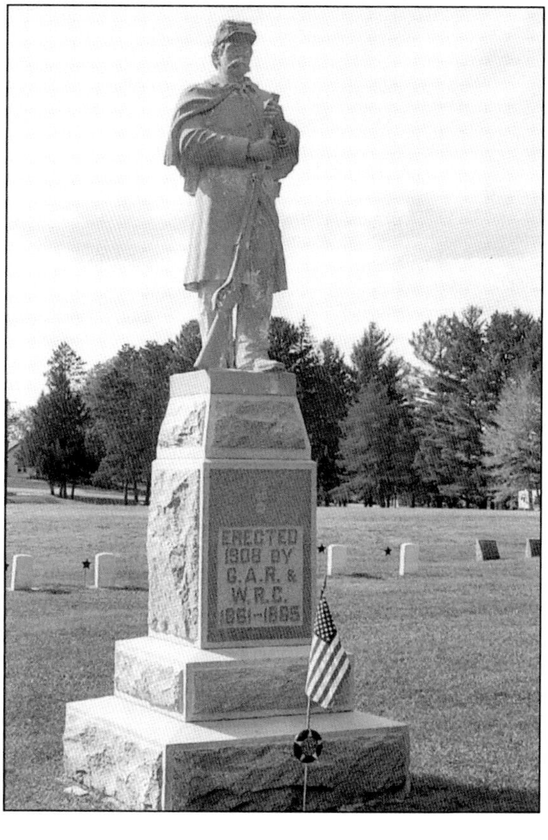

Members of Neillsville's Grand Army of the Republic (GAR) gathered for this photograph in front of the Neillsville Armory. The GAR had its first reunion in Neillsville at the Hubbard house on October 9, 1866, one year after they were mustered out of service from the Civil War. They met on the same day, October 9, every year thereafter, for Reunion Day, until the last veteran passed away.

This statue of a Union soldier in the Civil War was dedicated on July 10, 1908. He is wearing a cape overcoat with a musket and knapsack. The statue is in the Neillsville Cemetery in a place of honor. It was erected through the efforts of the GAR and the Woman's Relief Corps (WRC).

Pvt. Earl Ferris of Abbotsford was stationed in Lemans, France, in this 1919 photograph. He is seated on the left, and his friend is only identified as Charlie from Chipley, Florida. Ferris commented on the back that he purchased a dozen of these photograph postcards for 12¢, which were then sent home via Soldiers' Mail.

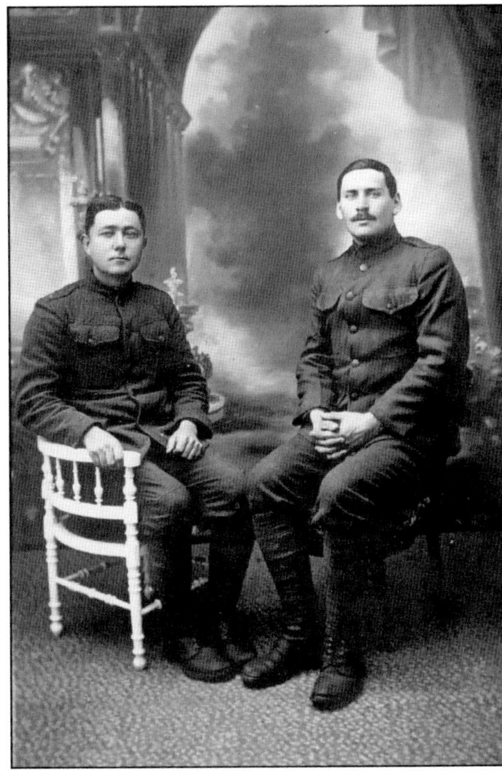

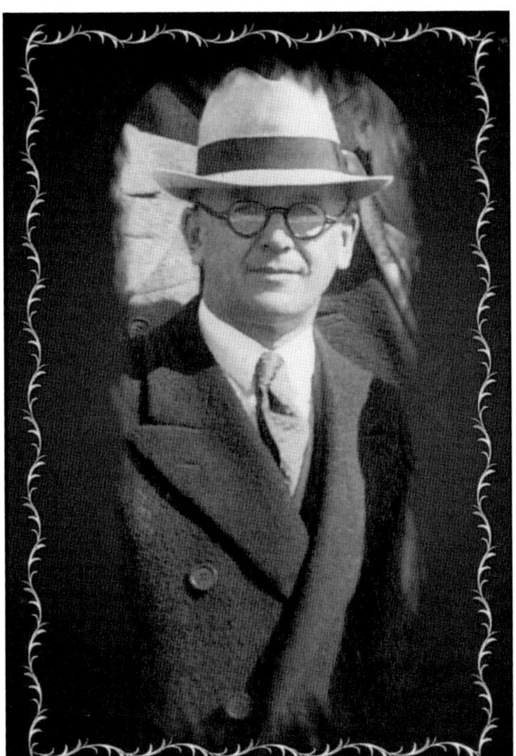

William Campman of Neillsville joined Company A, 3rd Infantry Regiment, Wisconsin National Guard at the start of the Spanish-American War. He was aide to Capt. J.W. "Tom" Hommel and accompanied Captain Hommel to the signing of the truce agreement in Puerto Rico. He died in 1982 at the age of 103, and was believed to be Wisconsin's last surviving Spanish-American War veteran prior to his passing.

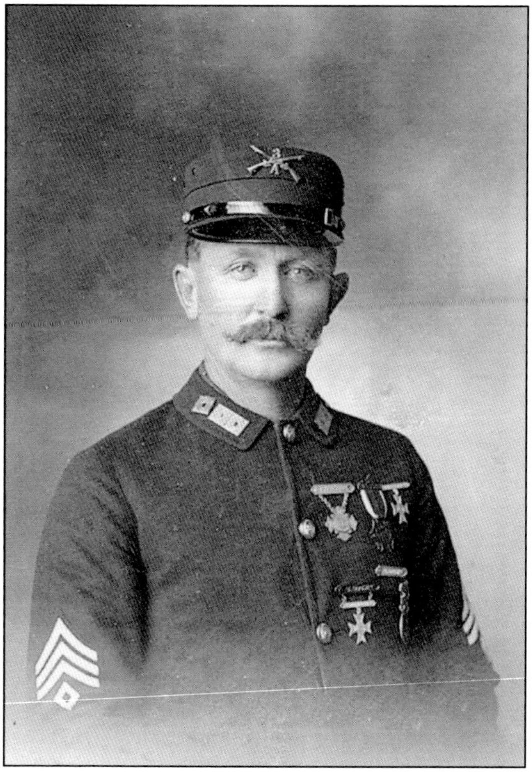

1st Sgt. Burton Wells served with the 3rd Infantry Regiment of the Wisconsin National Guard for 19 years. This unit was a forerunner to Neillsville's Service Company. During his service, Sergeant Wells won a medal for marksmanship. He served during a time when National Guard units had rifle competitions at their yearly encampments. The unit from Neillsville included highly regarded marksmen.

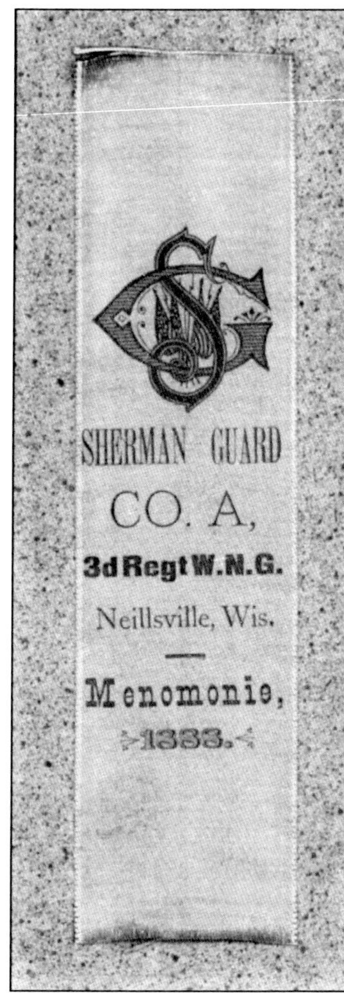

Company A of the Sherman Guard, Neillsville's unit, won this ribbon in an 1888 shooting skills competition in Menomonie. The following soldiers were noted as skilled shooters in Company A: Jacques, Eilert, Ludington, Lacey, and Pratt. Later, in 1893, Company A (now the Wisconsin National Guard) had three men on the state shooting team.

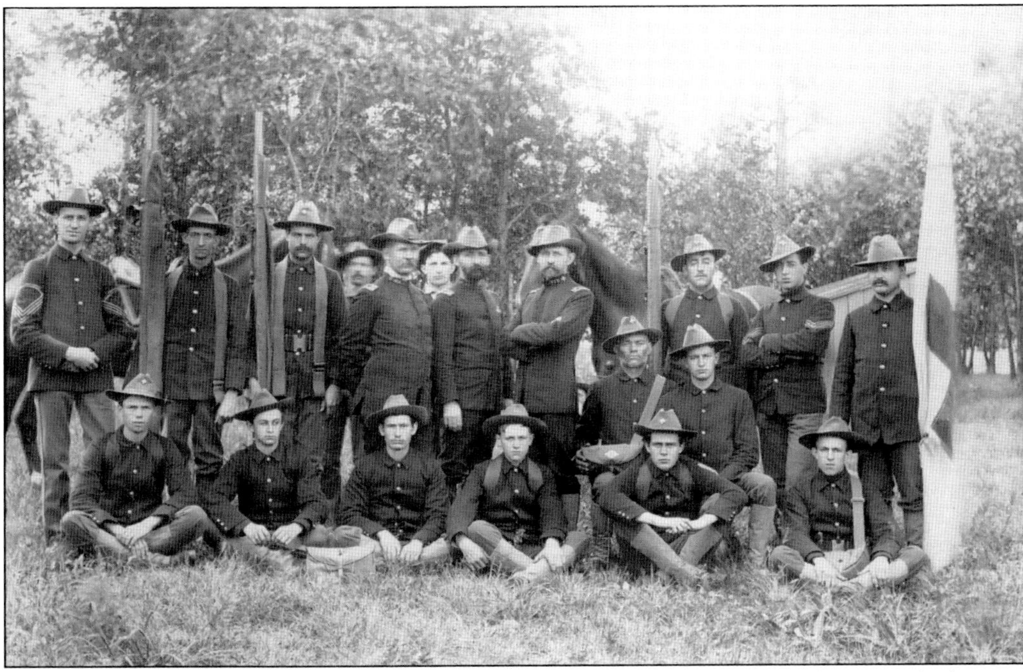

Company A, 3rd Infantry Regiment, Wisconsin National Guard, is seen here during its deployment for the Spanish-American War in 1898. The men have assembled and are awaiting orders. Of these 19 men, five have been identified. In the top row are, beginning second from the left, Charles Poole, William Horton, and Capt. J.W. "Tom" Hommel. Also in the top row, third from right, is William Farning. Kneeling below is Arnold Knoop.

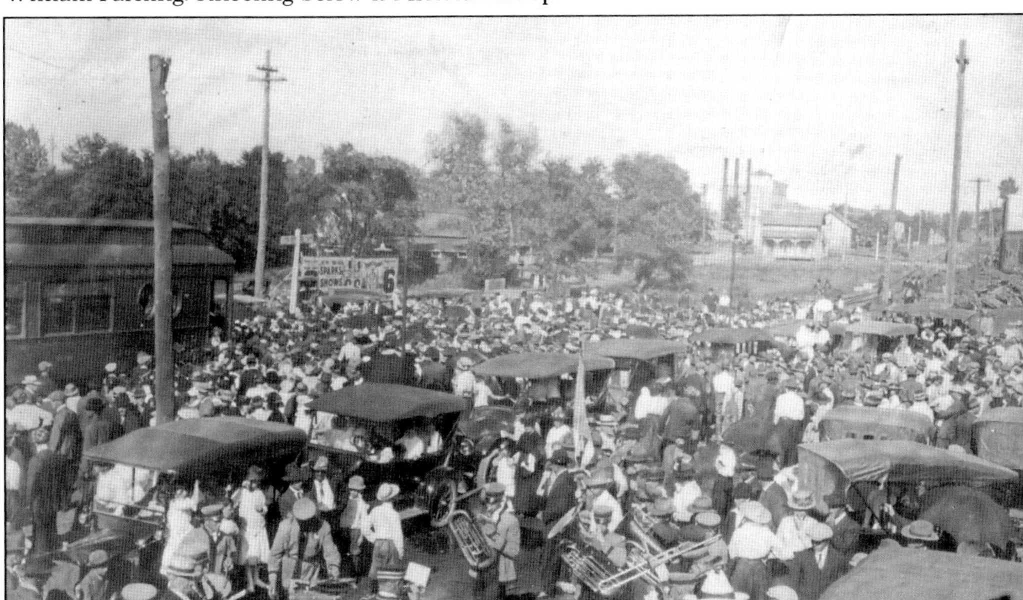

In May 1919, this crowd gathered near the depot in Neillsville to view the war trophies exhibited on a government train. The centerpiece of the attraction was a Whippet tank. The tank was unloaded and put through its paces on the streets of Neillsville, to the delight of the crowd.

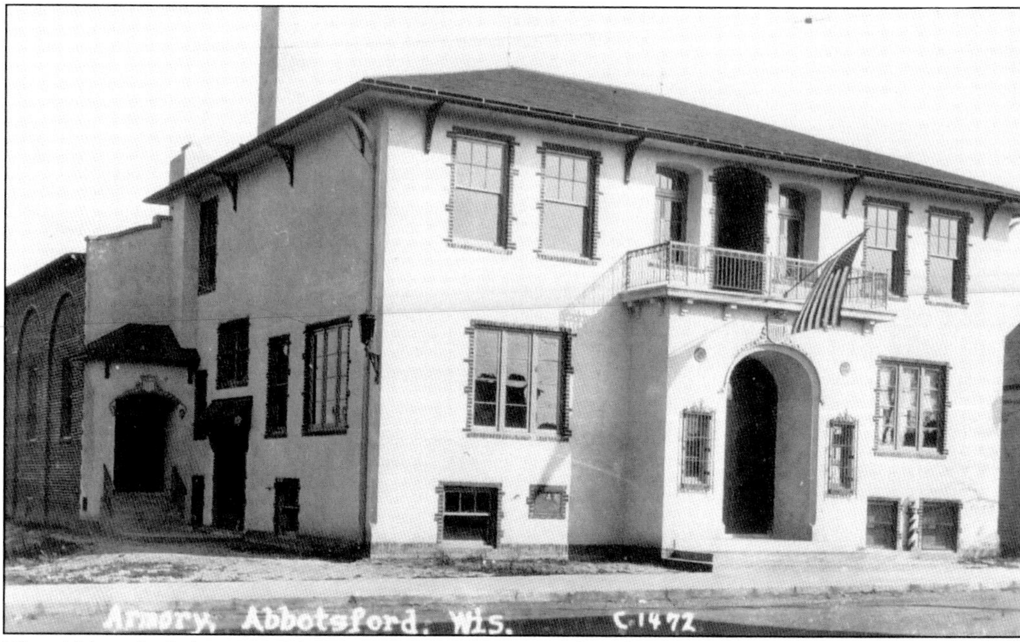

The Abbotsford Armory, like its counterpart in Neillsville, also functioned as a multipurpose building. It hosted high school graduations and class reunions as well as other civic functions. It is seen here around 1940. Today, it is part of the 32nd Infantry Brigade Combat Team, members of which were on active duty in Iraq.

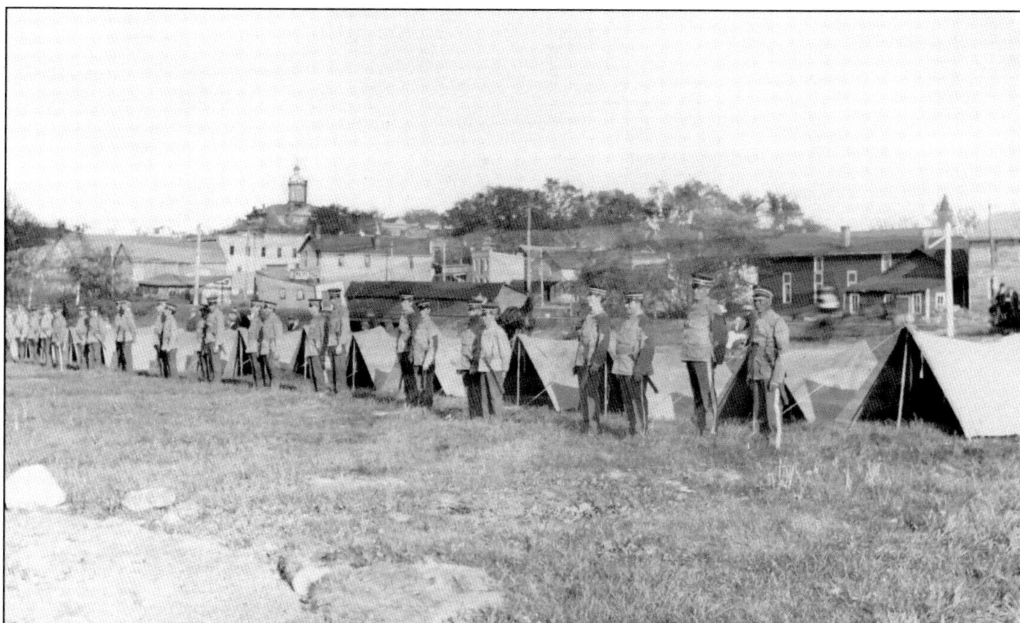

The Neillsville National Guard unit is assembled for inspection on a weekend drill held in Neillsville on the weekend of July 4, 1911. The unit camped near the depot, just north of Eighth Street. Behind them are the buildings on Seventh Street, with the dome of the courthouse and spire of the Congregational church visible. The unit also participated in the Neillsville Fourth of July parade.

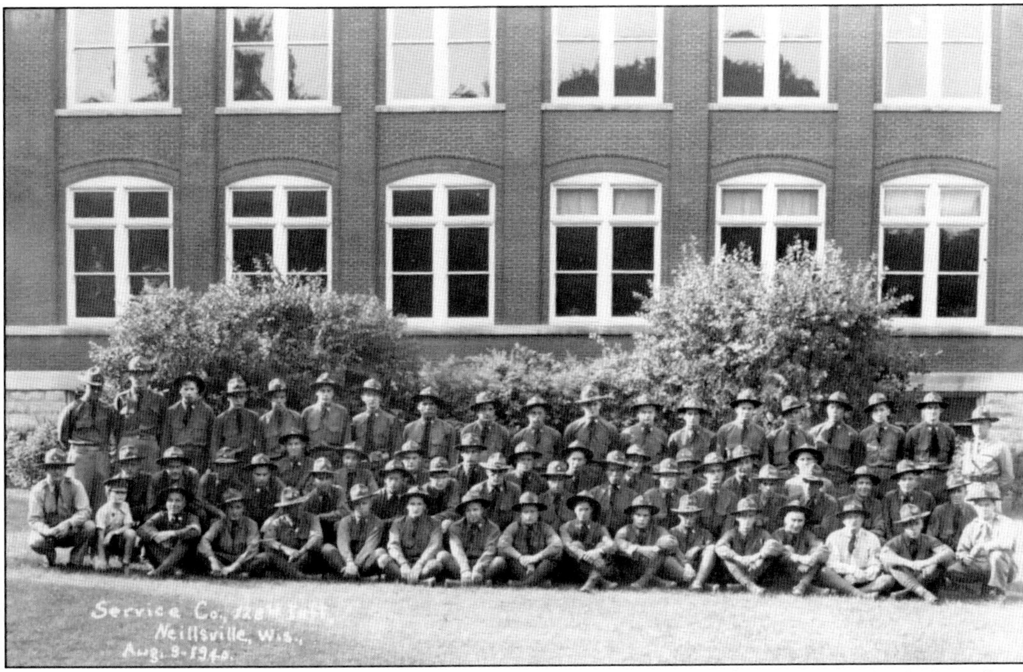

Service Company, 128th Infantry, gathered for this group photograph on August 9, 1940, in front of Neillsville High School. In the following days, the company departed for a 22-day encampment at Fort McCoy, Wisconsin. Two years later, men like these from all over the country were involved in World War II. Many of the men seen here served in the Pacific theater of operations.

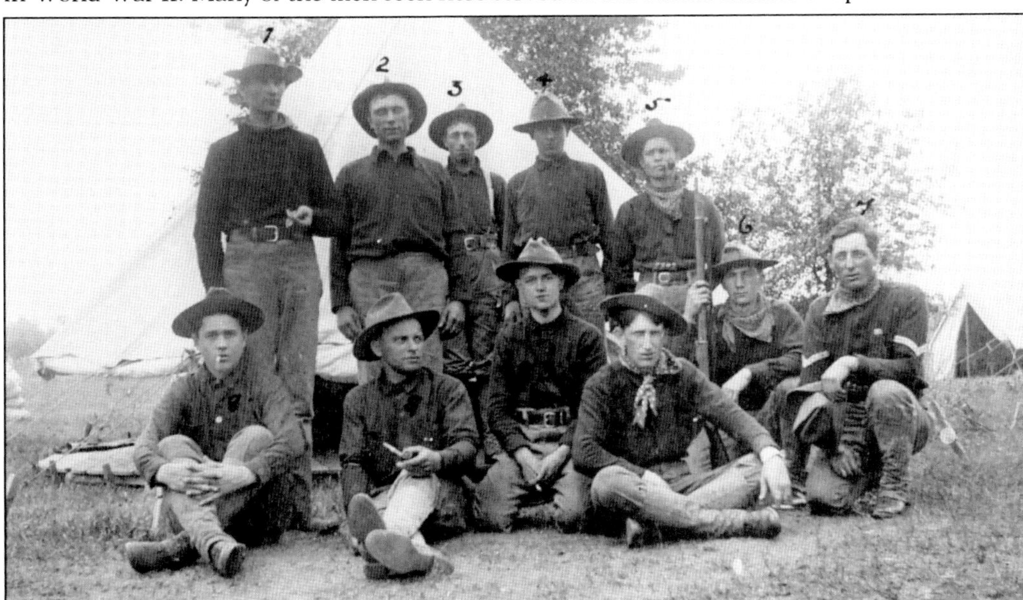

Members of Company A are seen here at their annual two-week encampment in 1905 at Camp Douglas, Wisconsin. From left to right are (first row) Richard "Buck" Dickenson, A. "Amus" Kaudy, Dell Potter, Harry "Spider" Francomb, Bert "Crazy" Hart, and William "Brody" Bradford; (second row) Bill "Fishook" Tragsdorf, Lt. Frank "Daisy" Burnett, Fritz "Fed" Ketel, Carl "Gunpowder" Doty, and Robert "Bobbie" Glass.

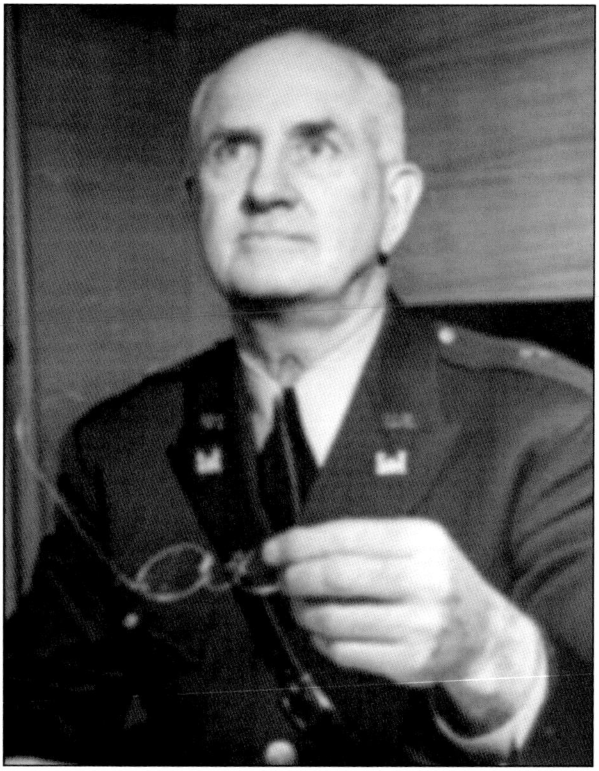

Maj. Gen. Clarence L. Sturdevant was a Neillsville native and a top-10 graduate from West Point's class of 1908. Honors status allowed him to choose his branch of service and assignment, and he chose the Army Corps of Engineers. He was the architect for the construction of the Alaska-Canadian (Alcan) Highway during World War II. This career soldier holds the highest rank ever attained by a Neillsville service member.

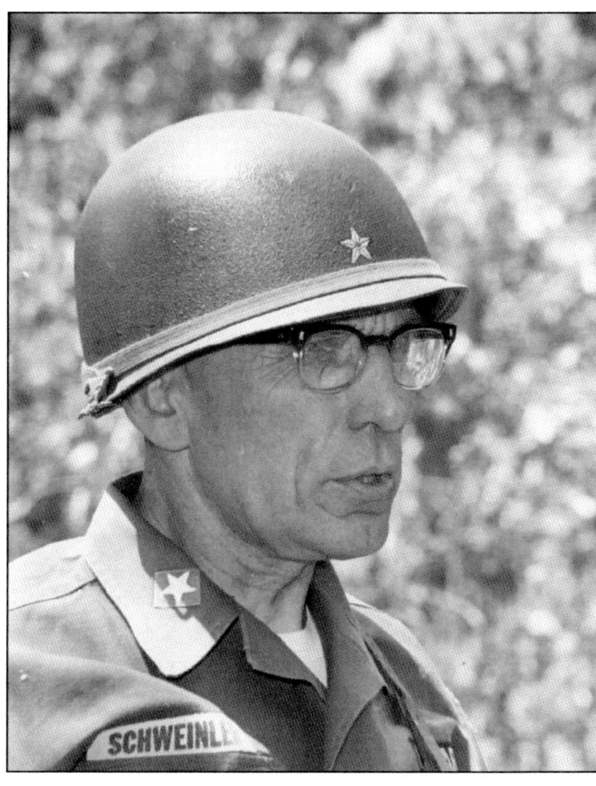

Brig. Gen. Francis Schweinler joined the Wisconsin National Guard in 1924 and retired in 1966. He was the director of the Tank Destroyer School at Fort Hood, Texas, and was later assigned commander of the 806th Tank Destroyer Battalion. He saw service in the South Pacific in World War II, and in the early 1950s, was assigned to Sen. Joe McCarthy as his press secretary.

Six

AGRICULTURE AND OUR PART IN AMERICA'S DAIRYLAND

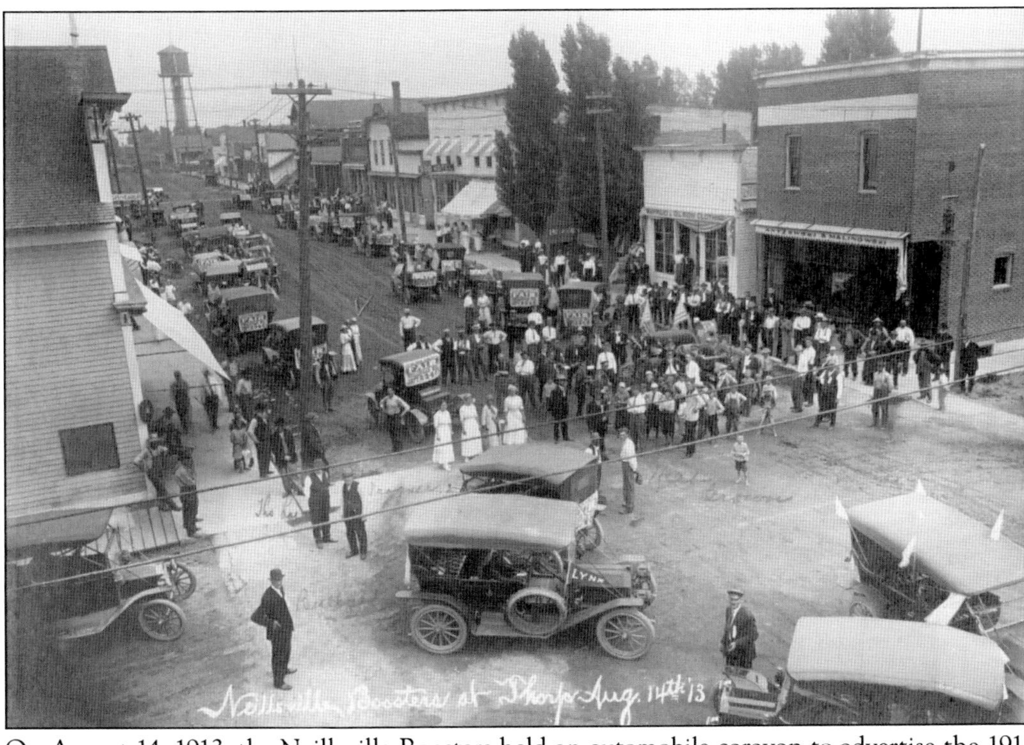

On August 14, 1913, the Neillsville Boosters held an automobile caravan to advertise the 1913 Clark County Fair, which was held September 2–5. The caravan traveled from Neillsville to Greenwood and Thorp. People were especially encouraged to attend that year, as lots were to be drawn for a new Ford automobile. Anna Greeler was the winner, and her lucky husband, Frank, drove their prize home.

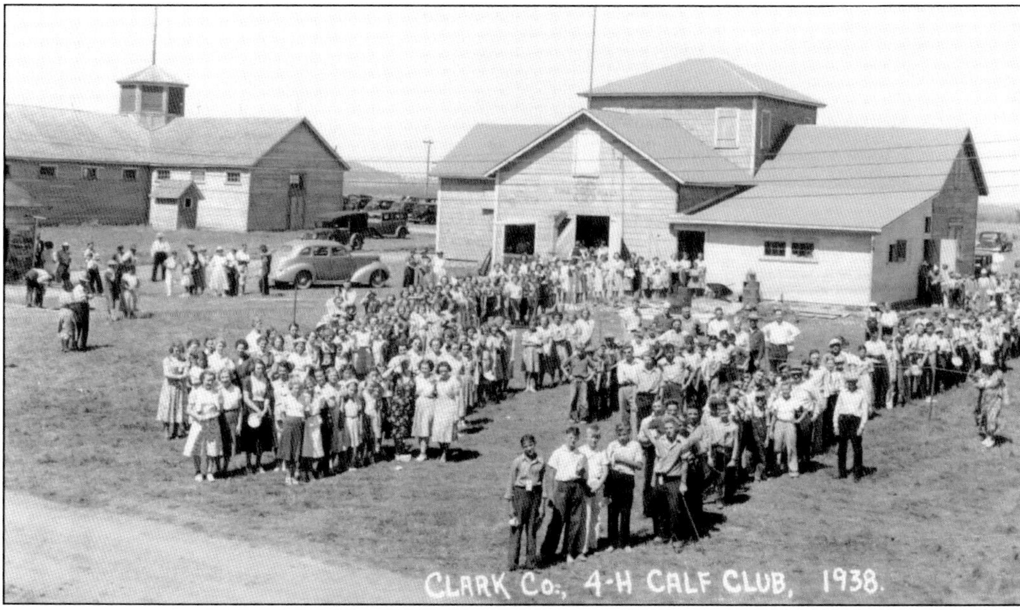

Clark County's 4-H program started with calf clubs, which were first organized by the school districts around 1916. Many children were raised on farms, and the club was a way for them to participate in the industry and learn life skills. Clark County had one of the first calf club exhibits, in 1918. It also had the largest stock barn owned by a fair society, and was the first to build a dormitory for fair campers.

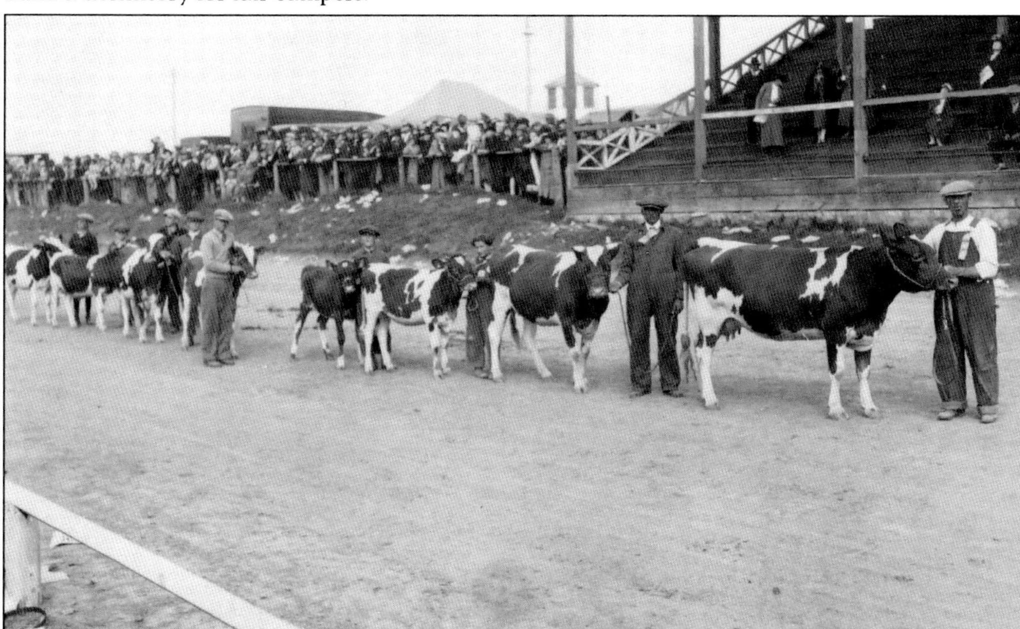

In the 1920s, showing and judging cattle was the highlight of the Clark County Fair for exhibitors and fair-goers alike. While young 4-H members exhibited their animals in the Junior Class category, adults exhibited their stock in the Open Class category. After judging, all of the animals were part of the stock parade in front of the grandstand at the fairgrounds. (Courtesy of UW Extension-Clark County.)

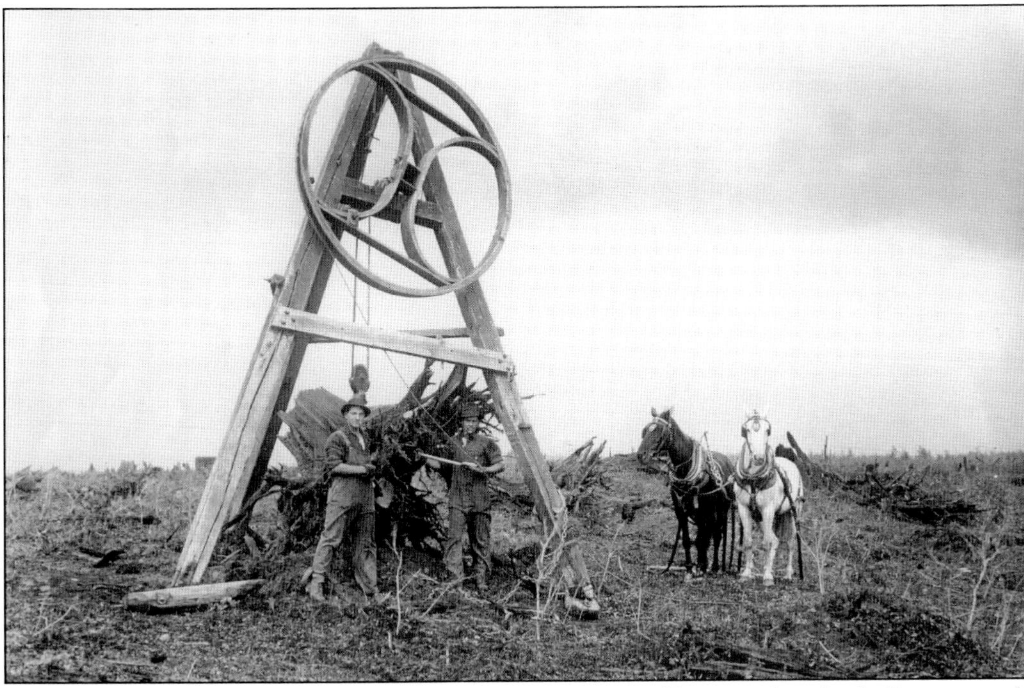

To prepare cutover land for farming, tree stumps were removed by several methods. Farmers could dig them out, pull them out with horses, blow them up with dynamite, or use a mechanical stump puller. In this early 1900s photograph, two men use a tripod stump puller, or "crearion," at a farm in Worden Township. (Courtesy of the Stanley Area Historical Society.)

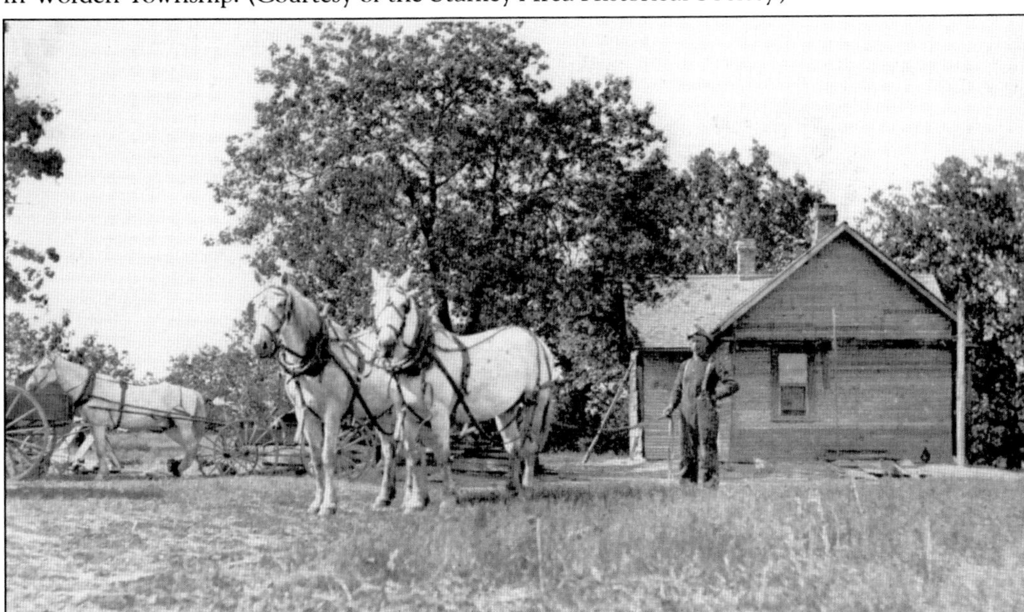

This view of a Curtiss area farm around 1900 reflects a simpler time. Farmers grew hay, corn, oats, or other grains that could be sold for cash or used to feed their stock. Dairy cows, pigs, chickens, and draft horses were the traditional farm animals. Eggs and milk were sold for cash, as were pigs and chicken meant for the meat market.

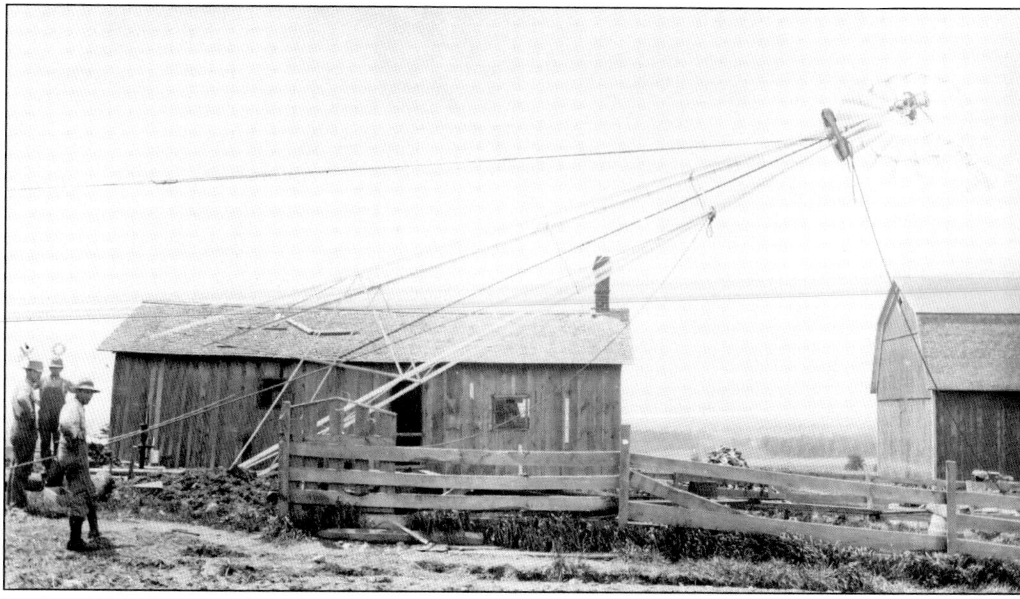

In this 1890 photograph, Edward Stelloh (left), Frank Stelloh (center), and an unidentified man raise a windmill into place using ropes, chains, and horsepower. Windmills produced energy to power the well pump and produce electricity for the barn or farmhouse in the days before electric cooperatives ran lines and brought electricity to everyone in the county.

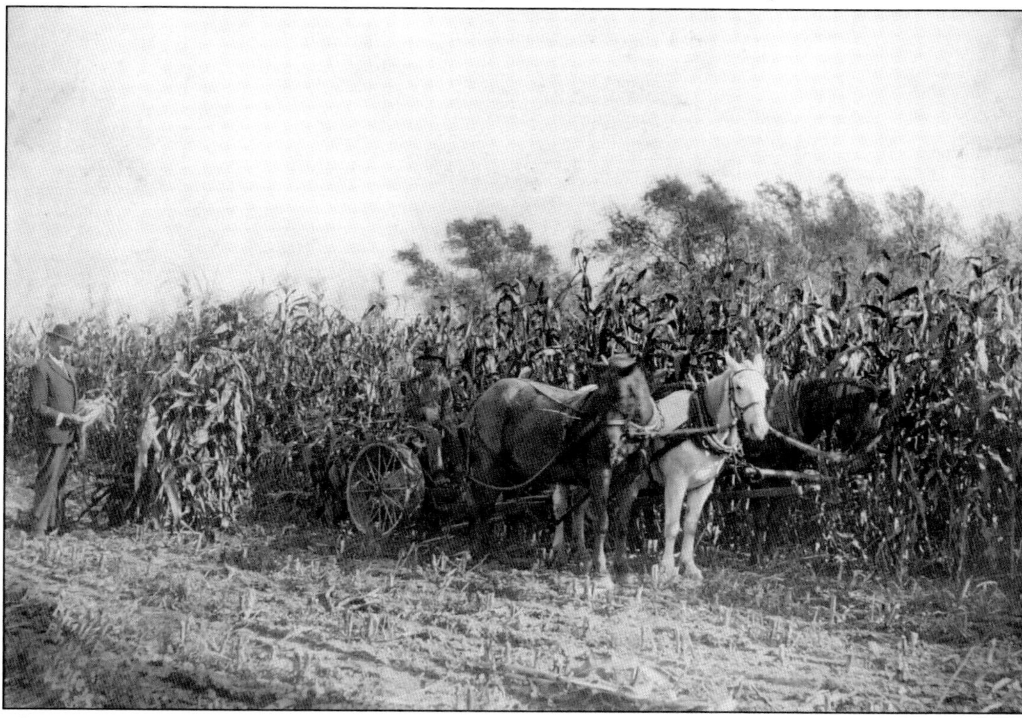

This cornfield was near Stanley, on the Andrew Samuelson farm. Here, in the early 1900s, Mr. Bridgeman (far left) checks an ear of corn for yield and quality. It took longer to harvest crops by hand, as cornstalks were hand-cut and loaded onto a horse-drawn wagon. (Courtesy of the Stanley Area Historical Society.)

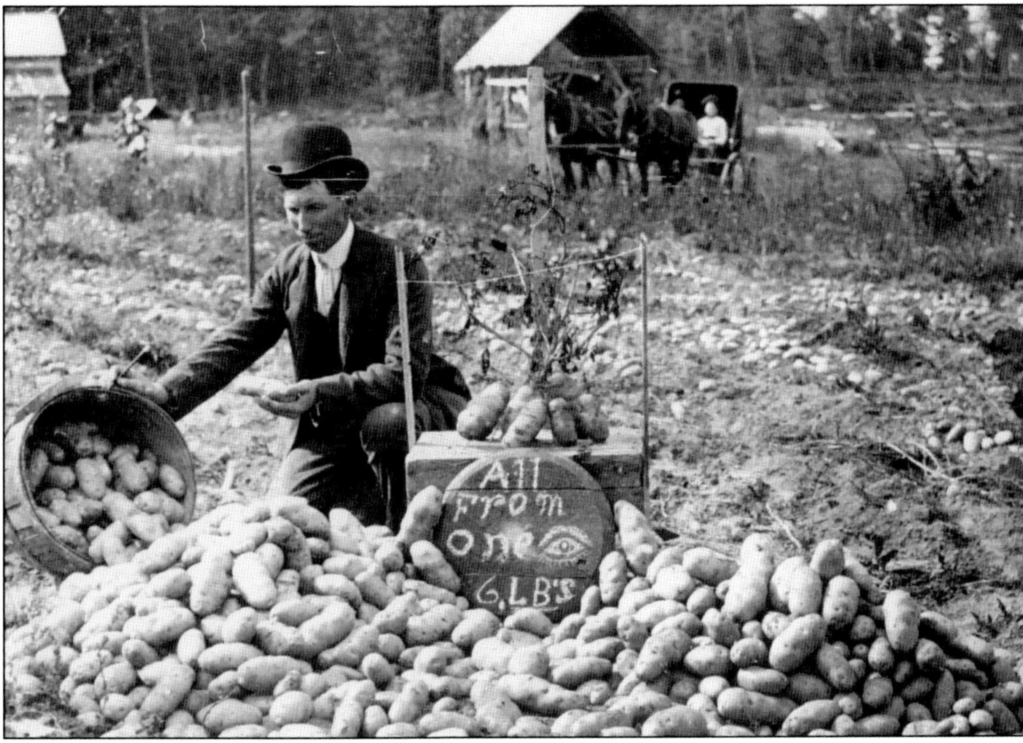

Efforts to sell cutover land prompted wealthy lumbermen, or their land companies, to circulate material like this photograph, which makes the claim that one planted potato eye produced all of the potatoes shown. (Courtesy of the Stanley Area Historical Society.)

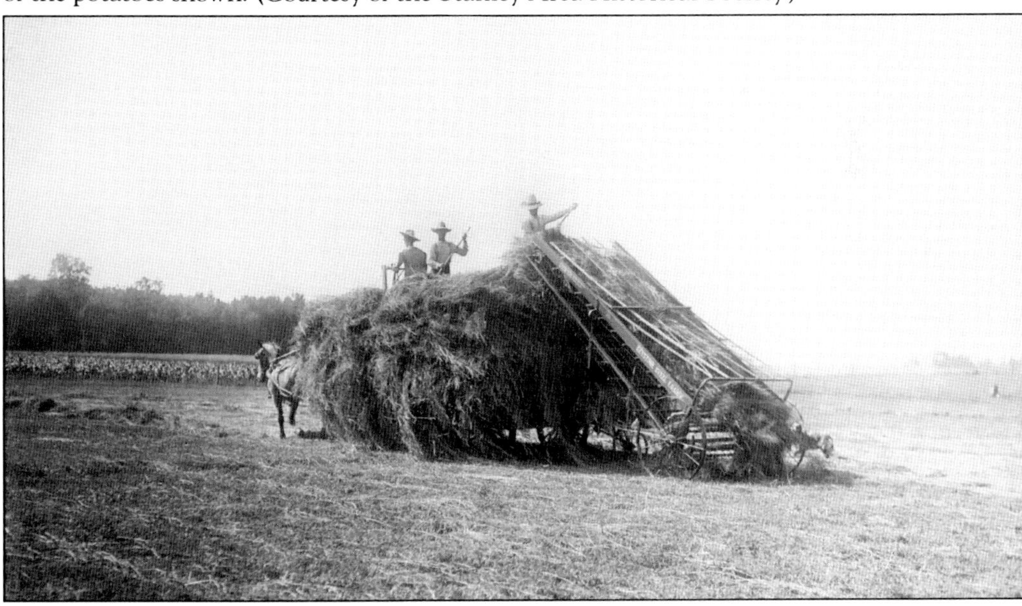

In the 1800s, men used pitchforks to toss hay up onto the wagon. By the early 1900s, a mechanical hay loader moved the cut hay up a conveyer to the top of the wagon. The men on top of the wagon would position the hay to keep the load stable and even. The modern hay loader was a welcome improvement for farmers. (Courtesy of the Loyal Area Historical Society.)

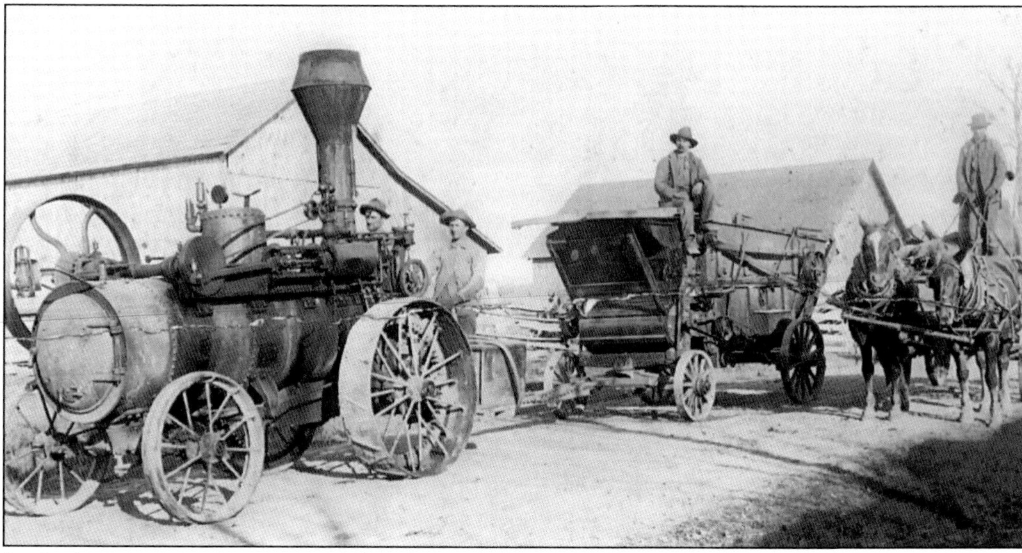

In the late 1890s, steam-powered threshing machines, or threshers, were becoming more popular. Farmers could thresh their own crops, and their neighbors' crops as well. Steam engines used long, flat belts to power the threshers. Grain stalks were hand-fed into the back of the thresher, and the grain was then separated from the stalk, with the grain going to a hopper and the stalk, or straw, saved for animal bedding.

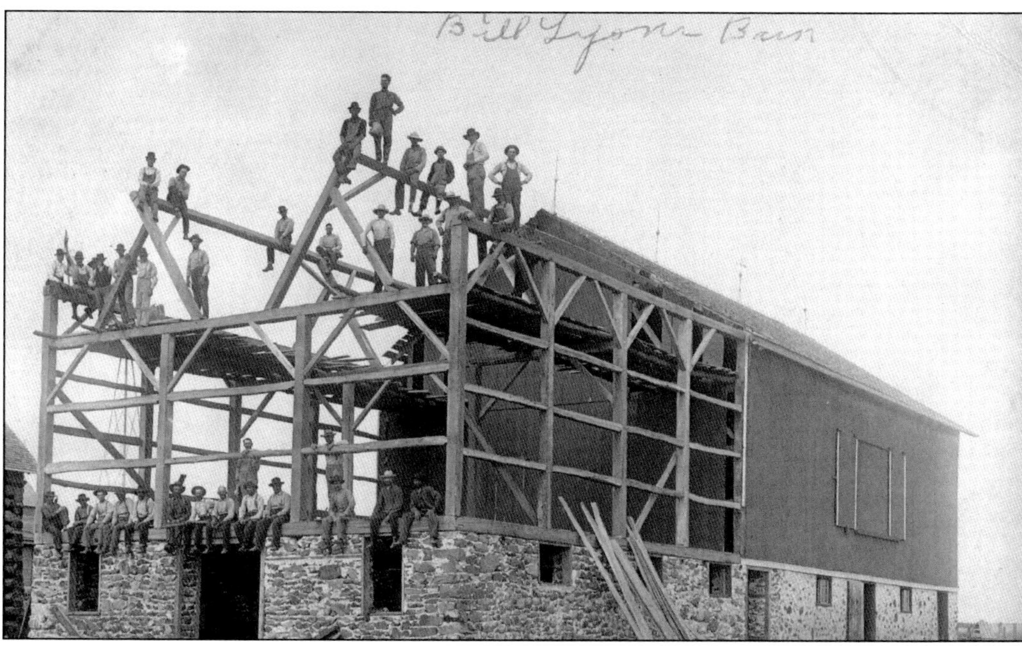

Many hands helped make farm work go faster. Around 1900, these friends and neighbors came to the Bill Lyons farm, near Riplinger, to help construct a new barn addition. These barn raisings were true community events. While the men were busy building the barn, the ladies gathered together to make meals for everyone there. (Courtesy of the Loyal Area Historical Society.)

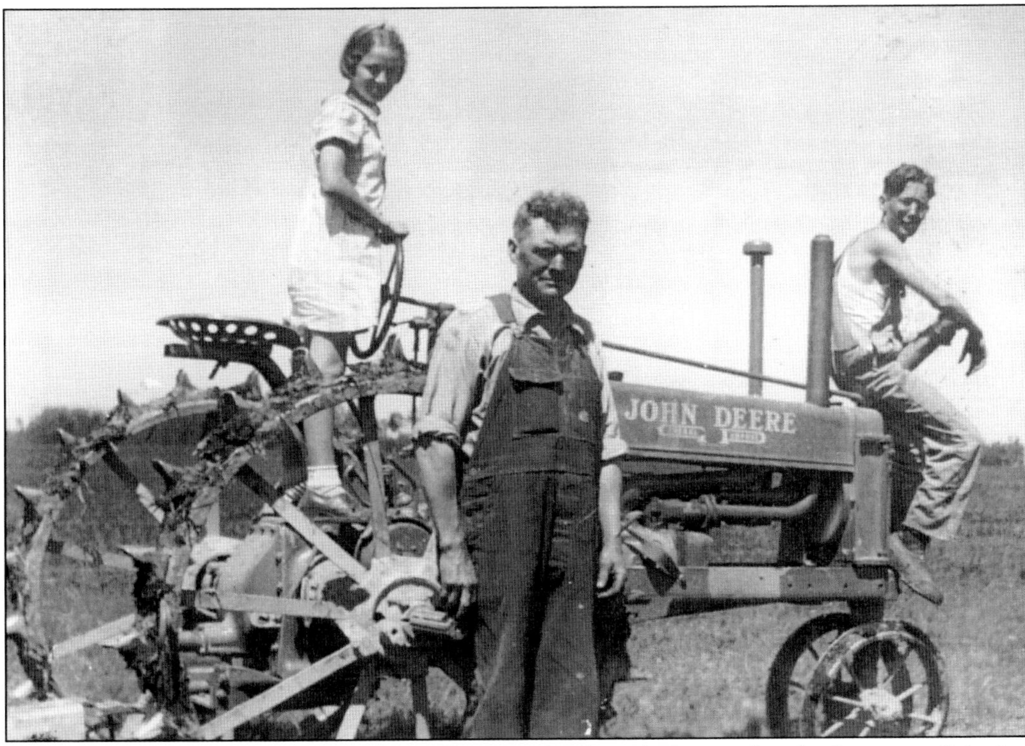

Today's John Deere farm tractors are like offices on wheels, with their enclosed cabs, air conditioning, computerized systems, and cell phone service. In the 1930s, however, tractors like this were not as comfortable, but they got the job done. Here, the Isenberger family, with daughter Betty, father Oscar, and son Harold, work together on their family farm near Stanley. (Courtesy of the Stanley Area Historical Society.)

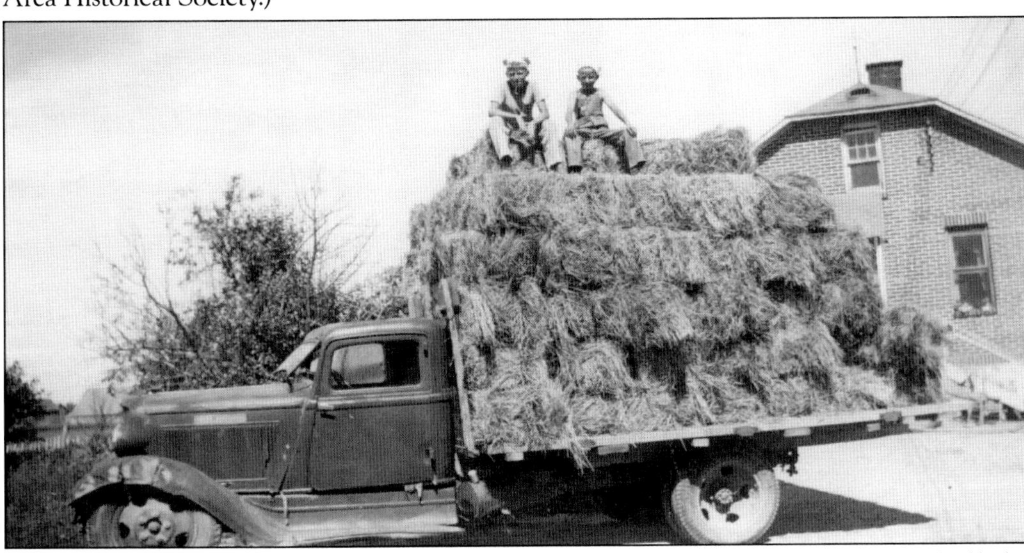

These two young men, Jerry Ohmski (left) and John Holewinski Jr. (right), sit on a load of baled hay in the bed of a truck near Thorp in the late 1940s. Using hay balers and twine made it easier to move hay, in small or large loads, wherever it was needed. (Courtesy of the Stanley Area Historical Society.)

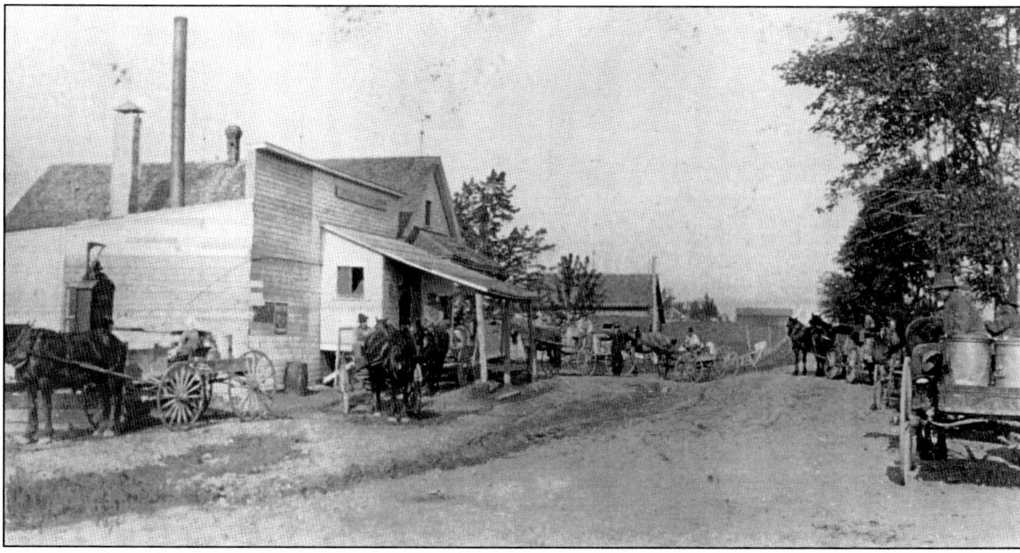

In 1916, the Clover Leaf cheese factory (left) receives milk deliveries from farmers at their town of Worden plant. Fresh milk was taken to the creamery, or cheese plant, every day. Farmers got credit for the quantity and quality of their deliveries, and were paid with what was known as a milk check at least once a month. (Courtesy of the Stanley Area Historical Society.)

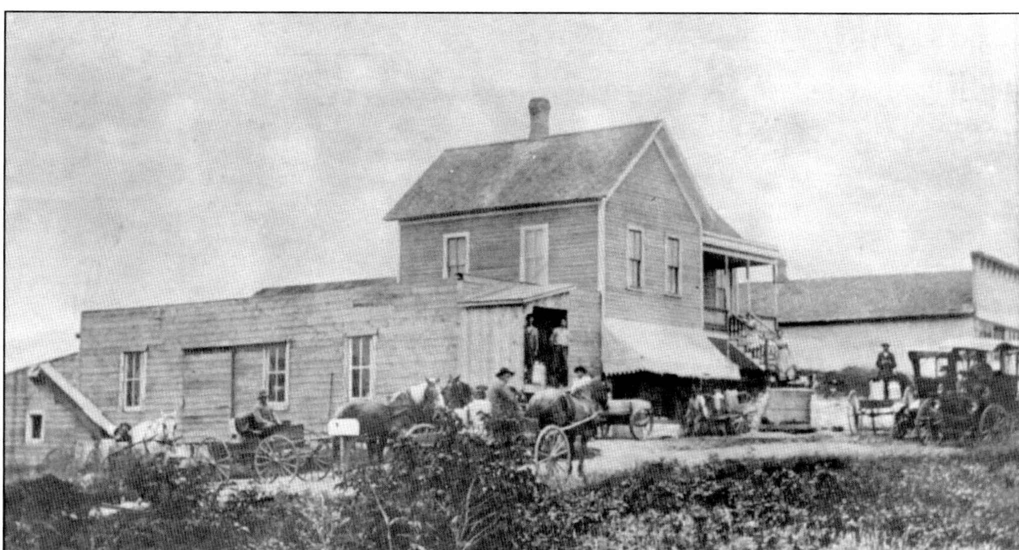

In 1906, the E.S. Boardman cheese factory at Eisvold had wagons lined up by the loading dock, waiting to offload their milk. Farmers had started using 30-gallon milk cans instead of 10-gallon cans, so the cheese plant needed ropes and pulleys to lift the heavy cans out of the wagons. Farmers took cleaned, empty milk cans home to use the next day. (Courtesy of the Stanley Area Historical Society.)

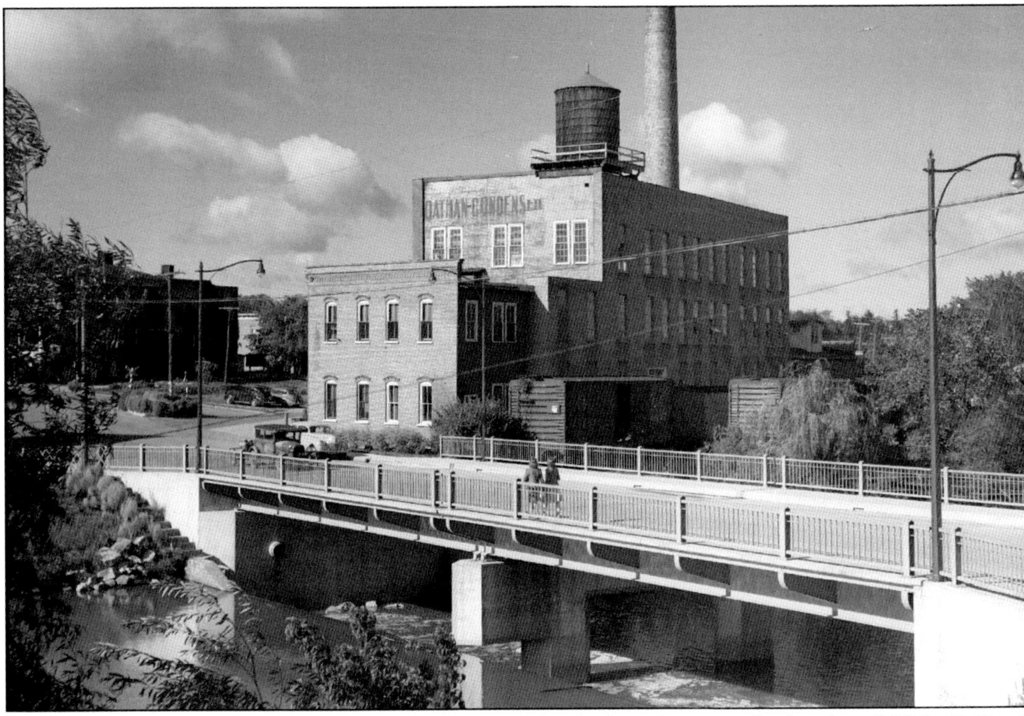

In 1916, the Oatman Condensed Milk Company built this plant on the banks of O'Neill Creek in Neillsville, the same site where James O'Neill built his gristmill in the 1850s. For the next 50 years, under various owners, this plant produced quality condensed milk that was used by homemakers, for baby formula, and by soldiers in World War II. Production ended in 1966, when the plant closed.

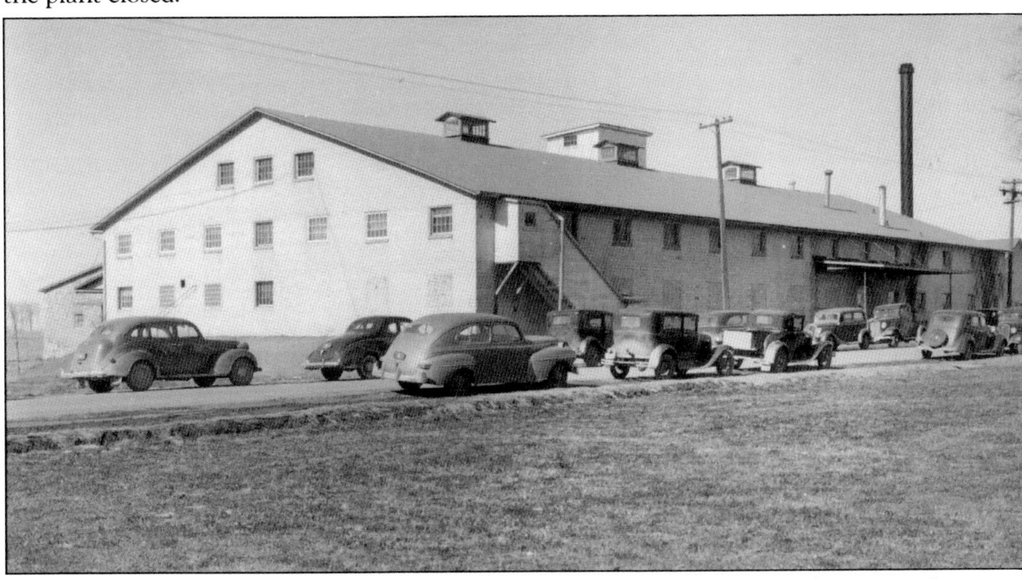

Blue Moon Foods Inc., located in Thorp and seen here in 1945, was known for its award-winning Gorgonzola and bleu cheese. They also made natural American cheese and their exclusive Gold'N Rich semi-soft cheese spreads. It started as a locally owned business, and over the years purchased many smaller cheese and dairy plants in northern Clark County.

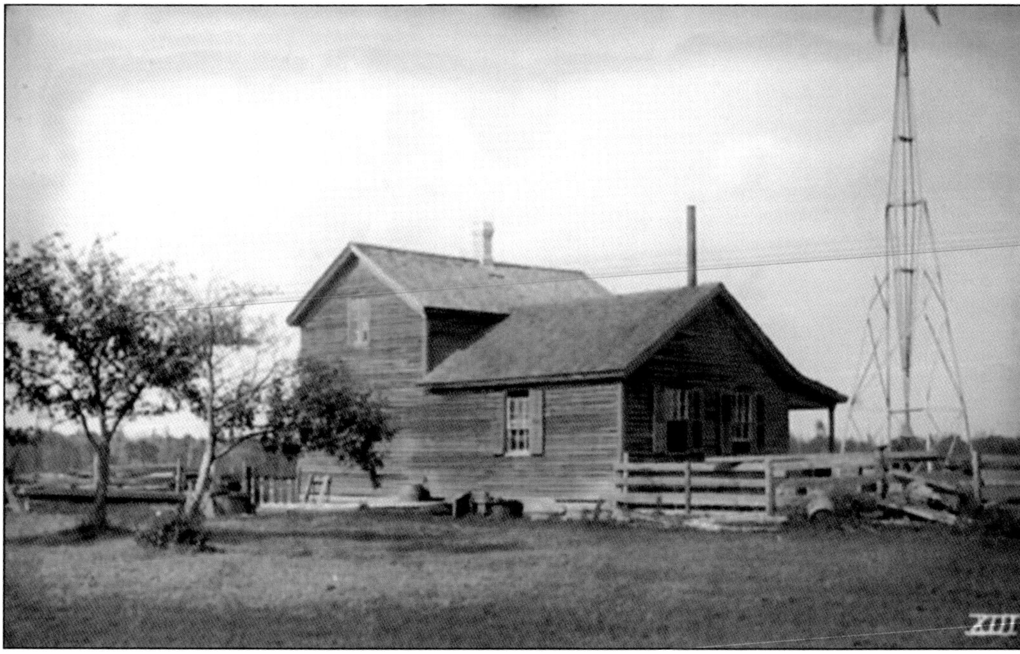

Colby cheese is a favorite of most cheese lovers, with its mild taste and versatility in all sorts of recipes. First made by Joseph F. Steinwand in his father's cheese factory in 1885, the cheese was named after the northern Clark County township of Colby, where the factory was built and where Steinwand's family lived. Colby has a historical marker honoring the creation and home of Colby cheese. (Courtesy of the Wisconsin Historical Society.)

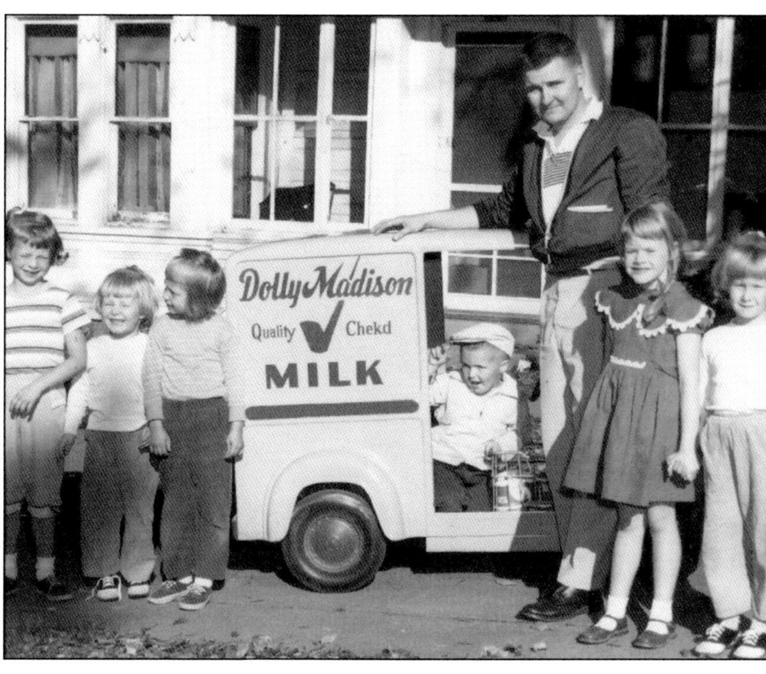

Dan Patey became the owner of Neillsville Dairy in 1958, a supplier of milk and milk products to residents, schools, and businesses in the area. He borrowed a miniature Dolly Madison milk wagon and used it on his delivery route, attracting the children seen here with him. They are, from left to right, Diane and Susie Kunkel, Marcie Seif, John Patey (in the wagon), Dan Patey, Ellen Blodgett, and Kathy Seif.

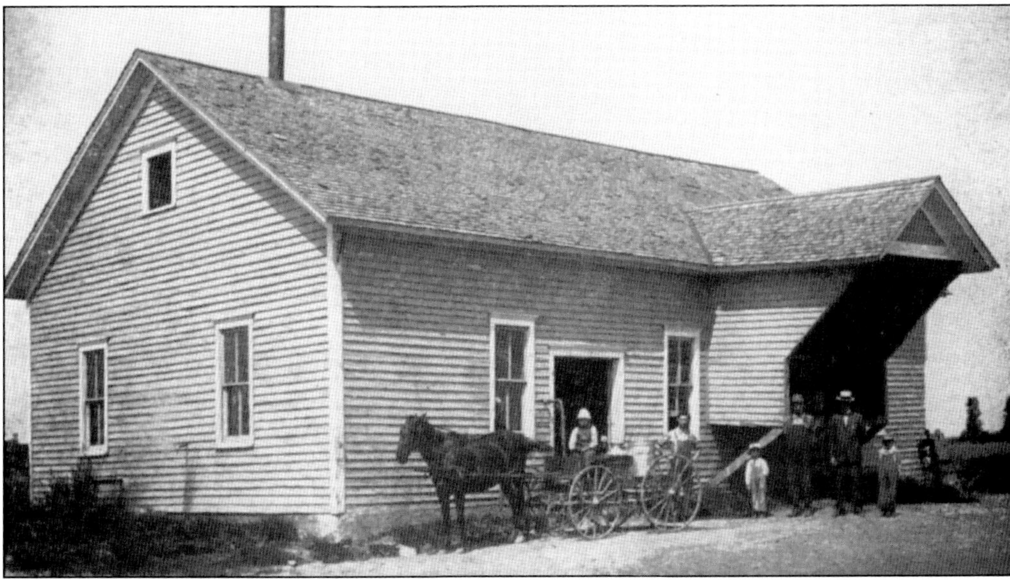

In 1904, John S. Wuethrich became the manager of the local cooperative creamery in Greenwood (above). About 10 years later, Wuethrich purchased the operations of and started the business that would become Grassland Dairy Products Inc. Born in Switzerland in 1883, Wuethrich was a master butter and cheese maker and a pioneer in the dairy industry. Today, Grassland Dairy Products has grown from this small creamery into the world's largest butter producer. Their three plants receive more than three million pounds of milk each day and produce more than 42,000 pounds of butter every hour. Residents of Clark County see tankers like the ones below delivering milk to the Greenwood plant each day. The company is known as the Butter People. Chances are, the little packets of butter on your restaurant table came from Greenwood, Wisconsin. (Courtesy of Grassland Dairy Products, Inc.)

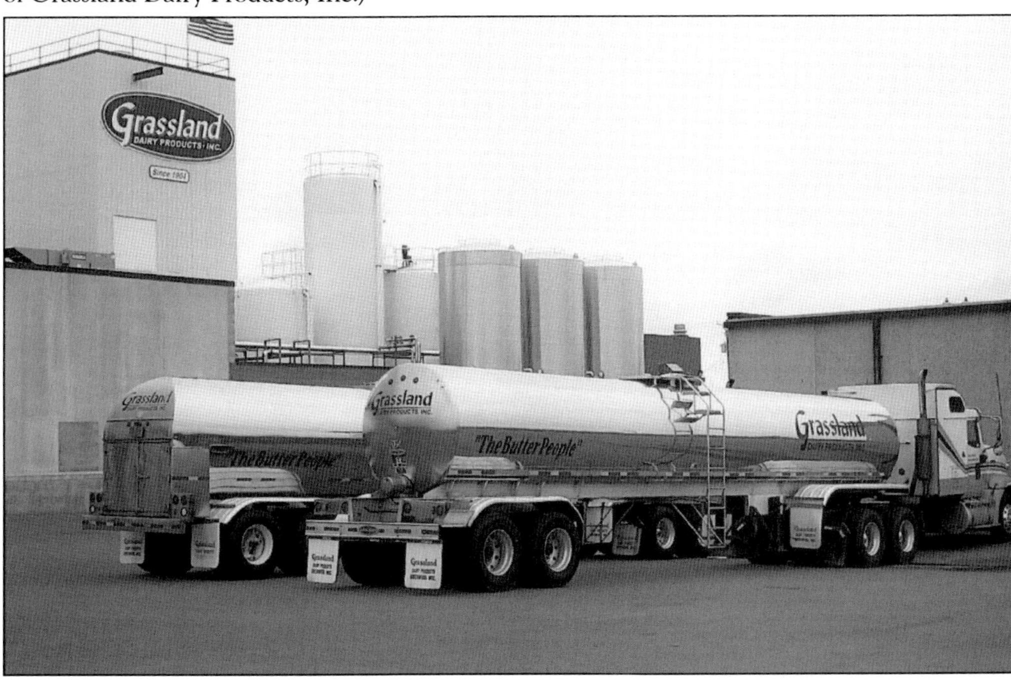

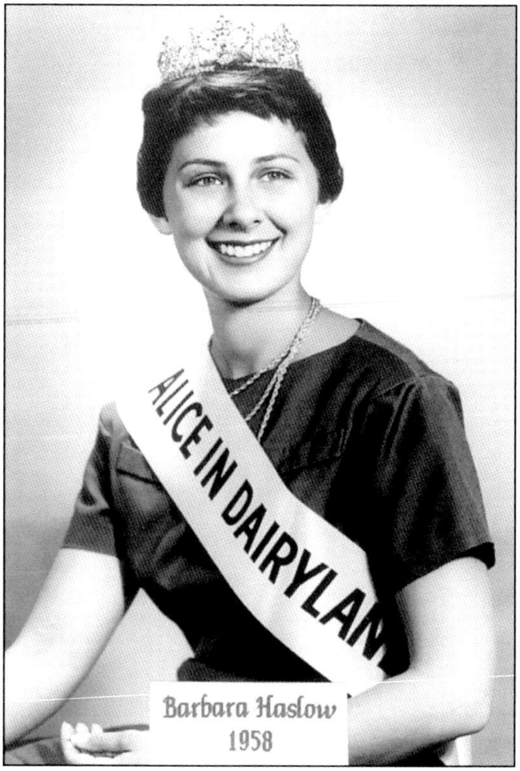

In 1948, as Wisconsin was celebrating 100 years as a state at the Centennial Exposition in West Allis, the very first Alice in Dairyland was crowned. In 1958, Barbara Haslow of Chili, seen here, became Alice—Wisconsin's ambassador for the state's agricultural industry for the next year. Clark County will proudly host the Alice in Dairyland competition in 2014. (Courtesy of the Wisconsin Department of Agriculture, Trade, and Consumer Protection.)

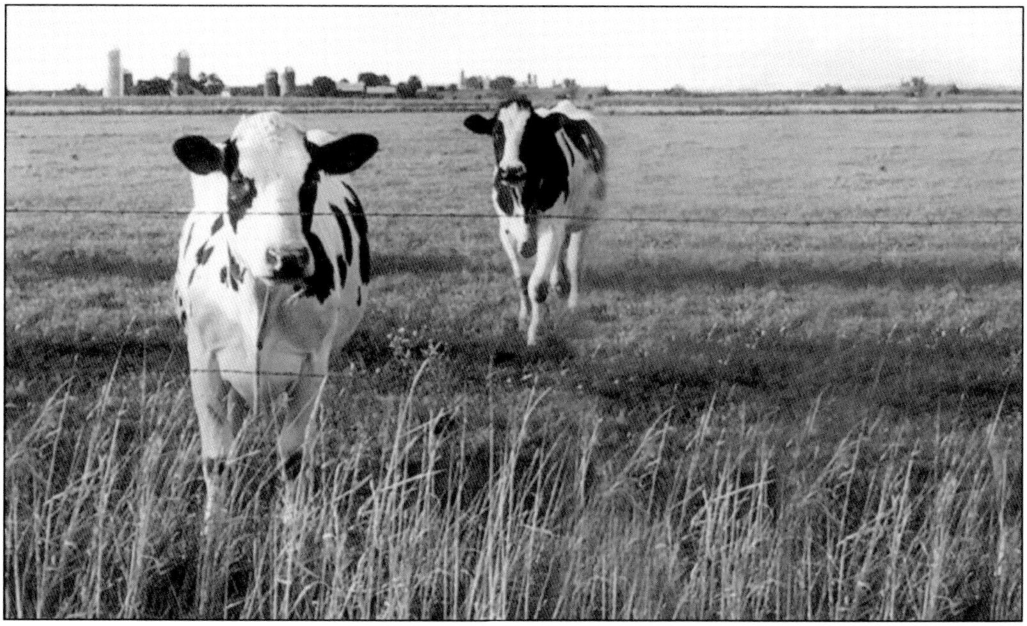

Today, Clark County's 66,000 cows each produce an average of 20,000 pounds of milk, which is used to produce cheese, butter, and milk products. With award-winning Clark County cheese makers like Holland's Family Cheese, LaGrander's Hillside Dairy, Lynn Dairy Products, Nasonville Dairy, North Hendren Co-op, Welcome Dairy, and Grassland Butter, our local cows will be kept busy for many years to come. (Courtesy of the Clark County Economic Development Corporation.)

Seven

Entertainment and Recreation

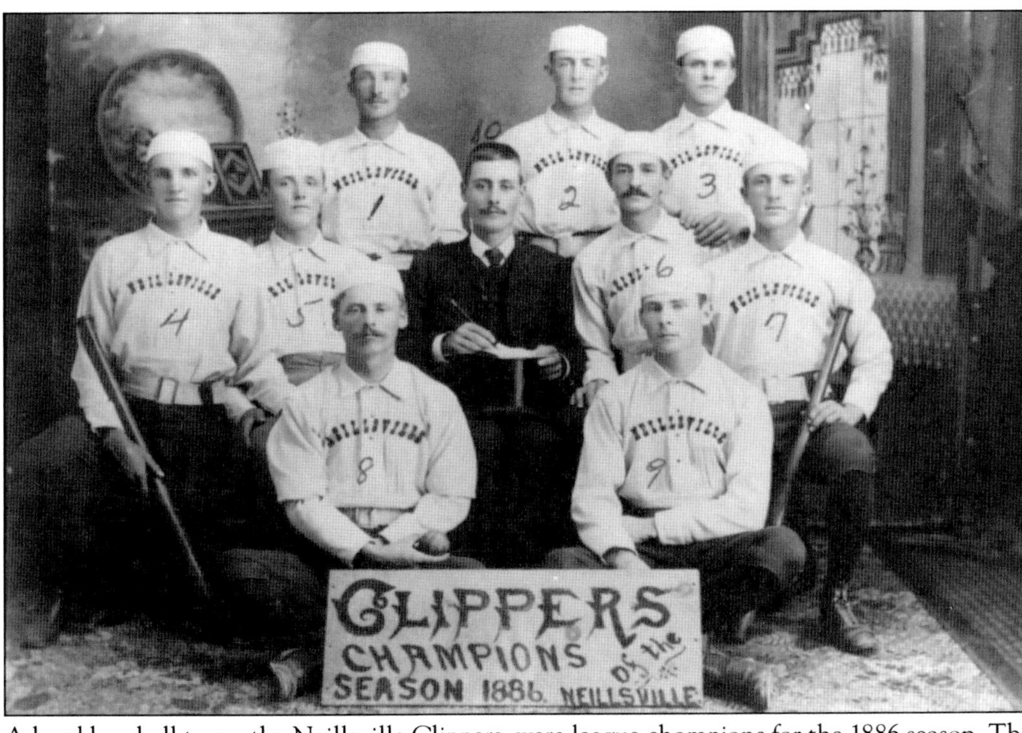

A local baseball team, the Neillsville Clippers, were league champions for the 1886 season. The team included, in numbered order, unidentified (1), Frank Hewett (2), unidentified (3), Ed Gates (4), A.B. Marsh (5), Gus Klopf (6), George Huntizicker (7), Frank Eryly (8), unidentified (9), and coach George Ure (10).

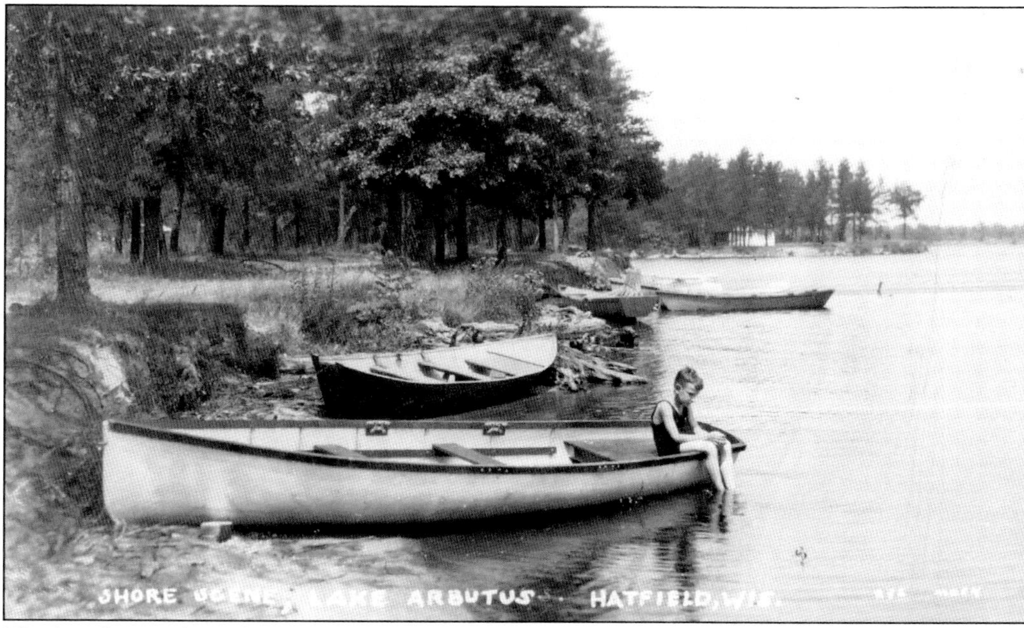

The beach at Lake Arbutus, in Hatfield, is a common gathering place for residents of southern Clark County and the many tourists who visit each year. The area surrounding the lake is a popular swimming, boating, fishing, and camping area with access to the ATV trails of Clark County Forests. Hatfield proudly boasts a population of 50 in the winter and 5,000 in the summer.

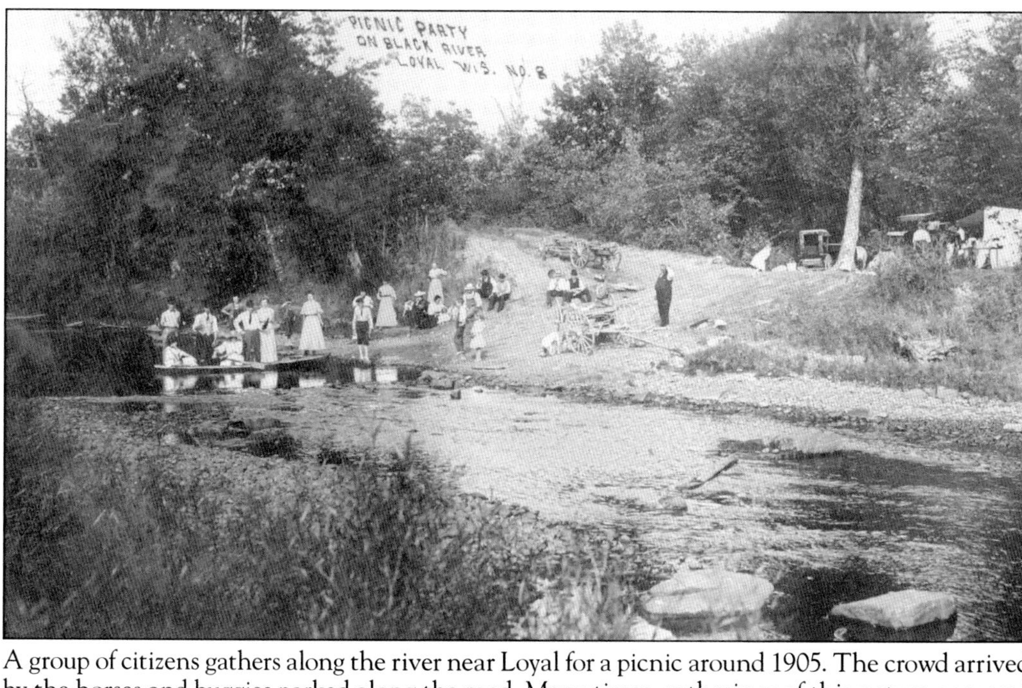

A group of citizens gathers along the river near Loyal for a picnic around 1905. The crowd arrived by the horses and buggies parked along the road. Many times, gatherings of this nature occurred on Sundays, either as a church service, a baptism, or just a social time with a picnic lunch.

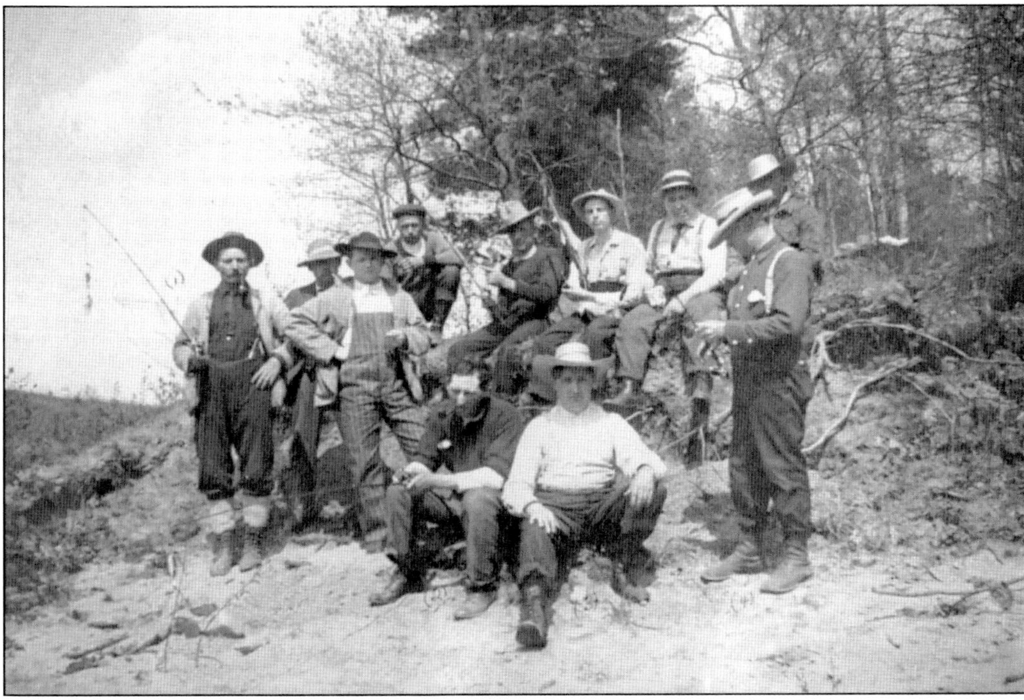

Neillsville fisherman gathered along the banks of the Black River for this photograph, dated August 13, 1905. Only four members of the group are identified. In no particular order, they are Charlie Gates, William Bradford, Fritz Neverman, and either Bill Huntley or Bill Dahnert.

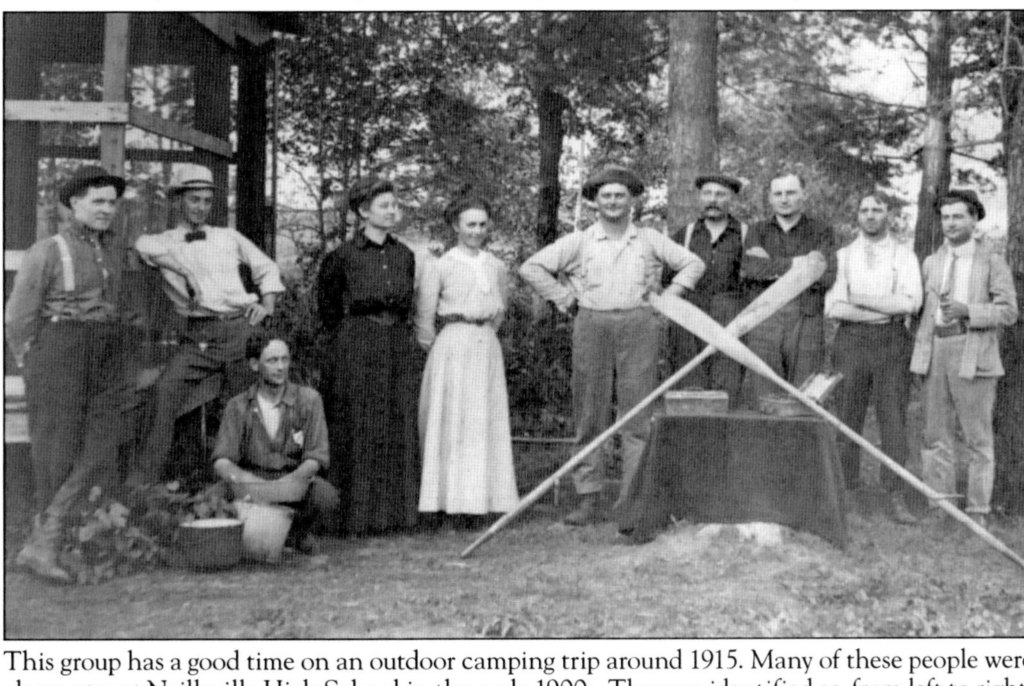

This group has a good time on an outdoor camping trip around 1915. Many of these people were classmates at Neillsville High School in the early 1900s. They are identified as, from left to right, H. Albright, Clarence Klopf, E. Dixon, Anne Rude, Mandy Kutchera, G. Rude, Carl Rabenstein, Ed Schoengarth, E. Crosby, and unidentified.

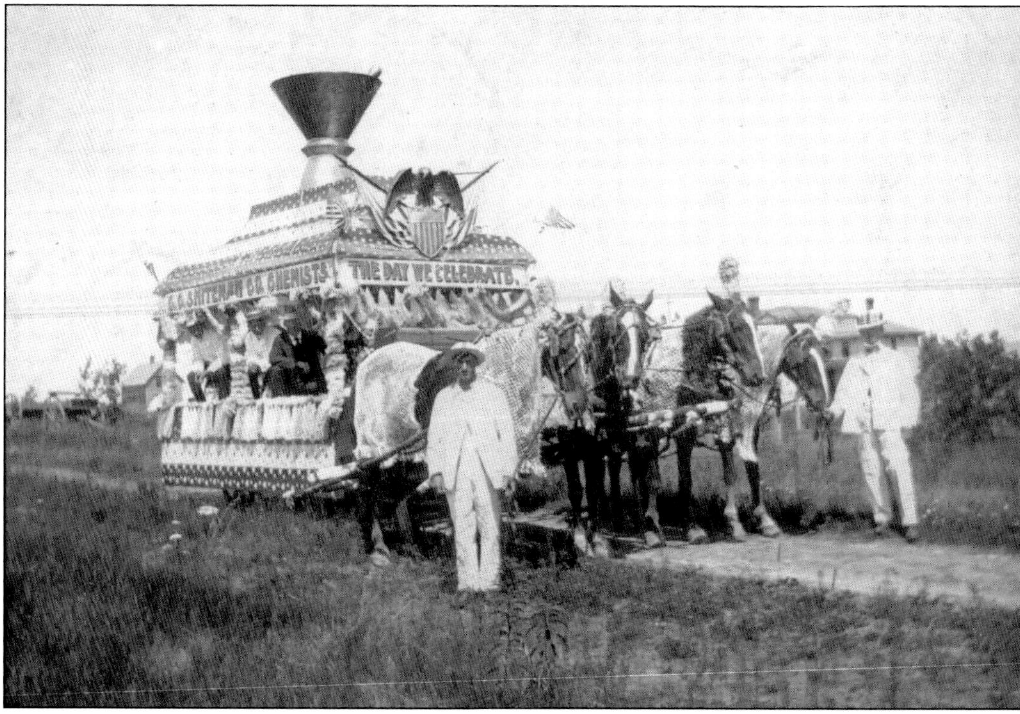

Parades were a way to celebrate important events in the community and in our history. Each year, Neillsville held a Fourth of July parade, with the entire community turning out for the festivities. Other events, like high school homecomings and military sendoffs and returns, also called for great parades. Both of these photographs show Fourth of July parades. The float above was sponsored by C.C. Sniteman of Neillsville around 1900. The mortar and pestle on the float mimic the same design feature found on the sign in front of Sniteman's drugstore. Below, flowers decorate every available spot on a parade automobile. The automobile likely carried notable citizens, elected officials, or the parade marshal and his family.

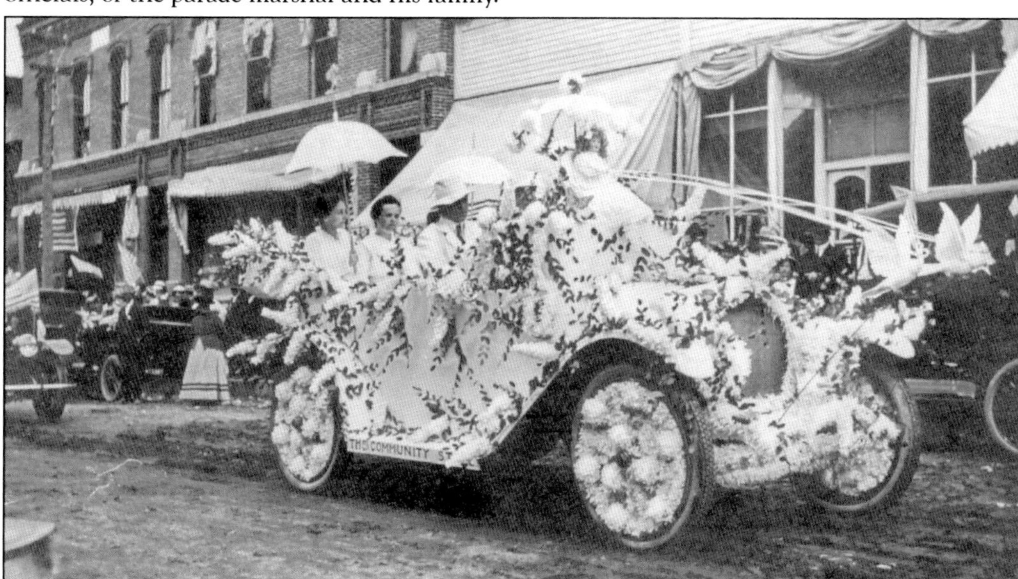

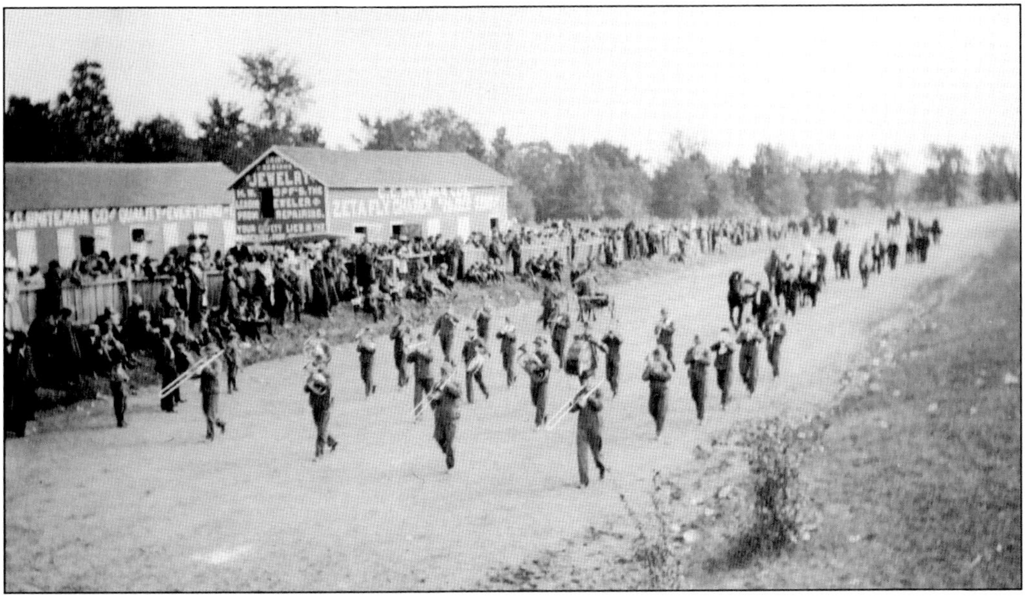

County fairs have been a gathering place for people for more than 100 years. Above, a marching band leads the entries for a horse race onto the track at the fairgrounds. The fair's Midway is seen below in the 1940s. The Midway featured games to test skills, food to delight every taste, displays of the latest technologies, and most of all, a social gathering place for people of the county to be entertained. Past county fair events, like horse racing and horse pulls, have given way to current events like modified truck and tractor pulls and mud bog racing. (Courtesy of UW Extension-Clark County.)

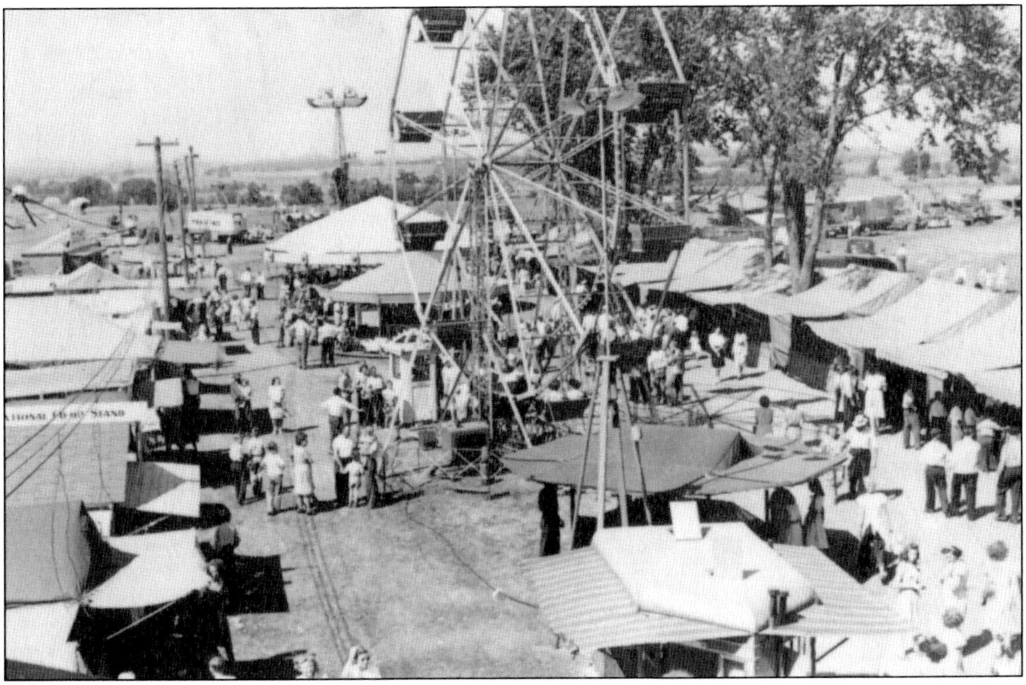

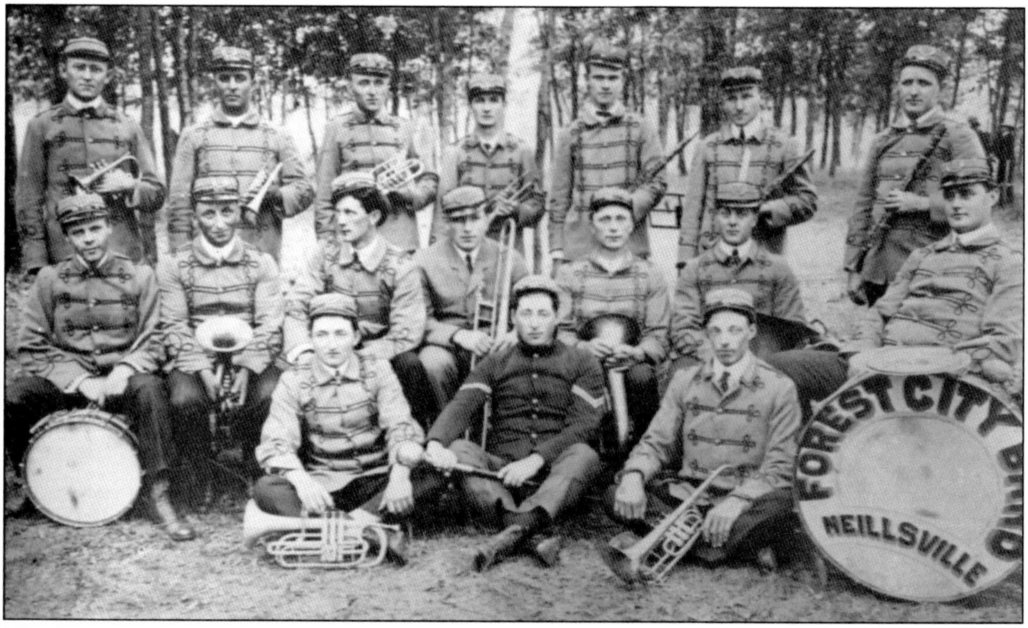

The Forest City Band, so named because of the many trees in the area, provides music for a Masonic picnic at Merrillan in 1905. From left to right are (first row) Otis Beardsley, Bill Bradford, and John Huntley; (second row) Thurmo Luethe, Fred Bullard, Ernest Dixon, Ernst McIntire, Frank Burnett, unidentified, and George Rude; (third row) Paul Walk, Ern Ayers, Arthur Haugen, unidentified, John Rude, Oscar Schoengarth, and Fred Neverman.

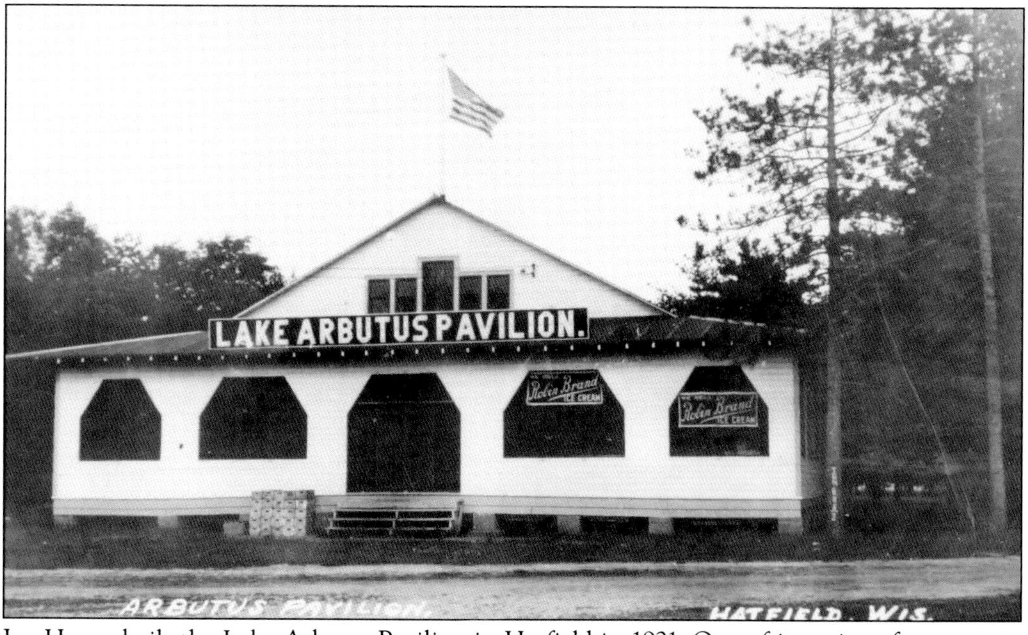

Joe Hanus built the Lake Arbutus Pavilion in Hatfield in 1921. One of its unique features was a floating-floor design that provided a bounce, or spring, when danced upon. It was repurposed by Joe and Violet Vieau into a roller-skating rink in 1939 and renamed Vieau's Recreation Center. Today, it is again a roller-skating rink, but using the building's original name, the Lake Arbutus Pavilion.

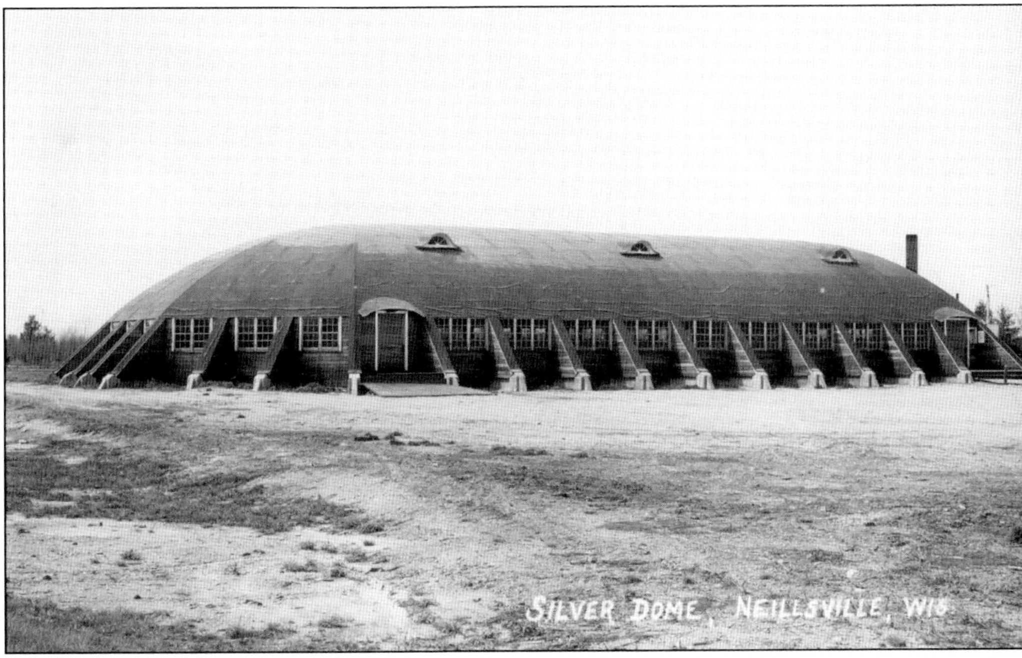

The Silver Dome Ballroom is located five miles west of Neillsville on Highway 10. In 1929, when the Keller brothers began construction on it, they never dreamt that their building would one day be listed in the National Register of Historic Places. It took four years to build, and its most unusual feature is its lamella truss roof. Over the years, bands from every genre of music have performed on its stage. It has hosted Duke Ellington, Gene Autrey, George Jones, and the Grass Roots, as well as many local bands and orchestras over the years. The ballroom is still in use today, hosting wedding dances and reunions. Natives of the surrounding area of Clark County have fond memories of dancing to their favorite music at the Silver Dome.

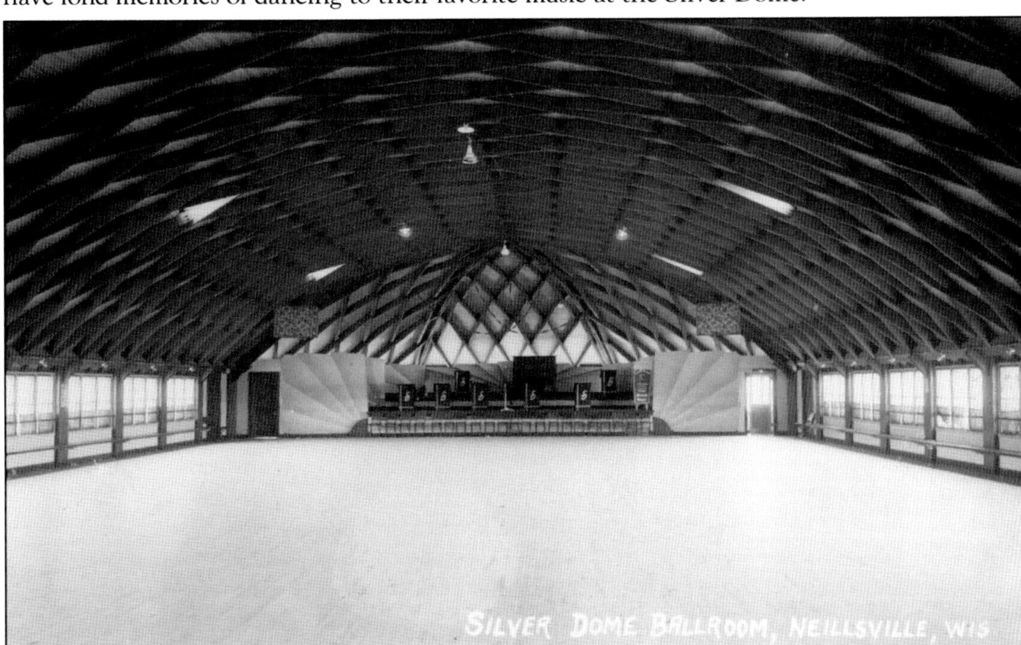

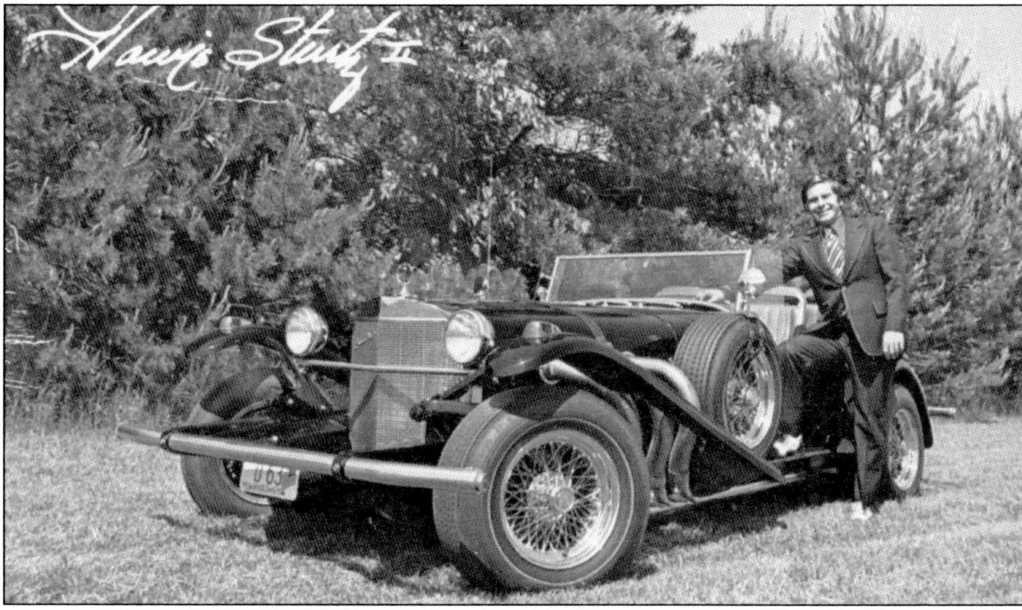

Howie Sturtz, a local bandleader, is seen here with his Excalibur car, which he loaned to Johnny Cash to use in a commercial. Sturtz and his orchestra played waltzes, foxtrots, and polkas in the area for more than 50 years, at fairs, wedding dances, proms, and homecomings. The Howie Sturtz Orchestra had its own TV shows, recorded many albums, and along the way, was named Wisconsin Band of the Year nine times.

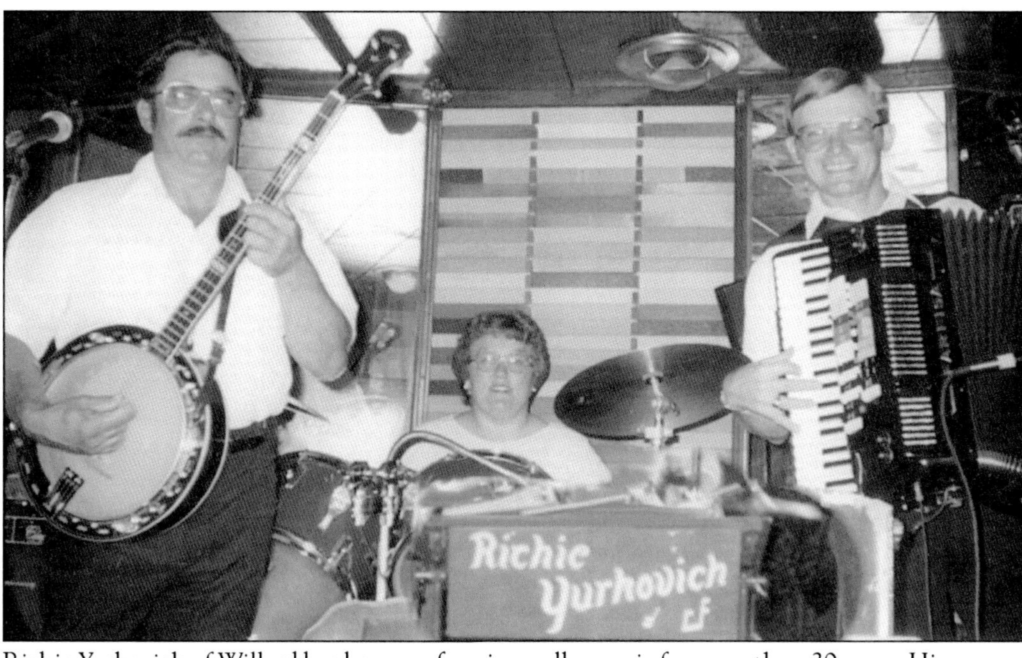

Richie Yurkovich of Willard has been performing polka music for more than 30 years. His current band, Polkalarity, includes, from left to right, Chico Gregorich, Gabe Yurkovich, and Richie Yurkovich. Polka music, originally brought to this area by German and Slovenian immigrants, continues to be a favorite music genre for dances, parties, and festivals. (Courtesy of the Willard Historical Society.)

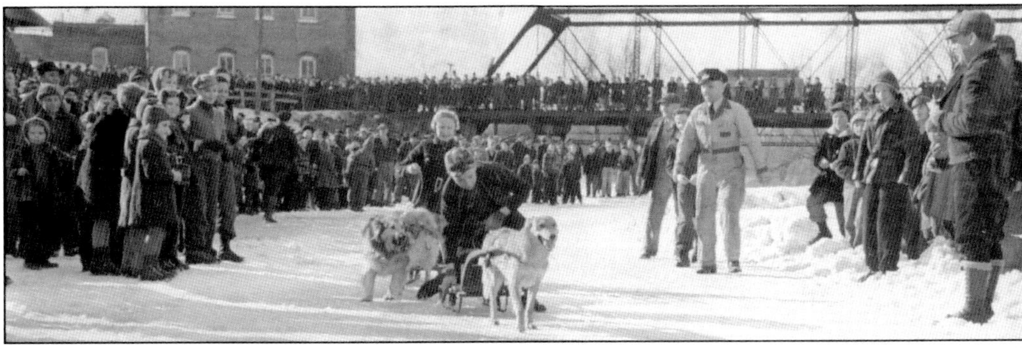

Winter Carnival has been a tradition in Neillsville since the first event in 1938. In 1939, people gathered on the Hewett Street Bridge and on both banks of O'Neill Creek to watch dogsled racing. Other events that year were wood chopping and log sawing. Many old-time loggers turned out for these events, showing the skills they honed in the woods when logging was the major industry.

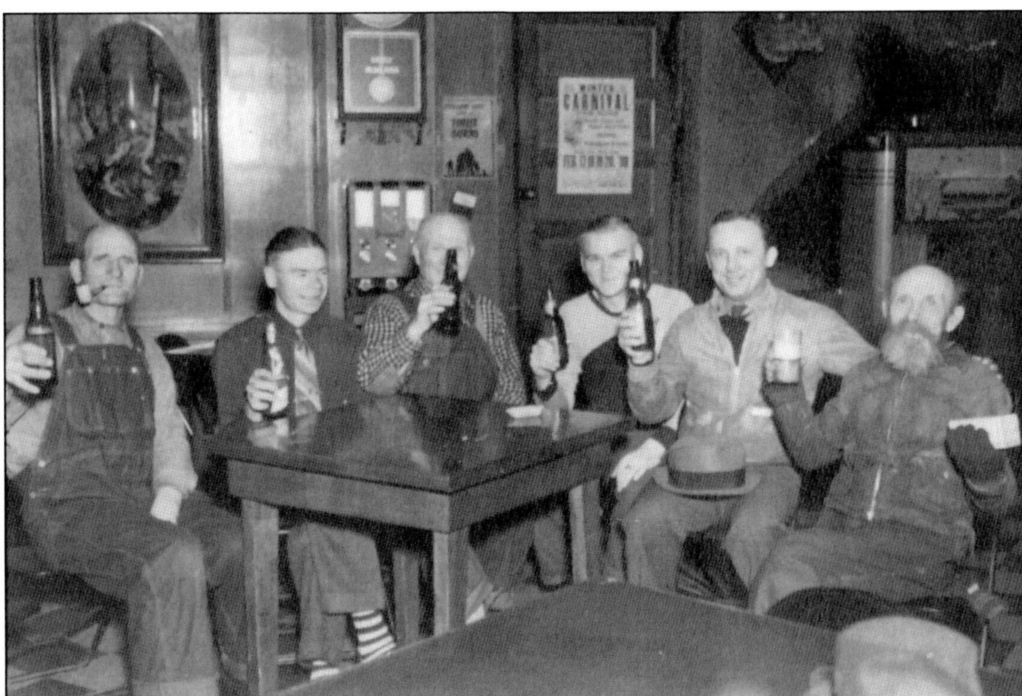

With a 1938 Neillsville Winter Carnival poster in the background, these six men gather in a local tavern to make a toast. Just five years earlier, this would not have been possible, as Prohibition was in place until January 1933. Today, certain Winter Carnival events take place in taverns or community halls. People participate in sheepshead, cribbage, or dirty clubs tournaments, and in pool and dart tournaments.

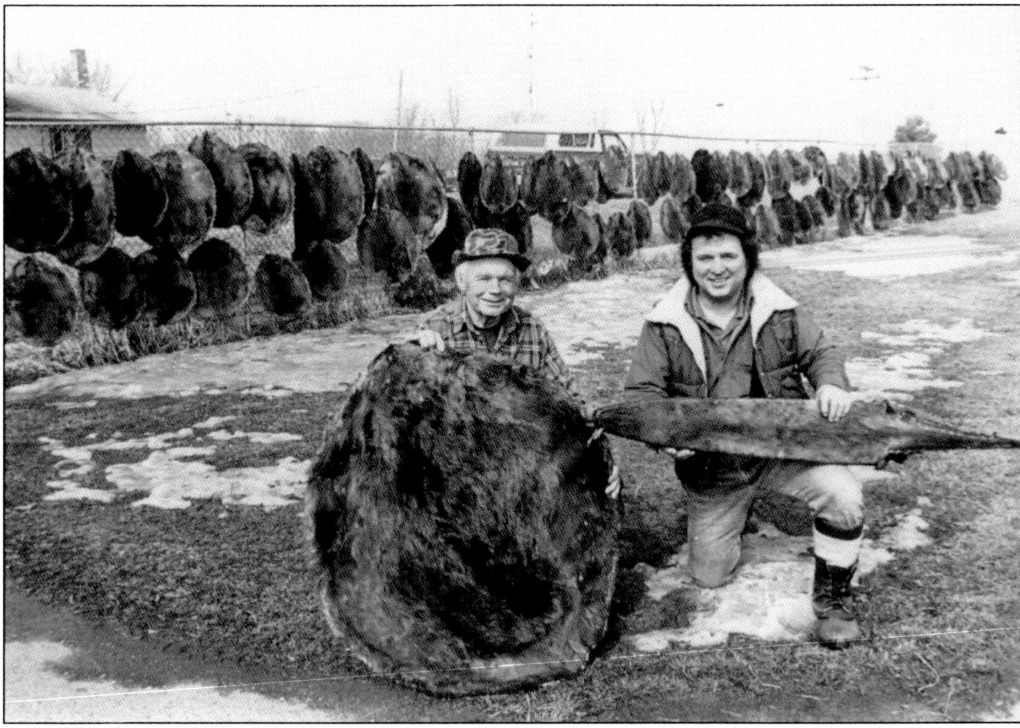

Willard Beaver Days, celebrated on the third weekend in March each year, includes a parade, a queen coronation, and a display of the beaver hides trapped in the Willard/Rock Dam area. The festival grew out of a complimentary pancake breakfast with local maple syrup to thank the community for all they do. Seen here are two of the event's founders, Bill Stabnow (left) and Bing Perko (right). (Courtesy of the Willard Historical Society.)

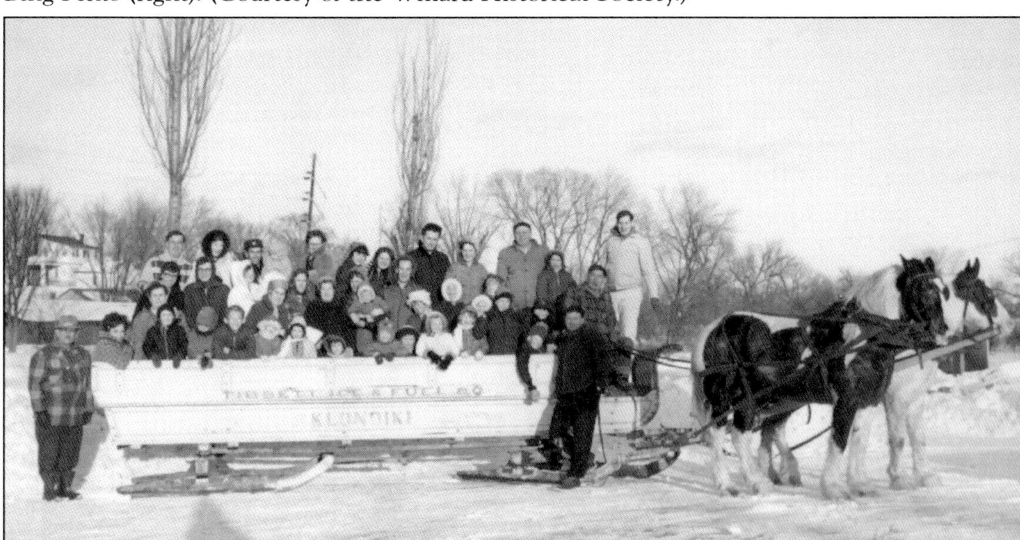

The George and Jack Tibbett families are all loaded into the family's beloved Klondike sleigh in this 1960s photograph. Pulled by a team of horses on the frozen O'Neill Creek in Neillsville, the family is bundled up for a sleigh ride in the same sleigh that was used in the W.B. and W.F. Tibbett lumber camps in the early 1900s. (Courtesy of the Dick and Joanne Tibbett collection.)

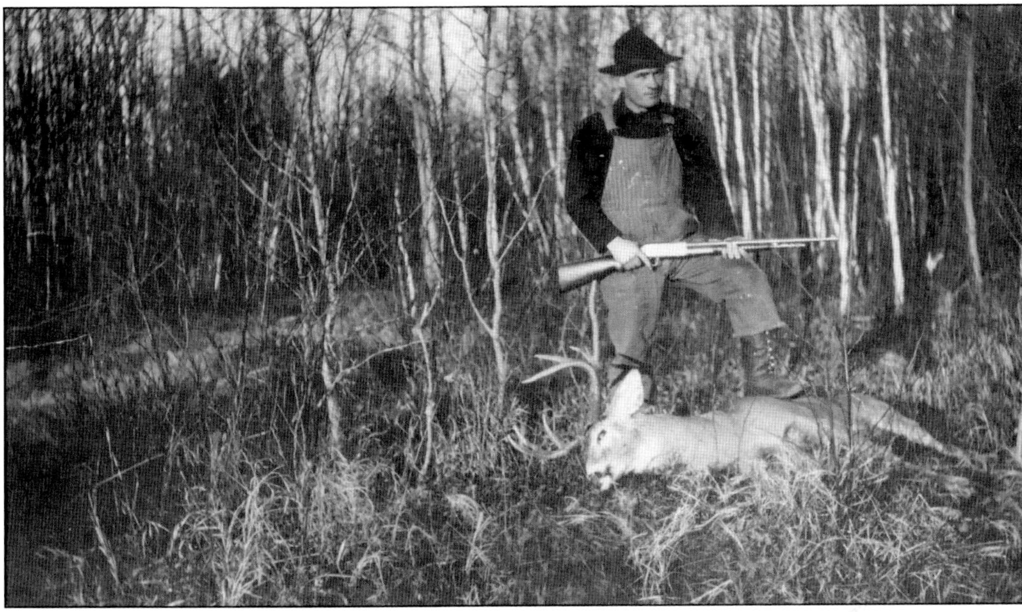

The dominant color in Wisconsin during the week of Thanksgiving is blaze orange, as hunters head into the woods for the annual deer-hunting season. This 10-point buck was shot by a Granton area hunter in 1915. Undoubtedly, this hunter told stories for years to come about the one that did not get away.

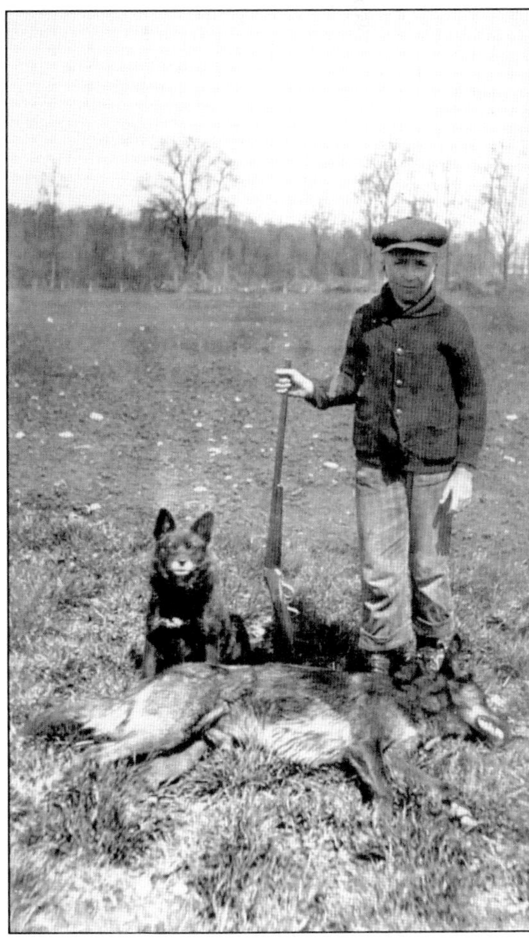

Young Art Garbisch of Granton used this Winchester single-shot .22 to down a wolf around 1930. Wisconsin wolf bounties ended in 1957, when the state's wolf population was nearly extinct, and wolves were then added to the list of protected species. As the years passed, the wolf population began to recolonize, and in 2012, the Wisconsin Department of Natural Resources once again allowed a limited-quota wolf-hunting season.

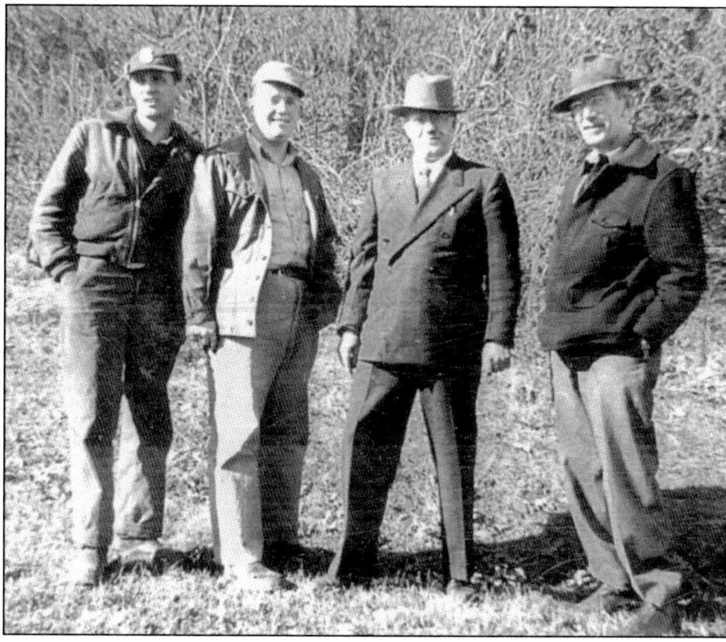

The Bruce Mound Ski Area is located in southern Clark County, about 15 miles from Neillsville. Work was begun by members of the Half Moon Ski Club in 1948, who spent many of their free summer days clearing brush and trails to bring the ski hill to life. The original organizers were, from left to right, Jim Hauge, Pink Van Gordon, Herb Smith, and Dr. Milton Roskrans, all of Neillsville. (Courtesy of the *Clark County Press.*)

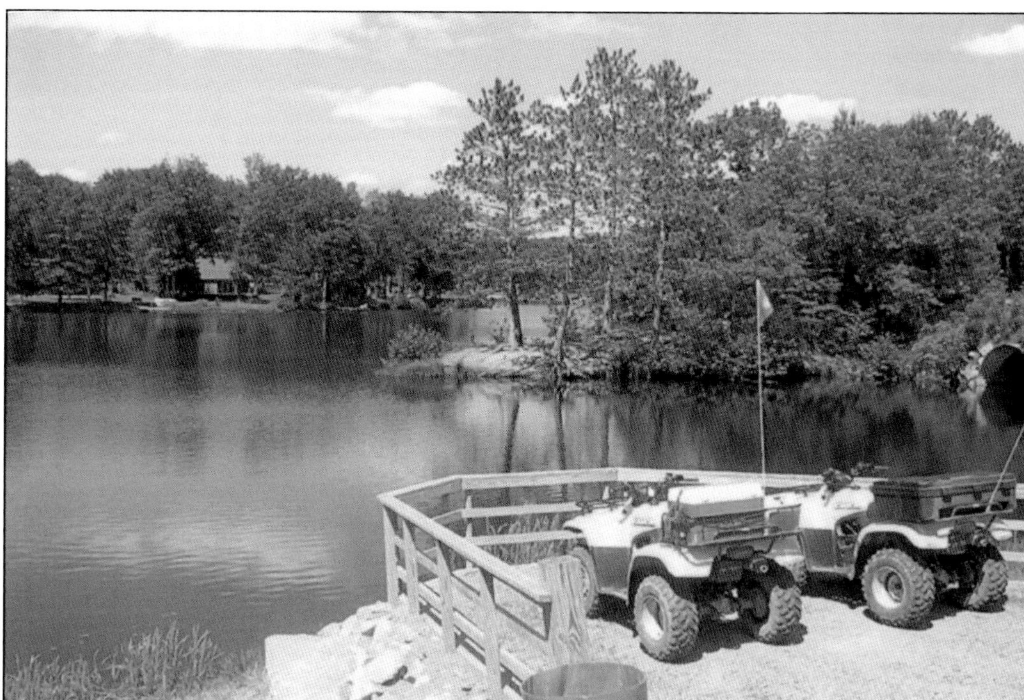

Summer in Clark County is ATV time. Clark County's 133,000-acre forest supports 82 miles of interconnecting trails. Five campgrounds and six parking lots provide access to its trails. The trail system is considered one of the finest in the upper Midwest. On summer weekends, riders from Wisconsin, Minnesota, Iowa, and Illinois enjoy the vistas of central Wisconsin. (Courtesy of Norm and Ann's Campground.)

Eight

Unique Clark County

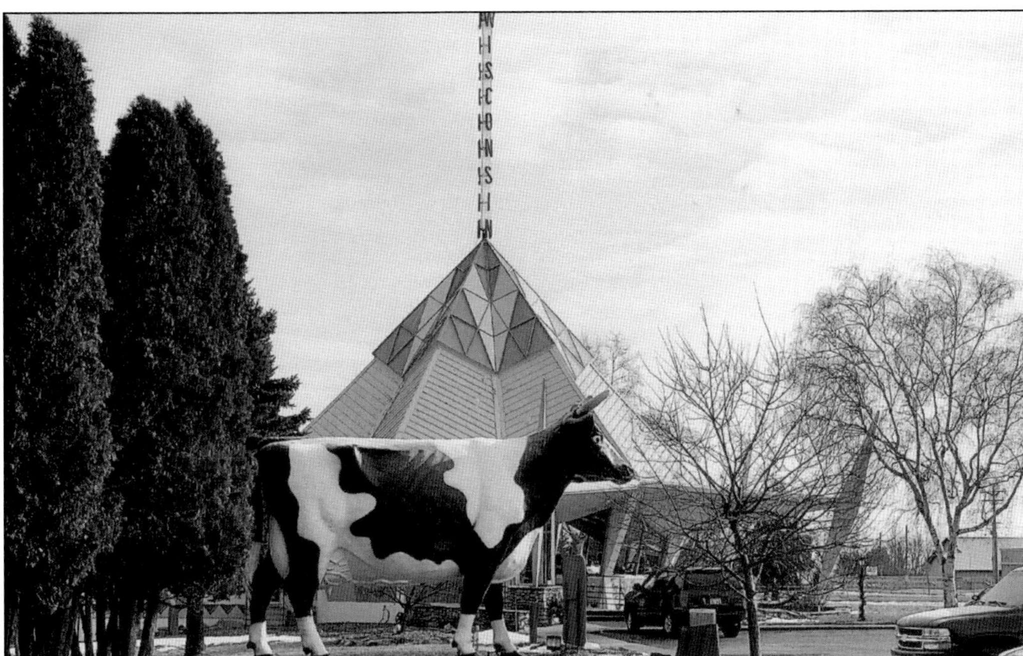

Wisconsin's exhibit at the 1964 New York World's Fair was the Pavilion, seen here, and a tractor-trailer with the world-record block of cheese in it. Ivan Wilcox of Boscobel bought and dismantled the exhibit, and then sold it to WCCN Radio in Neillsville. The Pavilion is now home to WCCN/WPKG Radio, and Chatty Belle, the world's largest talking cow. (Courtesy of the Central Wisconsin Broadcasting Corporation/WCCN.)

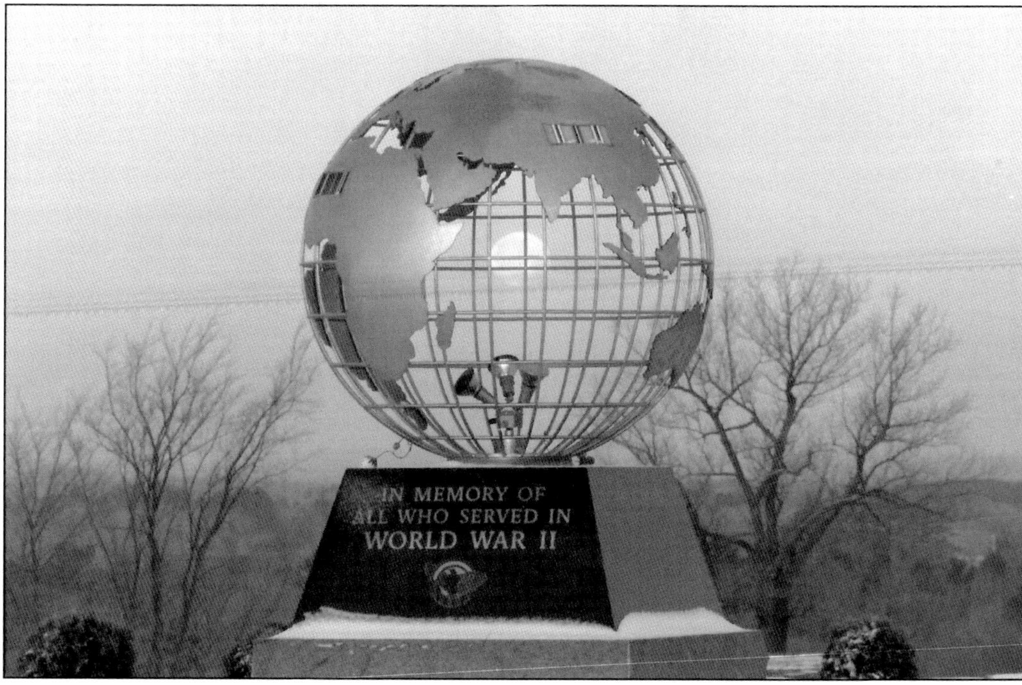

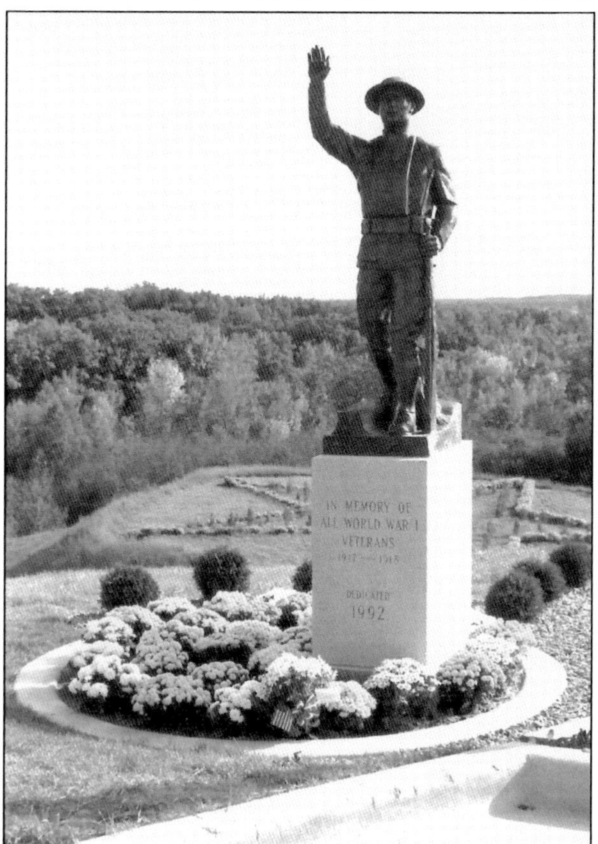

The Highground is a volunteer, nonprofit organization located three miles west of Neillsville along Highway 10, on 148 acres that border a glacial moraine and offering spectacular views of thousands of acres of farmland and forests. The original goal of the Highground was to create a place honoring Wisconsin's Vietnam veterans. Over time, the organization has evolved into a memorial park that pays tribute to the service of our fallen men and women, honors the survivors of military service, and also acknowledges the people who supported their loved ones while they were away and after they returned. The World War II globe memorial (above) and the World War I doughboy memorial (left) are just two of the many tributes at the Highground. (Courtesy of the Highground.)

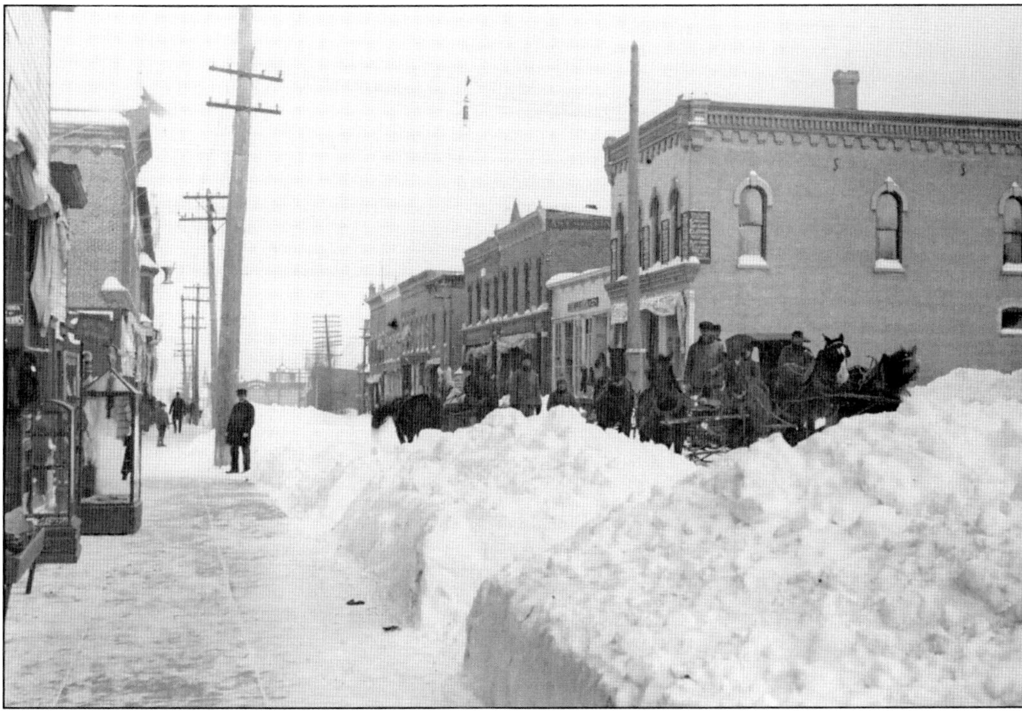

The merchants along Hewett Street in Neillsville have dug themselves out after the snowstorm of December 27–28, 1904. This blizzard produced 26 inches of snow in 24 hours, a record that still stands today. In the era before the automobile, shoveled snow was left in the streets until warmer weather or sunshine melted it away.

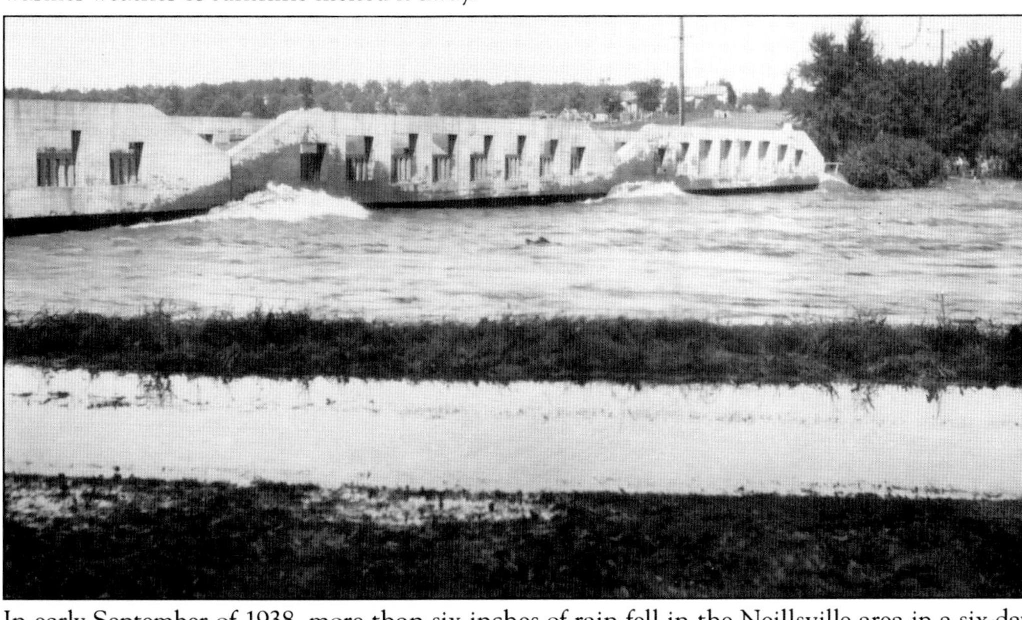

In early September of 1938, more than six inches of rain fell in the Neillsville area in a six-day period, causing widespread flooding and record river crests. Looking south across the river where the Grand Avenue Bridge crosses the Black River, this view shows the height the water reached. The bridge held as the water level rose to an unsurpassed record 23.8 feet above flood stage.

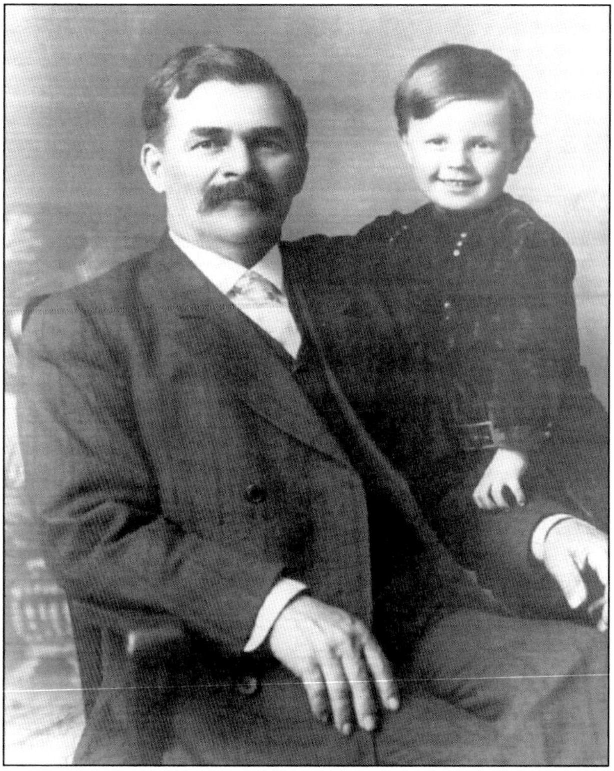

Robert Eunson, seen here with his son Dale, was Clark County's sheriff in 1909 and 1910. The family then moved to Montana and later to California. Dale Eunson grew up to be a writer, and published a story his father had told him many times growing up. The story, *The Day They Gave Babies Away*, became the movie *All Mine To Give*, the true story of Robert "Robbie" Eunson on Christmas Day, 1868.

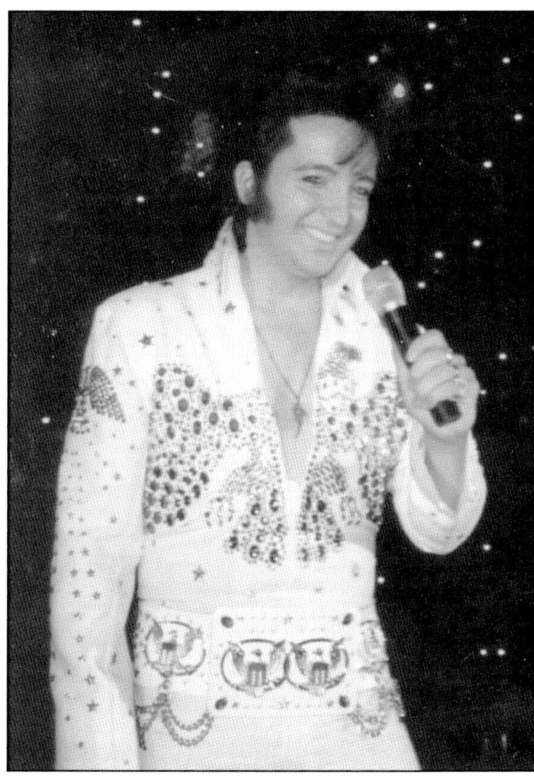

Gary "G.L." Wesley was born and raised in Willard. For 30 years, he has been performing as an Elvis Presley impersonator. His favorite song to perform is Elvis's version of "How Great Thou Art." He has performed locally as well as throughout the United States, Canada, and other locations worldwide. (Courtesy of the Willard Historical Society.)

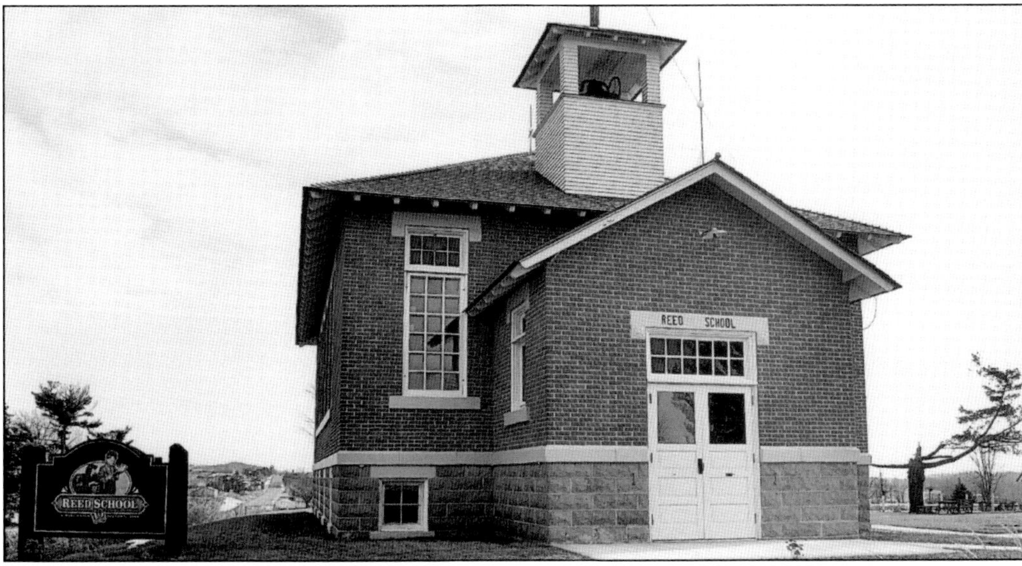

Reed School, one of Clark County's rural schools, east of Neillsville, is now a historic site operated by the Wisconsin Historical Society. Open for tours from May to October, Reed School was restored and is operated by a foundation established by Gordon Smith, who attended class here while staying with relatives in 1939. He always felt that those few weeks changed his life forever.

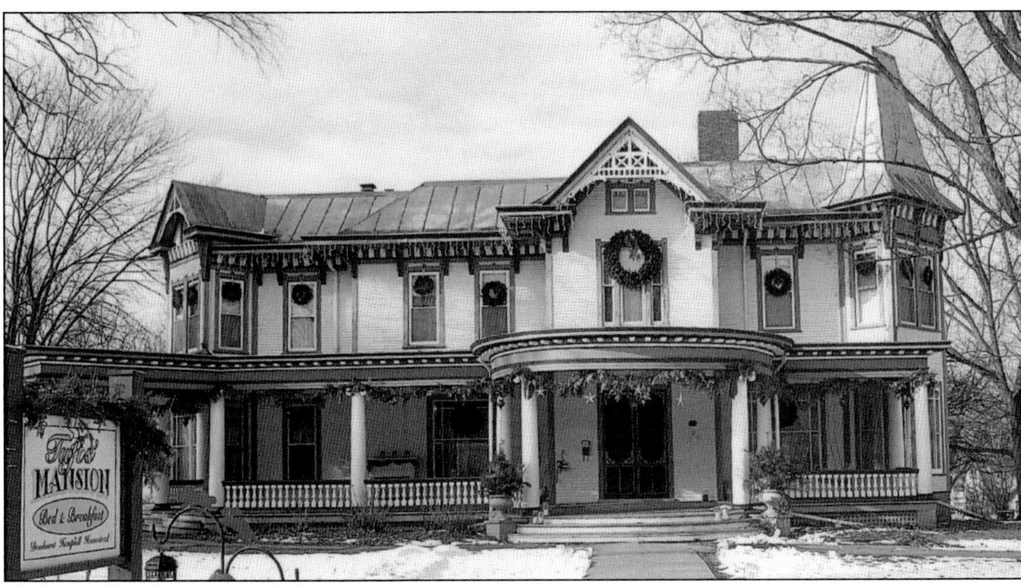

The Tufts' Mansion, named for its last owners, Col. William B. and Jennie Tufts, is a bed and breakfast and a museum located in Neillsville. The mansion, operated by the Voss family, was built in 1879 and features a beautiful front porch and a carriage house. It is one of many grand Victorian homes and other historical places in Clark County.

DISCOVER THOUSANDS OF LOCAL HISTORY BOOKS FEATURING MILLIONS OF VINTAGE IMAGES

Arcadia Publishing, the leading local history publisher in the United States, is committed to making history accessible and meaningful through publishing books that celebrate and preserve the heritage of America's people and places.

Find more books like this at
www.arcadiapublishing.com

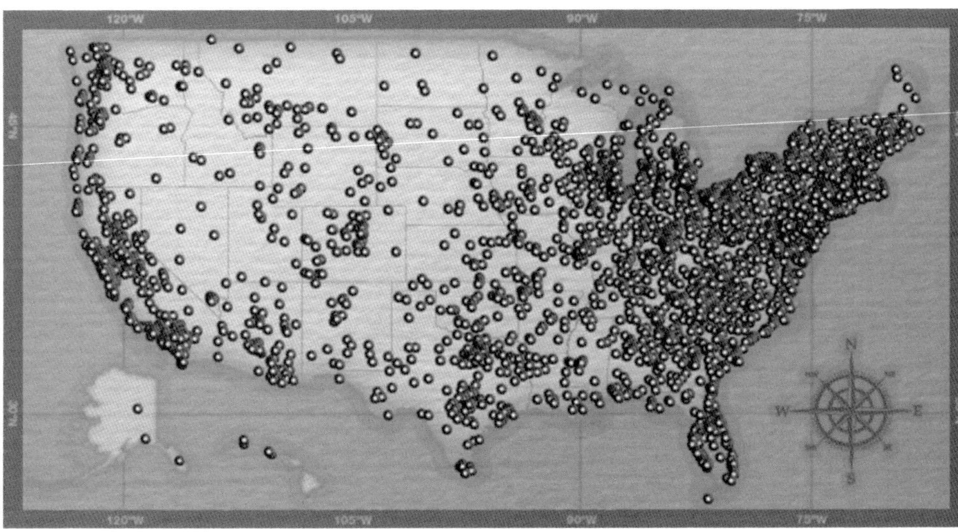

Search for your hometown history, your old stomping grounds, and even your favorite sports team.

Consistent with our mission to preserve history on a local level, this book was printed in South Carolina on American-made paper and manufactured entirely in the United States. Products carrying the accredited Forest Stewardship Council (FSC) label are printed on 100 percent FSC-certified paper.

MADE IN THE USA